www.wadsworth.com

www.wadsworth.com is the World Wide Web site for Wadsworth and is your direct source to dozens of online resources.

At *www.wadsworth.com* you can find out about supplements, demonstration software, and student resources. You can also send email to many of our authors and preview new publications and exciting new technologies.

www.wadsworth.com
Changing the way the world learns®

Sex and Religion

CHRISTEL MANNING
Sacred Heart University

PHIL ZUCKERMAN
Pitzer College

THOMSON
™
WADSWORTH

Australia • Canada • Mexico • Singapore • Spain
United Kingdom • United States

THOMSON

WADSWORTH

Publisher: *Holly J. Allen*
Religion Editor: *Steve Wainwright*
Assistant Editors: *Lee McCracken, Anna Lustig*
Editorial Assistant: *Barbara Hillaker*
Marketing Manager: *Worth Hawes*
Advertising Project Manager: *Bryan Vann, Vicky Wan*
Print/Media Buyer: *Judy Inouye*

Permissions Editor: *Kiely Sexton*
Production Service: *Shepherd, Inc.*
Copy Editor: *Jennifer Coker*
Cover Designer: *Yvo Biezebos*
Cover Image: *Michael Escoffrey/Art Resource,* NY
Cover and Text Printer: *Malloy*
Compositor: *Shepherd, Inc.*

For more information about our products, contact us at:
Thomson Learning
Academic Resource Center
1-800-423-0563
For permission to use material from this text or product, submit a request online at http://www.thomsonrights.com.
Any additional questions about permissions can be submitted by email to thomsonrights@thomson.com.

Library of Congress Control Number:
ISBN 0-534-52493-1

Thomson Wadsworth
10 Davis Drive
Belmont, CA 94002-3098
USA

Asia
Thomson Learning
5 Shenton Way #01-01
UIC Building
Singapore 068808

Australia/New Zealand
Thomson Learning
102 Dodds Street
Southbank, Victoria 3006
Australia

Canada
Nelson
1120 Birchmount Road
Toronto, Ontario M1K 5G4
Canada

Europe/Middle East/Africa
Thomson Learning
High Holborn House
50/51 Bedford Row
London WC1R 4LR
United Kingdom

Latin America
Thomson Learning
Seneca, 53
Colonia Polanco
11560 Mexico D.F.
Mexico

Spain/Portugal
Paraninfo
Calle Magallanes, 25
28015 Madrid, Spain

Contents

About the Authors

Miriam Williams Boeri
Education: PhD, Sociology, Georgia State University Atlanta, Georgia; MA, Sociology, Georgia State University Atlanta, Georgia; BS, Communications, Kennesaw State University, Kennesaw, Georgia.

Miriam Williams Boeri is Assistant Professor of Sociology in the Department of Sociology, Geography, Anthropology and Criminal Justice at Kennesaw State University in Kennesaw, GA. She also conducts ethnographic research on drug use and abuse for Rollins School of Public Health at Emory University in Atlanta, GA. She is author of *Heaven's Harlots: My Fifteen Years as a Sacred Prostitute in the Children of God,* as well as journal articles on new religious movements and drug abuse. Born in Pennsylvania, and having lived in Europe for fifteen years while raising five children, she now lives in Atlanta with her husband and youngest son.

Barbara Geller
Education: PhD, Religion, Duke University; MA, Religion, Duke University; BA, Religion, Princeton University.

Barbara Geller is Professor of Religion at Wellesley College in Wellesley, MA, where she teaches courses in post-Biblical Jewish history and history of Judaism, women in the Biblical world, Jews and Christians in the Roman Empire, and archaeology of the Biblical world. Her research and publications focus on Late Antique Jewish history. She resides in the Boston area with her human and feline family.

Klaus J. Hansen
Education: PhD, History, Wayne State University; Diploma, Archival Stud., Harvard; BA, History, Brigham Young University.

Klaus Hansen has had academic appointments at Ohio State University, Utah State University, and Yale University. In 1968 he joined the history department at Queen's University, Kingston, Ontario, Canada, where he attained the rank of professor. His academic specialty is the history of American thought and culture. He is the author of *Mormonism and the American Experience* as well as several other books and articles on religion, sexuality, race, and the liberal tradition. Born in Germany, he was educated at the Herder Gymnasium in Forchheim before immigrating to the U.S. with his family.

Anthony F. LoPresti

Education: PhD, Theological Ethics, Boston College; MA, Theology, Boston College; BS, Mathematics, Georgetown University.

Anthony F. LoPresti is Assistant Professor of Religious Studies at Salve Regina University in Newport, RI, where he teaches courses in sexuality, marriage, and a variety of undergraduate courses. A husband and father of three children, he has written articles and given public addresses on the Christian understanding of sexuality to groups of teenagers, young adults, and mixed audiences.

Christel Manning

Education: PhD, Religious Studies, University of California Santa Barbara; MA, Relig. Stud., UCSB; BA, Economics, Tufts University.

Christel Manning is Associate Professor of Religious Studies and Chair of the Department of Philosophy & Religious Studies at Sacred Heart University in Fairfield, CT, where she teaches courses in world religions, new religions, and religion, gender and sexuality. She is author of *God Gave Us the Right: Conservative Catholic, Evangelical Protestant, and Orthodox Jewish Women Grapple with Feminism,* as well as several articles on women and religion and new religious movements. Born in California and raised in Germany, she now lives with her husband and daughter in New Haven.

Larry Poston

Education: PhD, History of Religions, Northwestern University, Evanston, IL; MA, History of Religions, Northwestern University, Evanston, IL; MA, Missiology, Trinity Evangelical Divinity School, Deerfield, IL; BA, Religious Education, Grace College of the Bible, Omaha, NE.

Larry Poston is Chair of the Department of Missiology and Religion and Professor of Religion at Nyack College in Nyack, NY. He and his wife Linda lived for several years in Saffle, Sweden, where Larry taught at the Nordic Bible Institute. He is the author of *Islamic Da'wah in the West: Muslim Missionary Activity and the Dynamics of Conversion to Islam* and *The Changing Face of Islam in America,* as well as numerous articles.

Rita Dasgupta Sherma

Education: PhD, Religious Studies, Claremont Graduate University; MA, Women's Studies in Religion, Claremont Graduate University; BA, Business Administration, Ottawa University.

Rita Dasgupta Sherma is Visiting Assistant Professor of Asian and Asian American Studies at Binghamton University in Binghamton, NY. She is Senior Research Associate at Berghoffer Institute, and Chair, Board of Distinguished Visiting Scholars, Dharma Association of North America. She has presented in a wide variety of academic forums on issues related to gender and religion, religion and ecology, and Hindu studies. She is the author of numerous essays and articles on women and religion, ecofeminism, religious pluralism, and Hindu theology.

Alan Sponberg

Education: PhD, Chinese Language and Literature (Buddhist Studies), University of British Columbia; MA, South Asian Studies, University of Wisconsin/Madison; BA, Philosophy, School of International Studies, American University, Washington, DC.

Alan Sponberg is Professor of Asian Philosophy and Religion, and Academic Chair of the Asian Studies Program at the University of Montana, where he teaches courses in Buddhism and comparative ethics. He has also taught at Princeton, Stanford, and the Buddhist Library of Singapore. His research and publications focus on Buddhism in various cross-cultural contexts, ranging from the transmission of early Yogacara into medieval China to contemporary Buddhist revival and neo-traditionalist movements in both Asia and in the West. Beyond his interests in the history of Buddhism, he practices as an ordained member of the Western Buddhist Order.

Douglas Wile

Education: PhD, East Asian Languages and Literatures, University of Wisconsin; BA, Comparative Literature, University of Wisconsin.

Douglas Wile is Professor of Chinese Language and Literature and Chairman of the Chinese Division of the Department of Modern Languages at Brooklyn College–CUNY, where he also teaches Asian Religions in the Program in Religions. Prof. Wile teaches Chinese Philosophy and Medical Chinese in the MA Program at Pacific College of Oriental Medicine and is the author of six books and numerous articles on Chinese martial arts history, self-cultivation, sexology, and religion.

Phil Zuckerman

Education: BA, Sociology, University of Oregon; MA, Sociology, University of Oregon; PhD, Sociology, University of Oregon, 1998.

Phil Zuckerman is a professor of sociology and religious studies at Pitzer College, where he teaches courses in social theory, deviance, sociology of religion, and sex and religion. He is the author of *Invitation to the Sociology of Religion* and *Strife in the Sanctuary: Religious Schism in a Jewish Community,* and the editor of *Du Bois on Religion.* Born and raised in Southern California, Phil lives with his wife, Stacy, and their two daughters.

Sex and Religion

Chapter 1

Sex and Religion: An Introduction

Phil Zuckerman and Christel Manning

Sex and religion[1]—two of the most powerful, passionate, and poetic aspects of human existence. Both the sacred and the sexual have been of paramount symbolic and practical importance for all societies. Every culture grapples and dances in its own ways with the seemingly universal questions of what it means to be intimate with other humans and what it means to be intimate with the otherworldly. The rapture of sexual union and the rapture of communion with the divine are strikingly similar in their power and transcendence, and there isn't a religion on earth that hasn't constructed barriers and/or bridges between these two experiences. As sociologist of religion Meredith McGuire has observed, "all religions have attempted to interpret sexual themes or experiences. Religious symbolism frequently deals directly with themes of sexuality. Important parallels exist between spiritual and sexual ecstasy."[2]

Religion is an endlessly varied and ever-nebulous phenomenon, and one finds numerous approaches to—and multiple understandings of—sex and sexuality within its rubric. As Bryan S. Turner remarks, "religious orientations to human sexuality have occupied a variety of positions along a continuum between total denial and orgy."[3] Indeed, there is no one specific religious approach to sex, nor one specific approach to sex within any one given religion. Rather, the relationship between sex and religion involves a myriad of perspectives, paradigms, contradictions, and debates.

Some religions (or aspects within them) can be described as comparatively "sex positive." By "sex positive," we mean that sensual, erotic activity involving the consensual pursuit and/or actualization of gratifying bodily pleasure is understood as natural and acceptable, even holy. Conversely, some religions (or aspects within them) can be described as "sex negative," that is, sensual, erotic activity involving the consensual pursuit and/or actualization of gratifying bodily pleasure is understood as unnatural and unacceptable, even sinful. Sex-positive religious traditions construct sex as potentially sacred, holy, and divinely lauded, whereas sex-negative religious traditions construct sex as essentially profane, evil, and inimical to that which may be understood as divine.[4]

For a wonderfully clear and "ideal-typical" illustration of these two divergent religious approaches to sex, we need only look at the case of the Shakers and the Oneida Perfectionists.[5] The Shakers and the Oneida Perfectionists were two relatively small Christian sects that arose and thrived during the nineteenth century in the Northeastern United States. Both were devout communal religious movements that stressed faith, pious living, love and worship of God, study of the Bible, and so on. The Shakers viewed *all* sexual activity as inherently sinful. The founder of the Shakers, Ann Lee, was convinced that carnal lust was the ultimate source of sin and thus taught that complete celibacy was required of those wishing to live holy lives. Conversely, the Oneida Perfectionists viewed sexual activity as natural, pleasurable, and acceptable to God. The founder of the Oneida Perfectionists, John Humphey Noyes, taught that "the outward act of sexual connection [was] the most noble and comely of all" acts.[6] He believed that the "natural instinct of our nature demands frequent congress of the sexes" not merely for biological purposes of procreation, but for social as all well as "spiritual" purposes.[7]

Of course, the unique case of the Shakers and Oneida Perfectionists represents a rare historical example of mutually exclusive, polar opposite religious approaches to sex. We know that most religions do not fit neatly into such distinct boxes that can be clearly labeled "sex positive" or "sex negative."

More often than not, the relationship between a given religion and its approach to sex is somewhere in between sex positive and sex negative, ever fluctuating and changing, and always subject to debate and reinterpretation. It is preferable then to think of sex positive and sex negative distinctions in the vein mentioned by Turner above, as existing on imagined polar ends of a continuum within which religions fall, but seldom falling unambiguously or permanently at any one given extreme. Probing this continuum of religious approaches to sex and the various specific religious manifestations that flow and tread within its confines is the major goal of this book.

Sex and Religion in Union

As alluded to in the case of the Oneida Perfectionists, sometimes the sexual and the religious mesh directly and positively in sacro-sensual harmony. For instance, the earliest known religious writings, those from Sumeria, describe in sacred terms the erotic love between the popular goddess Inanna and her consort Dumuzi. And not only are some of the earliest religious writings (from Sumeria and elsewhere) laced with sacred sexuality, but sexual activity is suspected to have been part and parcel of ancient religious practice and expression.[8]

Some historians of religion have suggested that sexual expression and activity were widespread in ancient and indigenous religions. For instance, many have acknowledged the existence of so-called "temple prostitution," that is, the ancient religious practice in which female priestesses would initiate men, through erotic rites, into sacred mystery or fertility cults.[9] During such ceremonies, both giving and receiving sexual pleasure were viewed as important and central spiritual experiences.[10] Gerda Lerner[11] suggests that while the historical evidence is limited and open to much speculation/interpretation,[12] and while we may not be sure of the degree of volition or compulsion on behalf of the women involved, it is believed that sexual activities ensued within pagan temples "to honor the fertility and sexual power of the goddess." James Brundage speaks of the ancient Phoenician sex cults of Ishtar and Asarte and how their temples were served by "sacred prostitutes" who "provided worshippers with opportunities to experience the divine power of the goddess through the ministry of sexual pleasure."[13] According to Stephen Benko, it is understandable that sex was part of such early religious worship. As he says of ancient ritual promiscuity: "it was a religious act because in the act of intercourse male and female, albeit momentarily, became one and in orgasm came as close to divinity as humanly possible."[14]

Many Eastern religious traditions contain deeply entrenched erotic elements to this day, and nowhere has the connection between sex and religion been more intimate and pervasive than in India. Hindu temples, such as those at Khajuraho and Konarak, are well-known for their graphic depiction of sexual practices and positions. Hindu scriptures are perhaps unique in their inclusion and depiction of sexual scenes, stories, and erotic escapades between various gods and goddesses.[15] And Hindu culture also produced the ancient manual of the art of love-making, the *Kama Sutra,* which is said to have been originally recited by the God Shiva while he was enjoying intercourse with his lover Parvati.

Although sex maintains a strong presence within certain Indian religious traditions, in the West, things developed differently, especially within Christianity. As a result of the influence of various authoritative Christian theologians, sex lost its sacred aura and became largely understood as the soul's virtual nemesis.[16]

Sex and Religion in Conflict

Mark Twain, in his humorously sardonic collection of essays on religion titled *Letters from the Earth,* comments on the peculiar state of sexual and sacred estrangement:

> . . . the human being . . . naturally places sexual intercourse far and away above all other joys—yet he has left it out of his heaven! The very thought of it

excites him; opportunity sets him wild; in this state he will risk life, reputation, everything—even his queer heaven itself—to make good that opportunity and ride it to the overwhelming climax. From youth to middle age all men and all women prize copulation above all other pleasures combined, yet it is actually as I have said: it is not in their heaven; prayer takes its place.[17]

Twain's remark, of course, refers to the traditional Christian heaven, and many scholars have characterized Christianity as the world religion most antagonistic to sexual pleasure.[18] Ever since Western social scientists began scrutinizing the relationship between Christianity and sexuality, the conclusion has generally been one of a persistent, negative lament. Early feminist sociologist Marriane Weber charged that:

> In reaction against the sexual license of the late-antique cultural world, the church overemphasized the ideal of mastery of instinctive drives . . . The natural basis of the fellowship of husband and wife was relegated to the realm of the sinful, that was still admittedly allowed within marriage, but that was nevertheless even there worthy of no consecration. Remaining unmarried was esteemed the more perfect condition . . . Protestantism did again elevate marriage, as "God's work," over celibacy as "the work of man," but it too left sexual love with the stain of being an "evil desire," stemming not from God but from the devil. . . .[19]

Uta Ranke-Heinemann examines the writings of such Christian founding theologians as Paul, Ignatius, Jerome, Justin the Martyr, Tatian, Origen, Ambrose, Chrysostom, Augustine, and Aquinas, all of whom did their part in "welding Christianity and hostility to sexual pleasure into a systematic whole."[20] "Most of us still retain a deeply ingrained belief that sex is shameful," comments James Brundage;[21] he argues that the common and pervasive sex-negative attitudes and beliefs held by many in the West are largely the consequences of patristic and early medieval Christian teachings that held that "sex was a source of moral defilement, spiritual pollution, and ritual impurity; hence, the argument ran, human sexuality was something to be ashamed of because it was both a result and a source of sin."

Lawrence Obsorne has gone so far as to discuss Christian "sexual pessimism"— the linkage of sexual love with death.[22] In his compelling discussion of various strands within Christianity, from Gnosticism to Catholicism, Osborne reveals the depths to which human sex and sexuality can be vilified. The celibate is deemed holier and closer to God and more deserving of everlasting life than the sexually engaged, who is deemed sinful and closer to Satan and death. The same is true of the virgin compared with the nonvirgin. The body is viewed as a corrupting entity, a thing to be ashamed of, controlled, and ultimately condemned. Again from James Brundage: "Western Christendom has been more restrictive in its interdiction of sensual pleasure than most other human societies. Western Christians have commonly associated sensuality with sin, guilt, and fear of damnation . . . virtue has come to be identified with sexual abstinence [and] purity with rejection of sexuality . . . few [other religions] have carried fear of sexuality to the point of loathing and disgust, as Western Christians have done."[23]

Yet Christianity is not the only religion to separate the sacred from the sexual. The demise of indigenous, nature-based religions and the rise of the major world religions (Judaism, Christianity, Islam, Buddhism, and Classical Hinduism) was accompanied by a move toward asceticism in many cultures. Take Exodus 19 from the Jewish Torah, in which Moses, while instructing the Jews on how to get ready to meet their God, requires sexual abstinence as part of their holy preparation. Fatima Mernissi speaks of the Islamic perception of sexuality as a source of chaos that draws man away from God.[24] Or consider the many Indian and Asian religious traditions that developed out of Hinduism, such as Jainism and many Buddhist monastic orders, that conceptualize the pursuit and experience of sexual pleasure as antithetical to enlightenment, stressing celibacy as a requirement for religious purity and spiritual ascendancy. After all, one of the last major temptations Buddha successfully resisted and overcame while seeking enlightenment was sensual pleasure.

In the West, hostility toward sexual pleasure can be traced to Greek philosophical traditions. Neo-Platonism in particular developed a dualistic understanding of body and soul that was absorbed into both Judaism and Christianity. As noted earlier, Christianity is most obvious in its rigorous construction that the body and spirit are antithetical, the soul and flesh are at war, sensual pleasure is inimical to holiness, and vice versa. As Paul, the founder of Christianity, writes in Galatians 5:16, "Live by the Spirit, I say, and do not gratify the desires of the flesh. For what the flesh desires is opposed to the Spirit and what the Spirit desires is opposed to the flesh."

Most contemporary Americans, whether religious or not, definitely tend to view and experience sex and religion in terms of conflict and separation. Phil remembers the first time he considered teaching a class titled "Sex and Religion"—the overwhelming response was: "Huh?" Most people were either slightly confused as to what the two subjects could possibly have to do with one another or they reacted with outright disapproval and/or shock upon hearing the two words coupled in the same breath. And when he did teach the class, discussions and stories abounded from his students of the ways in which they struggled to somehow get beyond the almost insurmountable wall that they felt divided their sexuality from their religiosity. One particular student, "Regina," who had been raised in a fundamentalist Protestant home, dropped the class after two weeks and subsequently began a correspondence with Phil over e-mail. She wanted him to know that she had dropped the class because the subject matter, while fascinating, was simply too painful for her. As she explained:

> When I was a little girl my mother caught me masturbating. She told me that this was a TERRIBLE thing and if she ever caught me again, she would take me to the hospital. This really confused me. That was a time I could be by myself and feel relaxed. I didn't understand what was so bad about it. So I kept doing it, and my mother would threaten me with hell and the hospital and other such

things. I would try to stop, but couldn't, so then I thought that I was some sex monster or something. So I grew up and learned to restrict my masturbation times to when my parents weren't around. But then when I became interested in boys, the new problem was sex. "Regina, don't kiss boys, don't make love to them until you're married." That is the Christian way. She gave me books not unlike the one in the packet about a guide for Christian girls. Ok. So put those two things together and here is my problem at twenty-one years. I am still a virgin. I literally cannot have sex. I have developed something called vaginismus, where my vagina closes up when confronted with intercourse. It is almost as if my mother won't let me have sex. She plugged up my vagina. I've been to the gynecologist about this and they think that I was abused as a child. I told them that Christianity can be just as frightening for a child as sexual abuse.

"Sally," raised a Catholic, recalled how excruciating it was as a young teenager to confess her sexual experiences to her priest, who vigorously condemned such experiences; she developed a strong association of guilt with sex, even sex with her husband. Then there was "Mark," who had wanted to be a priest all his life but was kicked out of the seminary for failing to cease from masturbating. Phil's in-laws, who are born-again Southern Baptists, refuse to look at any photos or watch any movies that contain any form of nudity. Although these examples are merely anecdotal, scholarly research has uncovered the depth to which the dominant Western religious traditions serve as strong barriers to sexual expression and bodily enjoyment.

Numerous contemporary studies have shown that intense religiousness correlates strongly and consistently with decreased sexual experience and pleasure. Although many of these studies are limited in scope (often restricted to white, middle-class Christian North American college students), they do provide interesting evidence that the strongly religious, in terms of both belief and participation, are less likely to engage in a variety of sexual behaviors,[25] are less likely to engage in or enjoy oral sex,[26] and are less likely to have sex before marriage.[27] Furthermore, the strongly religious are more likely to condemn masturbation,[28] are more likely to feel guilty after sex,[29] are more likely to feel guilty after even fantasizing about sex,[30] and are more likely to condemn nontraditional sexual behaviors.[31]

The most comprehensive, thorough, and valid study of sex within the United States was conducted by Robert Michael and his colleagues.[32] This study revealed that while there was little difference between the religious and nonreligious in terms of frequency of intercourse over the course of the previous year or frequency of experiencing orgasm, the nonreligious are much more likely to think about sex more often than the religious, the nonreligious are more likely to have had more sex partners overall than the religious, the nonreligious are more likely to engage in sex for longer periods of time than the religious, and the nonreligious are more likely to have engaged in anal sex than the religious. As Paul Haerich has summarized, "previous work has so typically observed a negative relationship between religiousness and sexual permissiveness that it has recently been dubbed an 'empirical generalization.' "[33]

Holes in the Wall

Of course, it is important to remember that although there does seem to be a thick wall firmly established among most religions between the sexual and the spiritual, there are holes in the wall to be sure. Most religions, even the most restrictive or sex negative, do in certain instances view sex as having at least a somewhat positive function. Take Judaism: Sexual activity (albeit strictly within heterosexual marriage) is highly encouraged and even deemed holy at times.[34] Jewish law explicitly states that a man must fulfill his wife sexually, and failure to do so is grounds for divorce. The *Iggeret Hakodesh,* an authoritative rabbinic text from the thirteenth century, additionally states that a man should withhold his ejaculation until his wife reaches orgasm first.

As mentioned earlier, Hinduism's sacred literature is rife with eroticism. One of the most popular deities in India is Krishna—"master of the sport of love." The Puranas detail Krishna's sexual prowess; he makes repeated passionate love to his consort Rhahda (employing eight positions) and seduces a group of cowherd women, making love to all of them simultaneously all night long (employing sixteen positions), and "from the climaxing of love rose a beautiful outcry, and all the women fainted no sooner than they were united. They fell still and motionless, while goose bumps covered their limbs."[35] The foundational Upanisads of Hinduism also contain their fair share of sex-positive prose. The *Brhadaranyaka Upanisad* describes the creation of humans as stemming from sexual union. Sexual metaphors abound: "Her firewood is the vulva; her smoke is the pubic hair; her flame is the vagina; when one penetrates her, that is her embers; and her sparks are the climax. In that very fire gods offer semen, and from that offering springs a man."[36]

Concerning Christianity, although there is an undeniably large and compelling body of scholarship detailing the sex-negative aspects thereof, characterizing Christianity as totally and absolutely sex negative is clearly inaccurate and irresponsible. Although it is the only world religion to have a canonically asexual savior/messiah (Jesus),[37] and the only world religion to have an asexual founder (Paul), Christianity has never been uniformly negative on matters of sex. From its earliest beginnings, Christianity's sex-negative elements have always jostled with more sex-positive strains.[38] In I Corinthians 7:18, Paul openly declared the fundamentally sexual elements and rights within marriage: "The husband should give to his wife her conjugal rights, and likewise the wife to her husband. For the wife does not have authority over her own body, but the husband does; likewise the husband does not have authority over his own body, but the wife does. Do not deprive one another."

Many contemporary Christians believe that sexual pleasure (although strictly within heterosexual marriage) is an important part of a happy, healthy life.[39] Even the most conservative evangelical Christians advocate that a healthy sex life is an important part of Christian well-being. For instance, Timothy and Beverly LaHaye's best-selling manual for married Christian couples, *The Act of Marriage,* is quite explicit in terms of sexual information, instruction, and activities.[40]

Islam also contains many positive sexual elements. For instance, the Qu'ran speaks well of sex (again, strictly heterosexual and within marriage) and promises a sensual, erotic afterlife for men who live lives according to the laws of God. According to the *Hadith,* Muhammed despised celibacy and was known for his sexual prowess; it was said that he could satisfy all his wives and concubines (a total of fourteen) in one hour.

Even in Buddhism, there are the *Tantric* traditions (secret esoteric techniques of meditation) that bring together enlightenment and sexual ecstasy.

A Matter of Regulation

Thus far we have conceptualized the relationship between sex and religion in terms of "sex-positive" and "sex-negative" strains. We have spoken of sex and religion in union and in conflict. We have spoken of a wall of separation that exists between the sexual and the spiritual—and the various holes that permeate that wall. Clearly, on the matter of sex and religion, there is great diversity between, as well as within, religions.

But what all religions do have in common when it comes to sex is *regulation.* To varying degrees and concerning different aspects, all religions regulate sex in some manner. All religious groups establish various sexual guidelines, restrictions, proscriptions, and boundaries.[41]

For example, traditional Judaism blesses sex, but only sex between a man and woman who are married and are touching one another during appropriate times of the month, careful to avoid the impurity of menstruation. Official Catholicism affirms sexual relations between husband and wife, but the use of contraception is condemned.

Sexual regulation is often quite different for men than for women within a given religious tradition. For instance, early Mormonism allowed for one type of sexual life for married men, but quite another for married women; as God revealed to Joseph Smith: "if a man espouse a virgin, and desire to espouse another . . . if he have ten virgins . . . he is justified . . . But if one or either of the ten virgins . . . shall be with another man, she has committed adultery and shall be destroyed."[42] Within Islam, according to the Qu'ran, men may marry up to four wives; women, of course, may marry only one man. In the case of Hinduism, although the Upanisads mentioned earlier proscribe rituals and recitations for the positive enjoyment of sex, they also declare that if a woman refuses sex, a man "should beat her with a stick or with his fists and overpower her."[43]

No religious tradition is without some form of sexual regulation, even the most sexually liberal. For example, earlier we spoke of the Oneida Perfectionists. The Oneida Perfectionists conceptualized sex as natural and even spiritual. They practiced "free love"—a form of communal sex in which each member was sexually available to all. But even this seemingly sexually "free" religion wasn't totally free. The Oneida Perfectionists still regulated sex; the men of this community were instructed to have sex but to practice "male continence," known technically as *coitus reservatus* (not ejaculating). Also, sexual exclusivity was forbidden. If two people had a strong affinity for one another and wanted to remain each other's sole sexual partner, such a relationship was not allowed; the pair was broken up and their exclusive connection severed. And of course, sex with children was condemned, as was rape, incest, and homosexuality.

Grappling with homosexuality—often in terms of condemnation—is a prominent aspect of sexual regulation in almost every religious tradition; certainly in all major world religions.[44] Within ancient Judaism, according to Leviticus 20:13, male–male sex was an offense punishable by death. Today, however, many Jewish movements such as Reform and Reconstructionist Judaism are openly supportive of gay rights, and the Israeli government officially legalized homosexual relations in 1988. Within traditional Islam, according to the Qu'ran, homosexuality is an indecency worthy of punishment.[45] Unfortunately, Islam's condemnation of homosexuality currently enjoys tremendous hegemony, and openly gay/lesbian Muslim organizations are only barely beginning to emerge in the Muslim world.[46] Within the Christian scriptures, in Romans 1:32 those who practice such wickedness and evil as homosexuality "deserve to die." Of course, today there are many openly gay Christians and gay Christian congregations, as well as gay-supportive movements within a variety of Christian denominations such as Integrity (Episcopalian), Lutherans Concerned, Presbyterians for Gay and Lesbians Concerned, and Affirmation (United Methodist).[47] Buddhism's approach to homosexuality has been characterized as one of neutrality—with the ultimate issue of concern being one between sexuality and celibacy in general, rather than hetero versus homo, specifically.[48] Hinduism's various sources provide for much ambiguity concerning homosexuality, generally considering it a vice worthy of disapproval, but nowhere condemning it as harshly as traditional Judaism, Christianity, or Islam.[49] The Baha'i religion explicitly forbids homosexuality, considering it both unnatural and immoral.[50] Interestingly, most restrictions and condemnations of homosexuality focus on male–male sex, and either treat female–female sex less harshly or altogether ignore it.[51]

In almost every religion, "sex" is regulated to such a degree that it is essentially understood as that which takes place between a male and a female, generally within marriage. Controversial radio and television Jewish talk-show host Laura Schlessinger[52] has declared that "Holy sex is between husband and wife . . . Unholy sex is everything else," and this heterosexist, sex-only-within-marriage sentiment basically sums up the traditional sexual regulatory schemas of most religions, especially in the West.

Whether condemning homosexuality or incest, denouncing premarital sex or bestiality, encouraging multiple sexual partners or celibacy, lauding a variety of sexual positions or condemning masturbation, or encouraging or denouncing female sexual license, all religious traditions have some form of sexual regulation. And more often than not, that regulation is quite restrictive. Early Christian theologians such as Augustine regarded any sexual activity that was engaged in for the purpose of pleasure, even that between a husband and wife, as sinful. Biblical Judaism required that women be virgins upon marriage or possibly face the death penalty.[53] Islam forbids sex outside of marriage, especially for women. Catholicism to this day forbids its presumably most pious members (priests and nuns) from engaging in any sexual experiences at all. Within the Eastern traditions, such as Buddhism and Hinduism, those who choose the deepest spiritual paths must forgo sex altogether; celibacy is virtually welded to advanced piety.

Though ever-contested and internally debated, almost every religion tends to limit all sex to that which is hetero in nature and takes place only within marriage. Masturbation tends to be frowned upon, if not explicitly forbidden. Sexual indulgence for the sake of pure pleasure in and of itself is often condemned. The "virtuosos" (i.e., the priests, monks, nuns, lamas, gurus, and various leaders) of many religions worldwide forgo sex altogether. Seldom, if ever, is sex seen as a spiritual activity in and of itself. Rather, in most religious systems, sex is either tolerated or accepted, but only under specifically restrictive circumstances, or is simply forbidden or condemned altogether.

Explaining Restrictive Regulation

Why such strict sexual regulation? Why do so many religious traditions consider sex innately inimical to advanced spiritual enlightenment? Why does Paul's teaching that sex and prayer are mutually exclusive activities[54] enjoy such widespread, nearly universal hegemony?

According to Max Weber, sexual love is the "greatest irrational force of life,"[55] and as religions became more rationalized and intellectualized, this irrational force had to be controlled, harnessed, and ultimately overcome. James Brundage concurs, arguing that human sexuality is such a powerful, explosive force that it requires strict regulation by any group, religious in this case, seeking to establish authority.[56] Meredith McGuire speaks of the "chaotic power of sexuality" that religion must control in its effort to provide order in people's lives.[57] Thus, this theory views sex as a powerful, irrational, chaotic force that needs to be subdued/condemned, which explains why it developed as an antagonistic element in many religious systems.

One cannot help wondering though, if Weber and the others just mentioned don't have the causal sequence wrong. In indigenous religions (e.g., Native American or Australian cultures), sex was seen as a natural process, no more chaotic or irrational than eating or sleeping, and the coupling between men and women did not require legal or religious sanction (no vows, no contracts). It is only in the major world religions that sex requires such regulation. Could it be that these traditions see sex as chaotic and irrational *because* they would like to control it?

Others have argued that sexuality lost its sacred status with the decline of matriarchal societies and the increased dominance of patriarchal religion.[58] The degradation of sex is tied to the attempt to control women. Some scholars argue that men's desire to control women was motivated by fear. Ancient tribal cultures, though they connected the act of sex with reproduction, did not fully understand the reproductive process, and women were perceived to have magical powers closely tied to their sexuality. Female sexuality could lead to new life (the birth of a child) or to bleeding and death (menstruation), whereas men had no such powers. A woman's sexuality, therefore, was dangerous and had to be controlled.[59] Other scholars argue that the rise of patriarchy was motivated by more pragmatic concerns.[60] Sex in ancient tribal cultures was not always monogamous, and family ties were often traced through the maternal line. But once men understood their role in the reproductive process, they sought to lay claim to their own offspring.[61] The only way a man could be certain that a boy was his son was to regulate the sexual activity of women. Unregulated sexuality, therefore, was defined as dangerous. Whether it was fear or desire for heirs that gave rise to patriarchy, once sex is seen as dangerous, it is but a small step to label it evil.

The problem with this theory is its implication that patriarchal religion would always be ascetic. It is not! Indeed, the most famous example of a religion embracing sexuality, the *Kama Sutra,* was explicitly written for the benefit of upper-caste Indian males. The fact that ancient Hindu scriptures venerate goddesses and celebrate sexuality has not historically translated into empowerment for Indian women. If religions are antisexual because they are patriarchal, then why do some prosexual religions also oppress women?

Perhaps the antagonism between sex and religion can be traced to sex's linkage with the body. Many religions seek to commune with and emphasize the eternal, the immortal, the everlasting. The body is none of these things; the body decays, withers, dies, and eventually rots. Therefore, many religions see the body as impermanent and thus of lesser value than the soul, which is understood as eternal and transcendent. Anything associated with the body is subsequently deemed not only of less importance, but often unholy. Sex, of course, is deeply associated with the body. In fact, the body is its universe. Because most religions focus on the eternal, and because the body is not eternal, and because sex is ultimately a celebration of the body, it perhaps makes sense that religions would develop a hostility toward sexual activity, envisioning it as a feast of the impermanent, an indulgence of the transitory. As Paul writes in Romans 8:13, "For if you live by the flesh, you will die."

If the body draws the soul away from what should be its true ultimate concern, it is no wonder that many religions see sex as a distraction from or competition with spiritual matters. Buddhist monks were instructed to visualize decaying corpses while meditating to prevent contemplation of sexual fantasies that often distracted them. And when Phil once asked a Hare Krishna in Eugene, Oregon, why he practiced celibacy, he replied, "Sex is a distraction from the true source of real ecstasy," the latter being communion with his god Krishna.

Indeed, many religions view sex not only as a distraction, but as outright competition—and tough competition, at that. In sex, one derives overwhelming satisfaction directly from another person or from one's self, rather than from a god, spirit, religious leader, and so forth. Sex is so intrinsically powerful and visceral that it certainly could be viewed as ultimately threatening religious hegemony. After all, it is possible to "lose one's self" while experiencing sexual pleasure, to achieve a state of transcendence, to feel at peace, to feel released, liberated, and loved—all of which are often the manifest goals of religious systems. From this viewpoint, sex is conceptualized as an archrival that is natural and perhaps even more powerful than religion. Sex is the sugar to religion's NutraSweet.

But if sex and the body distract the soul from religious pursuits, then how is it possible for some religions (albeit the minority) to incorporate, assimilate, and synthesize sex into religious practice? In Hindu, Buddhist, and Taoist *tantra,* contemplating sexual images is not a distraction but sometimes the focus of meditation, and sexual activity itself may be performed as a meditative exercise. Given how much effort it takes to control sexuality in the more ascetic religions, one wonders why it is that these traditions became dominant.

Why the Relationship?

Whether existing in a state of harmony or hostility, sex and religion are inextricably tied. Sexual themes and teachings, be they positive or negative, permeate religious texts. Religious prayers, rituals, lamentations, dances, and other such activities can be, and often are, highly sensual—almost direct sublimations of the sexual urge. One's religiosity can greatly affect one's sexuality, be it in terms of liberation or restriction. One's sexuality can greatly affect one's religiosity, drawing some toward and others away from religion. No matter how one sets one's lens on the subject matter of sex and religion, it seems the two can't seem to get away from one another. Why?

To answer that, one first needs to explain religion, which of course is no easy task.[62] Yet if we survey the many theories of religion that have been provided, ultimately two basic explanations emerge: Religion is either what people receive from Above or it is what people create here on earth.[63] That is, religion can be understood as either a primarily genuine embodiment of transcendent revelation or as ultimately a human construction.[64] The former theory, that religion is something people receive from the holy "Other" is best represented by the texts and/or teachings of the religious: the Jewish Torah, the Christian Scriptures, the Qu'ran, the Book of Mormon, the Upanishads, the Adi Granth, and so on. The latter theory, which views religion as a social or psychological construction, is best represented by the works of Ludwig Feuerbach, Friedrich Nietzsche, Sigmund Freud, Karl Marx, Emile Durkheim, Peter Berger, Stewart Elliot Guthrie, Robert Hinde, Michael Shermer, and other social scientists.

How one explains the tight relationship between sex and religion will depend on how one explains religion. Thus, if one subscribes to the belief that religion is, at root, Revelation, then one would have to conclude that the reason religion and sex are so intimately tied is because god/the gods have a significant and pronounced interest in human sex and sexuality. That interest may be one of erotic voyeurism or ascetic condemnation. It may be concerned with love or with maintaining a particular social order. But either way, the gods care deeply about what we do with our bodies and how we experience (or don't, as the case may be) bodily pleasure.

On the flip side, if one believes that religion is, at root, a human construction, then the linkage of sex and religion makes perfect sense because being sexual and grappling with sexuality are intimately linked to being human. To be human is to be sexualized in one way or another. The social-constructionist viewpoint tends to see religion as one great human social and/or psychological projection. In other words, humans comprise the film and the projector, and religion is what gets projected onto the screen. Because sex—either resisting it or indulging in it—is an integral part of what it means to be human, the religious projection will obviously reflect that.

Overview of This Book

Religion and sex are forever connected—either because the gods are fixated on sex or because humans are fixated on sex. Whichever it is (and readers will have to make up their own mind on this), the relationship between sex and religion is fascinating, mysterious, and clearly deserving of explanation. This book will help you understand the nature of that relationship. You will learn about sex and religion in both ancient world religions (Hinduism, Buddhism, Confucianism, Taoism, Judaism, Christianity, and Islam) and new American religions (Mormons and The Family/Children of God). Although there are many new religious movements in the United States, we chose to include chapters on the Mormons and The Family/Children of God because they are religious movements that nonmembers and the popular media often associate with unusual sexual practices—polygamy (Mormonism) and prostitution (Children of God/The Family)—even though, in both cases, the official churches no longer endorse these practices. By directly covering these two religious movements, we seek to help separate fact from fiction and help readers to understand the relationship between these groups and so-called mainstream Christianity.[65]

In each chapter, you will learn about both the historical development and contemporary interpretations of religious beliefs and practices pertaining to sex. To ensure that each tradition is covered fairly and comprehensively, each chapter is written by an expert specializing in the study of that particular religion. Each chapter contains three sections. The first section begins with a brief introduction to the religion, including its origins, distinctive beliefs and practices, central texts, and the geographical distribution of the majority of adherents. The section then moves to a discussion of sex and religion, with primary emphasis on the contemporary context. It examines official religious teachings about sex as well as popular practices that may or may not be consistent with the former (e.g., Islamic law endorses polygamy but not the harem). The section explains contemporary challenges to these teachings and practices (e.g., feminism, gay rights, science, biblical criticism) and presents the major interpretive debates over how to respond to those challenges (e.g., liberals vs. conservatives, Protestants vs. Catholics, absolutist vs. situation ethics). The second section raises questions for further discussion, and the final section is a list of recommended readings and audiovisual resources.

Whether you are curious about the sexual practices of other religious cultures or simply want to know more about sex in your own religion, this book will answer some of your questions. In doing so, the book may help you make more informed decisions regarding your sexuality and/or your faith commitment, as well as develop empathy for the decisions made by others. If we have done our job right, the book will also raise new questions that will take you beyond what has been covered in these pages. So come join us on what promises to be a fascinating and thought-provoking journey!

ENDNOTES

1. While precise definitions of both "sex" and "religion" are virtually impossible to agree upon, we define religion as *beliefs, rituals, experiences, and institutions that humans construct based upon their understandings of the transcendent, holy, otherworldly, spiritual, or divine.* We define sex as *bodily experiences that humans conceive of as erotic, sensual, carnal, genitally related, or orgasmically significant.*

2. McGuire, Meredith. 1997. *Religion: The Social Context.* Belmont, CA: Wadsworth Publishing Company, p. 66.

3. Turner, Bryan S. 1991. *Religion and Social Theory.* London: Sage, p. 112.

4. See also Wright and D'Antonio's similar discussion of "restrictionist" vs. "liberationist" religious orientations to sex in "Families and New Religions" in *Religion and the Social Order,* edited by David Bromley and Jeffrey Hadden, 1993, Vol. 3A: 219–238. Greenwich, CT: JAI Press.

5. Foster, Lawrence. 1984. *Religion and Sexuality: The Shakers, the Mormons, and the Oneida Community.* Urbana, IL: University of Illinois Press.

6. Ibid., p. 80.

7. Ibid., p. 94.

8. See Benko, Stephen. 1993. *The Virgin Goddess.* Leiden: E. J. Brill; Brundage, James. 1987. *Law, Sex, and Christian Society in Medieval Europe.* Chicago: University of Chicago Press; Farnell, L. R. 1896. *The Cults of the Greek States.* Oxford: Clarendon Press; Tannahill, Reay. 1980. *Sex in History.* New York: Stein and Day; Weber, Max. 1946. "Religious Rejections of the World and Their Directions" in *From Max Weber,* H. Gerth and C. Mills (eds.). New York: Oxford University Press.

9. Dening, Sarah. 1996. *The Mythology of Sex.* New York: Macmillan.

10. Henshaw, Richard A. 1994. *Female and Male: The Cultic Personnel, the Bible, and the Rest of the Ancient Near East.* Alison Park, PA: Pickwick Press.

11. Lerner, Gerda. 1986. *The Creation of Patriarchy.* New York: Oxford University Press, pp. 129–130.

12. See Oden, Robert. 1987. *The Bible Without Theology.* San Francisco: Harper and Row Publishers.

13. Brundage, James. 1987. *Law, Sex, and Christian Society in Medieval Europe.* Chicago: University of Chicago Press, p. 11.

14. Benko, Stephen. 1993. *The Virgin Goddess.* Leiden: E. J. Brill, p. 69.

15. Dimmitt, Cornelia, and van Buitenen, J. A. B. 1978. *Classical Hindu Mythology.* Philadelphia: Temple University Press.

16. See Pagels, Elaine. 1988. *Adam, Eve, and the Serpent*. New York: Vintage Books; Ranke-Heinemann, Uta. 1988. *Eunuchs for Heaven*. London: Andre Deutsch.

17. Twain, Mark. 1938. *Letters from the Earth*. New York: Harper and Row, p. 17.

18. See Hamington, Maurice. 1995. *Hail Mary?* New York: Routledge; Harris, Kevin. 1984. *Sex, Ideology, and Religion*. Totowa, NJ: Barnes and Noble Books; Highwater, Jamake. 1990. *Myth and Sexuality*. New York: Penguin; Parrinder, Geoffrey. 1980. *Sexual Morality in the World's Religions*. Oxford, England: Oneworld Publications.

19. Quoted in Lengermann, Patricia, and Niebrugge-Brantley, Jill. 1998. *The Women Founders: Sociology and Social Theory 1830–1930*. Boston: McGraw-Hill, p. 216.

20. Ranke-Heinemann, Uta. 1988. *Eunuchs for Heaven*. London: Andre Deutsch, p. 62.

21. Brundage, James. 1987. *Law, Sex, and Christian Society in Medieval Europe*. Chicago: University of Chicago Press, p. 6.

22. Osborne, Lawrence. 1993. *The Poisoned Embrace*. New York: Pantheon Books.

23. Brundage, James. 1987. *Law, Sex, and Christian Society in Medieval Europe*. Chicago: University of Chicago Press, p. 8.

24. Mernissi, Fatima. 1987. *Beyond the Veil: Male–Female Dynamics in Modern Muslim Society*. Bloomington, IN: Indiana University Press.

25. Samuels, Herbert. 1997. "The Relationship among Selected Demographics and Conventional and Unconventional Sexual Behaviors among Black and White Heterosexual Men." *Journal of Sex Research*, 34(1): 85–92; Mahoney, E.R. 1980. "Religiosity and Sexual Behavior among Heterosexual College Students." *Journal of Sex Research*, 16(1): 97–113.

26. Herold, Edward, and Way, Leslie. 1983. "Oral-Genital Sexual Behavior in a Sample of University Females." *Journal of Sex Research*, 19(4): 327–338.

27. Beck, Scott, Cole, Bettie, and Hammond, Judith. 1991. "Religious Heritage and Premarital Sex: Evidence from a National Sample of Young Adults." *Journal for the Scientific Study of Religion*, 30(2): 173–180.

28. Gagnon, John. 1985. "Attitudes and Responses of Parents to Pre-Adolescent Masturbation." *Archives of Sexual Behavior*, 14(5): 451–466.

29. Wyatt, Gail, and Dunn, Kristi. 1991. "Examining Predictors of Sex Guilt in Multiethnic Samples of Women." *Archives of Sexual Behavior*, 20(5): 471–485.

30. Gil, Vincent. 1990. "Sexual Fantasy Experiences and Guilt among Conservative Christians: An Exploratory Study." *Journal of Sex Research*, 27(4): 629–638.

31. Bibby, Reginald. 1996. "Sex and the Single Parishioner." Paper presented at the Annual Meeting of the Society for the Scientific Study of Religion, Nov. 10 (Sunday) Nashville, Tennessee; Herek, Gregory. 1988. "Heterosexuals' Attitudes toward Lesbians and Gay Men: Correlates and Gender Differences." *Journal of Sex Research*, 25(4): 451–477.

32. Michael, Robert, Gagnon, John, Laumann, Edward, and Kolata, Gina. 1995. *Sex in America*. New York: Warner Books.

33. Haerich, Paul. 1992. "Premarital Sexual Permissiveness and Religious Orientation: A Preliminary Investigation." *Journal for the Scientific Study of Religion*, 31(3): 361–365.

34. Biale, David. 1992. *Eros and the Jews*. San Francisco: Basic Books.

35. Dimmitt, Cornelia, and van Buitenen, J. A. B. 1978. *Classical Hindu Mythology*. Philadelphia: Temple University Press, p. 129.

36. *Brhadaranyaka Upanisad* 6.2.13.

37. It must be acknowledged that there is a limited but important amount of scholarship that argues that Jesus was not asexual, but a very sensual, carnal, and even possibly sexual being. For instance, see *The Sexuality of Jesus* by William Phipps, 1996, Cleveland, OH: Pilgrim Press. However, the point here is that Jesus—as he is constructed in the canonical Gospels—is asexual. A compelling case could be made that he was possibly homosexually oriented, but even then, there is no direct canonical scriptural evidence of an actual homosexual sex taking place. Of course, the entire argument could be relatively moot if he never even existed at all, as many have recently argued; see *The Jesus Puzzle* by Earl Doherty, 1999, Ottawa, Canada: Canadian Humanist Press; *The Fabrication of the Christ Myth* by Harold Leidner, 2000, Tampa, FL: Survey Books; *The Jesus Mysteries* by Timothy Freke and Peter Gandy, 1999, New York: Harmony Books.

38. Pagels, Elaine. 1988. *Adam, Eve, and the Serpent*. New York: Vintage Books.

39. Taylor, Michael J., editor. 1972. *Sex: Thoughts for Contemporary Christians*. Garden City, NY: Doubleday.

40. LaHaye, Timothy, and LaHaye, Beverly. 1998. *The Act of Marriage: The Beauty of Sexual Love*. Grand Rapids, MI: Zondervan Publishing House. See also Grenz, Stanley. 1997. *Sexual Ethics: An Evangelical Perspective*. Louisville, KY: Westminster/John Knox Press; LaHaye, Timothy, LaHaye, Beverly, and Yorkey, Mike. 2000. *The Act of Marriage After 40: Making Love for Life*. Grand Rapids, MI: Zondervan Publishing House; Wheat, Ed, and Okes Perkins, Gloria. 1996. *Love Life for Every Married Couple*. Grand Rapids, MI: Zondervan Publishing House.

41. See Isaacson, Lynne. 1995. "Rule Making and Rule Breaking in a Jesus Community" in *Religion and the Social Order*, Vol. 5, Mary Jo Neitz and Marion Goldman (eds.). Greenwich, CT: JAI Press; Goldman, Marion. "From Promiscuity to Celibacy: Women and Sexual Regulation at Rajneeshpuram" in *Religion and the Social Order*, Vol. 5, Mary Jo Neitz and Marion Goldman (eds.). Greenwich, CT: JAI Press; Muncy, R. L. 1973. *Sex and Marriage in Utopian Communities*. Baltimore, MD: Penguin Books; Wagner, J. editor. 1982. *Sex Roles in Contemporary American Communes*. Bloomington, IN: Indiana University Press.

42. Doctrines and Covenants 132: 61–63.

43. *Brhadaranyaka Upanisad* 6.4.7.

44. Comstock, Gary David, and Henking, Susan. 1997. *Que(e)rying Religion*. New York: Continuum; Swidler, Arlene, editor. 1993. *Homosexuality and the World Religions*. Valley Forge, PA: Trinity Press International.

45. *Al Nisa* 4:13.

46. Duran, Khalid. 1993. "Homosexuality and Islam" in *Homosexuality and the World Religions*, Arlene Swidler (ed.). Valley Forge, PA: Trinity Press International. It should be noted, however, that in the United States, there does exist one major openly gay/lesbian Muslim organization, Al-Fatiha, with chapters in major cities across the country.

47. Ellison, Marvin. 1993. "Homosexuality and Protestantism" in *Homosexuality and the World Religions,* Arlene Swindler (ed.). Valley Forge, PA: Trinity Press International.

48. Cabezon, Jose Ignazio. 1993. "Homosexuality and Buddhism" in *Homosexuality and the World Religions,* Arlene Swidler (ed.). Valley Forge, PA: Trinity Press International.

49. Sharma, Arvind. 1993. "Homosexuality and Hinduism" in *Homosexuality and the World Religions,* Arlene Swidler (ed.). Valley Forge, PA: Trinity Press International.

50. Parrinder, Geoffrey. 1980. *Sexual Morality in the World's Religions.* Oxford: Oneworld Publications.

51. Jordan, Mark. 1997. *The Invention of Sodomy in Christian Theology.* Chicago: University of Chicago Press; Cabezon, Jose Ignazio. 1993. "Homosexuality and Buddhism," in *Homosexuality and the World Religions,* Arlene Swidler (ed.). Valley Forge, PA: Trinity Press International; Boyarin, Daniel. 1993. *Carnal Israel.* Berkeley, CA: University of California Press; Faure, Bernard. 1998. *The Red Thread: Buddhist Approaches to Sexuality.* Princeton, NJ: Princeton University Press.

52. Schlessinger, Laura. 1998. *The Ten Commandments: The Significance of God's Laws in Everyday Life.* New York: Cliff Street Books.

53. See Deuteronomy 22:13–21.

54. I Corinthians 7:5.

55. Weber, Max. 1946. "Religious Rejections of the World and Their Directions" in *From Max Weber,* H. Gerth and C. Mills (eds.). New York: Oxford University Press, p. 343.

56. Brundage, James. 1987. *Law, Sex, and Christian Society in Medieval Europe.* Chicago: University of Chicago Press, p. 1.

57. McGuire, Meredith. 1997. *Religion: The Social Context.* Belmont, CA: Wadsworth Publishing Company, p. 66.

58. Eisler, Riane. 1995. *Sacred Pleasure.* San Francisco: Harper-Collins; Stone, Merlin. 1976. *When God Was a Woman.* San Diego: Harcourt Brace and Company.

59. Ruether, Rosemary Radford. 1983. *Sexism and God-Talk.* Boston: Beacon Press.

60. Tannahill, Reay. 1980. *Sex in History.* New York: Stein and Day.

61. Engels, Frederick. 1972. *The Origin of the Family, Private Property and the State.* New York: International Publishers.

62. Thrower, James. 1999. *Religion: The Classical Theories.* Washington, D.C.: Georgetown University Press; Guthrie, Stewart Elliott. 1996. "Religion: What is it?" *Journal for the Scientific Study of Religion,* 35(4): 412–419.

63. Randall Collins, 1992. *Sociological Insight.* New York: Oxford University Press, p. 30.

64. Zuckermanm Phil. 2003. *Invitation to the Sociology of Religion.* New York: Routledge; Thrower, James. 1999. *Religion: The Classical Theories.* Washington, D.C.: Georgetown University Press.

65. In future editions, we hope to include chapters on non-Christian new religious movements, such as Wicca, Scientology, and Hare Krishnas/ISKCON. Unfortunately, the authors we had wanted to write these chapters were not available.

Chapter 2

Hinduism

Rita Dasgupta Sherma

Contemporary Western perceptions of Hindu sexuality range from the hedonistically erotic to the aridly ascetic. There is a tendency to view Hindu sexual mores in light of *tantric* sex, the *Kama Sutra,* and the late guru Rajneesh's "love communes" on the one hand, or through the halo of saintly celibacy that surrounds figures such as Mahatma Gandhi, monastic gurus, and meditating yogis, on the other. The actual facts of Hindu sexual mores and gender roles are, of course, far more complex. Gender and sexuality are viewed in relation to, and in continuum with, the natural laws of the cosmic order. It is not simply a question of sex as sin or sacrament, but a question of how a most powerful energy, a creative potency, can be harnessed and channeled for a community's well-being in material life and an individual's liberation in spiritual life.

To examine the place and position of sexuality in the Hindu ethos, therefore, it is first necessary to understand the Hindu conception of the relationship between the divine order and the human order. I will explore this connection historically in the following section after a brief overview of the Hindu theological framework.

The Hindu Religion

With over 800 million adherents, Hinduism is considered a major world religion. But for many Hindus it is not a religion so much as a way of understanding and acting harmoniously with the nature of reality. The term "Hindu," coined by the Persians, is not an indigenous term. Traditionally, no clear demarcations existed between the traditions now labeled "Hindu" and other Indian spiritual paths.

18

The different Hindu theologies do diverge, but they also share commonalities based on shared metaphysical and organic categories. Some of the shared conceptions of important Hindu theological traditions include:

1. The existence of a positive Ultimate Reality (Brahman) that is eternal, the source of all manifestation, immanent in the cosmos, yet unconditioned by it.

2. The twofold nature of Brahman: The Hindu conception of the Divine is bilevel and represents the two-stage experience of the Divine that is reported by Hindu mystics. First, Brahman as Ultimate Reality transcendent of the manifest cosmos that is without any characteristics whatsoever (*nirguna*) and is described only as Being-Consciousness-Bliss (*satchitananda*), which is descriptive of the experience of Nirguna Brahman that the sages are said to have known. Second, Brahman as the creative agent behind the universe of forms and phenomena is Brahman *with* characteristics (*saguna*). Saguna Brahman is closer to a theistic conception and can be equated to the English word "God." This two-stage experience of the Divine is integrated into the vision of most major Hindu theologies, even if there are distinctions in the details.

3. A transphysical or "Higher Self" (*paramatman*) that is related to Brahman as sparks of a fire are related to the fire itself. The *paramatman* is sometimes referred to as the "oversoul."

4. The possibility of transcending the limitations of normal cognition and experiencing the self as the *paramatman,* rather than identifying the self with the ego (this is the goal of liberation, or *mukti, moksha*).

5. The necessity of spiritual practice—such as ritual worship, the chanting of sacred sounds (*mantras*), yoga, and meditation—for catalyzing liberation.

6. The cyclic nature of the cosmos: The cosmos is manifest, sustained, reabsorbed, and recreated as an eternal cycle of Brahman's self-manifestation and withdrawal.

7. Rebirth as containing the potential for the evolution of the individual soul and of human culture: Rebirth is associated with the possibility of spiritual growth and with the law of *karma* (action). This law teaches that all actions have consequences that teach the Self lessons that need to be learned. To gain total insight into the true nature of the Self is to have a proper understanding of the nature of reality—for the same Brahman pervades both—and to overcome the need to learn from embodied life experience.

8. The importance of virtuous conduct for spiritual growth: Virtuous conduct is required of both the ordinary householder and the renunciant who has given up material life to seek liberation.

9. Acceptance of different theological interpretations: Because Brahman is ultimately ineffable, no rigid dogma can capture the totality.

10.   Spiritual development, or the movement toward enlightenment and
liberation as the ultimate goal of life.

Religion, for many Hindus, is a Western concept that involves a fixed starting point with a specific and self-conscious historical stance; clear-cut and
exclusive dogma; a self-understanding that is grounded in the specificities of
doctrine; and a distinction between activities or arenas deemed sacred and
those deemed secular or profane. Hindus are often uncomfortable with the
designation "religion" because Hinduism does not fit very well with the above
categories. Hindu categories evince greater fluidity between the mundane
activities of human life and the patterns of the divine and cosmic orders.

Historically, there has been a sense of continuity between Ultimate Reality
and conventional reality. Thus, ordinary activities such as sexuality have had
significance over and above the lives of the individual performers. To act in
harmony with the understood order of the cosmos was to become part of that
order. To live a life properly grounded in the knowledge that the Self is an
extension of the greater whole was not just helpful for one's spiritual development, but also important for the proper functioning of the greater order.

A Historical Overview of Hindu Attitudes toward Sexuality

The origins of Hinduism are rooted in three cultural spheres: that of the Indus
valley civilization that thrived in northwest India from about 2500 B.C.E. to
1500 B.C.E.; the traditions of the Sanskrit-speaking peoples who call themselves *Arya,* or "noble ones"; and the cultures of the indigenous Dravidian
and tribal peoples.

There is controversy about the origins of the Sanskrit-speaking peoples
(Aryans) and their relationship to the Indus civilization. Because Sanskrit is part
of the Indo-European linguistic family and is related to both Latin and Farsi,
the language of Iran, some speculate that Aryan tribes arrived in south Asia
around 1500 B.C.E. and slowly migrated across the fertile plains of north India,
replacing the Indus civilization and its influences. However, no archaeological
or textual evidence supports this theory. The other possibility that has been
considered is that the Sanskrit culture was an offshoot of the Indus civilization
and is native to the region. Whatever the facts of the matter may prove to be,
the traditions now called Hindu were formed through the interaction and synthesis between the Aryan and the non-Aryan cultures in South Asia.

As the Sanskrit-speaking Aryans spread over India, they encountered and
assimilated the religious methods and ritual practices of earlier, indigenous
peoples. The Aryans were originally nomadic and venerated celestial divinities. They sought to bring to earth, through their fire-based sacred rites, the
fecundity and munificence that existed in the celestial realms. They composed
the earliest Hindu scriptures, the four-part Veda. The period of 1200 B.C.E. to
about 900 B.C.E. is thought to be the era of the composition of the Veda and is
referred to as the Vedic age; it is characterized by a highly ritualized way of
life centered around the sacrificial fire in which offerings of milk, clarified
butter, grains and so forth were placed.

Family life was paramount, and marriage was necessary for the proper maintenance of the fire rituals. In the early Vedic period, women were active participants with their husbands in the sacrificial rights and rituals that were the foci of Vedic religion. Women seemed to have access to education and religious initiations. They were also joint owners (*dampati*) with their husbands of the household and property. Because fecundity—both human and agricultural—was associated with wealth, and therefore prized, a woman's sexuality, as the harbinger of fertility, was an auspicious thing. It is significant that a woman had the right to perform the sacrificial rites alone, if her husband was away on a journey, and certain rites, particularly those which pertained to the harvest or fertility of the soil, could be performed by women alone at any time.

Sexuality during the Vedic age was associated with the powers of creation. An organic continuum was believed to exist between the cosmos and the body; the same processes flowed through both. As this passage from the *Rig Veda* [10.129] indicates, sexual metaphors were used to explain the workings of creation:

> In the beginning was darkness swathed in darkness;
> All this was but unmanifested water.
> Whatever was, that One coming into being,
> Hidden by the Void,
> Was generated by the power of heat [*tapas*].
>
> In the beginning this [One] evolved,
> Became desire [*kama*], first seed [*retas,* lit. semen] of [the] mind.[1]

Deity was seen as inherently dyadic, and great importance was attached to the notion of the complimentarity of the masculine and the feminine for the proper functioning of the cosmos and the human community. As such, the forces of nature and the innate potencies of both human and natural worlds were deified and venerated in the form of "divine couples."

By the post-Vedic period, attitudes toward sexuality and, by corollary, women's status, suffered a downturn. As a response to the excessive ritualism that came to characterize the religiosity of the late Vedic age, an ascetic and mystical era dawned with the Upanishadic period. The Upanishads, composed between the eighth and fifth centuries B.C.E., are part of the concluding section of the Vedic corpus and are therefore referred to as the Vedanta (the end of the Vedas). However, with their philosophical reflection, metaphysical insights, an emphasis on meditative knowledge of the identity of Ultimate Reality (Brahman) and the eternal Self (Atman), the Upanishads are a marked departure from the late Vedic preoccupation with effecting a continuation between the ritual and cosmic orders for the sake of material well-being.

The era of the late Upanishads coincides with the rise of ascetic movements, including the Buddhist and Jain monastic institutions in the first millennium B.C.E. Attitudes toward sexuality changed with the shift in emphasis from the organic worldviews of the Vedas that had focused on the enhancement of abundance and fertility to the metaphysical worldview of ascetic and renunciate movements that centered on the transcendence of physicality and materiality. In order to facilitate identification with the transphysical self, the body was at times described as a foul and repulsive state that must not be taken to be the true self. The following verse from the *Maitri Upanishad* [I.3] is an example of this viewpoint:

> O Revered One, in this foul-smelling, unsubstantial body, a conglomerate of bone, skin, muscle, marrow, flesh, semen, blood, mucus, tears, rheum, feces, urine, wind . . . what is the good of the enjoyment of desires? In this body which is afflicted by desire . . . separation from what is desired, union with the undesired . . . old age, death, disease, sorrow and the like, what is the good of the enjoyment of desires?[2]

The *Maitri Upanishad* [VI.10] goes on to say that a *yogi,* a true practitioner of the contemplative sciences (*yoga*), is one who shuns the stimuli of the senses: "Even as there is no one to touch the sensual women who have entered into an empty house, so he who does not touch objects of sense that enter into him is a renouncer, a contemplator [*yogi*], a performer of self-sacrifice."[3]

By 200 C.E., the first written systemization of the principles of *yoga* appear in the *Yoga Sutras of Patanjali.*[4] This text is highly revered and forms the basis for many of the later yoga traditions that evolved in India, including Hatha Yoga. The *Yoga Sutras* lay out in terse statements the fundamental eightfold path of yoga, which includes moral injunctions and ethical restraints as well as guidelines for postures, breathing, cleansing, concentration, and meditation. But the text also intends to encourage a clear sense of distinction between the true self (eternal and free) and the body/mind complex (ephemeral and bound). *Yoga Sutra* 2.40 states: "From the practice of purification, aversion to one's own body is developed. And thus aversion extends to contact with other bodies." Texts such as these, intended for study by renunciants, display negative perceptions not only of sexuality but, as above, of embodiment itself.

The two opposing impulses represented respectively by the organic and the metaphysical worldviews have been in creative tension throughout Hindu history. Attempts to affect an accommodation between the two views are visible in Hindu social institutions such as the four stages of life (the *ashramas*). These stages are student, married householder, forest-dwelling hermit, and wondering ascetic sage. Celibacy characterizes three of the four stages, but the most important stage—on which the other three depend—is married life with its attendant sexuality and procreation.

One of the first and most important efforts at reconciliation between world-engagement and world-renunciation is the *Bhagavad Gita* (the "Song of the Lord"), the best loved and most influential of all Hindu scriptures. The *Gita* is part of the *Mahabharata,* which, at over 100,000 stanzas, is most likely the longest poem ever written. Along with the *Ramayana,* it is considered one of the two great Hindu epics. The initial composition of the *Mahabharata* probably dates to the fourth century B.C.E., but amendments may have been added until as late as the third and fourth centuries C.E. An incarnation of God, Krishna is a divine hero of the *Mahabharata* and the "Lord" whose song is the *Gita.*[5]

The most important message of the *Gita* is that there is no opposition between action *in* the world and renunciation *of* the world, as long as all action is undertaken in a spirit of virtuousness, and enacted without desire for the fruits of the action, as an offering to God. Sexual action is also just an "action" and is only a source of problems when it arises from a wrong mind-set and is enmeshed in selfish expectations. Of sex that is governed by nonattachment and virtuous conduct, Krishna says: "I am the strength of the strong . . . I am sensual pleasure (*kama*) that is not in opposition to righteous conduct (*dharma*)."[6]

The concept of *dharma* is best understood in reference to its root *dhr,* "to sustain" or "to uphold." The epic *Mahabharata,* an important source for Hindu ethics, proclaims that *dharma* is so termed because it sustains the world.[7] That is, actions that nurture, support, and maintain the well-being of the world are perceived as *dharmic.* The linking of sensual pleasure and *dharma* in the *Gita* is highly significant and lays the groundwork for the later Hindu acceptance of sexuality's intrinsic, and not merely instrumental, value within the framework of a *dharmic* relationship.

The other major epic, the *Ramayana,* is the story of Rama, prince (and later, king) of the state Ayodhya, and his devoted wife Sita. It is a very important source of values for familial interactions and marital relationships. The epic poem is loved not only in India, but all over Southeast Asia, and annual Ramayana dance and drama performances feature performers from Thailand, Cambodia, and even Indonesia. The story of the *Ramayana* begins with the self-banishment of Rama, a prince of Ayodhya and heir to the throne, in fulfillment of a promise made by his father to the youngest of his four queens. Rama's loving wife, Sita, and his loyal brother, Lakshmana, join him in his long exile to the forest. During the sojourn in the forest, Sita is kidnapped by a demon king. Rama, after many trials, manages to rescue his beloved wife and destroy the demon king Ravana. But, in response to rumors about Sita's possible infidelity with Ravana, Sita must undergo an ordeal by fire to prove her innocence. She comes out unscathed, proving her purity, and the couple return to Ayodhya to rule. Later redactions show a further abandonment of Sita by Rama after she conceives their twin sons and an eventual reconciliation between the sons borne to her and their father, Rama.

Whereas Westerners find the narrative problematic from the viewpoint of feminist hermeneutics, many Hindus view it very differently. They perceive Sita's survival of her trials and steadfast loyalty in terms of feminine courage, valor, and strength. Sacrifice is a unifying thread through the story. Rama sacrifices for his father; Lakshmana for his brother; Rama's father for one of his wives; and Sita for her husband. But does Rama sacrifice for Sita? He does rescue her from Ravana at great peril to his life; but is he merely defending his honor as a husband and king? It depends on the interpreter. Madhu Kishwar, a preeminent Hindu activist for women's rights, has long argued that the model that Sita represents appeals to women not because women are masochistic, but because it holds up an ideal of human action that goes beyond calculating, self-seeking behavior. She qualifies her assertions, however, with warnings about the dangers of one-sided sacrifice, affirming that placing the welfare of others before one's own needs creates social networks of caring, but only when there is mutuality between the sexes; without mutuality, such sacrifice leads to negative consequences for women.

With the dawn of the Epic and Puranic period, the idea of the divine couple was reintroduced through the mythic imagination. The Puranas, composed over a long period of time (estimated to be fourth to twelfth centuries c.e.), are a collection of dramatic stories that focus on the feats of kings, heroes, and celestial deities. In these texts, theology, including theodicy and cosmology, are explained by way of mythic narratives. The most important divinities in the Puranas are Vishnu and Siva, two deities, among others, mentioned in the Vedas. Some Puranas extol Mahadevi, the Great Goddess, as Mother of the Universe and as Brahman. But, Siva and Vishnu gained great importance over time and eventually came to represent the two major visions of God in Hindu theology. For some, Vishnu is Brahman personified (Saguna Brahman, the theistic God). For others, it is Siva who represents the theistic God, experienced as Creator, and Supreme Being that is capable of giving and receiving love.

The Puranas present a profoundly personal perception of Deity. God (whether represented by Siva or Vishnu) is incomplete without his Shakti (literally, "power"), his feminine aspect. Shakti is inseparable from God (Saguna Brahman) as his creative capacity and dynamic activity. It is through God's Shakti that all creation is enacted. A common thread visible in the many accounts of creation in the Puranas is the active involvement of the feminine divine in material creation. The *Brahma Purana,* for example, narrates: "Then the beings created did not reproduce. [Thus] having divided his own body into two parts, he became half male and half female. He [the male part] begot from her [the female part] various kinds of beings."[8] The *Vayu Purana* presents a similar story, but the male principle is Rudra (Shiva), and his Shakti is identified with Mahadevi, the Great Goddess. This theme is repeated throughout the Puranas, which are a very important category of scripture for ordinary Hindus, most of whom will never read the Vedas but are very familiar with the dramatic narratives of the Puranas and the two epics.

The linking of the feminine with materiality and creativity in the Puranas has significance for Hindu women. On one hand, such a correlation bestows on the feminine a great power that is feared and worshipped in the form of the feminine divine, human women gurus, and female spiritual adepts. Maternality and nurturance are also greatly revered. Women in leadership positions in India—whether religious or secular—adopt a maternal stance toward their clientele or audience. Hence, an internationally known guru such as Amritananda Mayi, who has never had children, portrays herself as a world-mother. In theistic Hinduism, although the divine feminine, as the power and dynamism of God, is not distinct from God but is related to the Supreme Being as the power to burn is related to a raging fire, she is represented separately for purposes of worship as the celestial feminine or the divine consort. Much of ancient Hindu art focused on the complex details of iconography of the celestial feminine that contained networks of meaning. Nevertheless, the masculine and feminine principles are meant to be understood as part of one another; the artistic rendering of this can be seen in the Ardhanarishwara (literally, "half-female Lord"), a depiction of Shiva as half male and half female, that is meant to graphically inform the viewer of the inclusion of both sexes within the being of God.

That aesthetics hold an important place in the Hindu order of life is evidenced by highly developed systems and theories of sculpture, dance, drama, poetics, and literature. *Kama* encompasses physical love and sensual pleasure as well as the theory and appreciation of aesthetics. The position of *kama* on the map of Hindu psychology is best understood when placed in juxtaposition with the stated goals of human life. The four aims of life (*purusharthas*) are duty/virtue (*dharma*), sensual/aesthetic pleasure (*kama*), economic well-being (*artha*), and spiritual liberation (*moksha*). A complex of meanings is associated with the term *dharma,* and it is always context specific, but for the present purpose it will suffice to interpret *dharma* as virtuous, dutiful conduct in keeping with the social, familial, moral, and ritual obligations enjoined by tradition. *Dharma*'s relation to *moksha,* the ultimate aim, is facilitative; a *dharmic* life makes it easier to move toward the path of renunciation and surrender required during the final stage of life, and for Hindu theism, non-*dharmic* action precludes God's liberative grace. *Dharma*'s relation to *kama* and *artha* is regulative; it sets the limits within which sensual pleasure and prosperity can be pursued.

These correlations, however, are ideals. It was recognized that dutiful and virtuous behavior was not always the best conduit to sensual pleasure. The high value accorded the science of sensual pleasure (*kama shastra*) is attested by the existence of textual treatises that deal exhaustively with the characteristics of a refined life and the minutiae of amorous encounters of all kinds.

The *Kama Sutra* and similar works such as the *Ananga Ranga* and the *Ratirahasya,* though not religious in genre, were in keeping with the Hindu ordering of life's aims as inclusive of sensuality and aesthetics. Although marriage was a norm and ideal for all who were not renunciants, ancient Indian society was pragmatic about the different possibilities and characteristics of love outside of conjugal life. As Geoffrey Parrinder notes in his study of sexuality: "In ancient Indian society, the sexes could mingle more freely than they did later [after Islamic and British influences], there was pre-marital and extra-marital sexual relationship, and while marriage was normal. . . . [women] were not secluded as they were in zenanas and harems under Muslim rule."[9]

Arguably the world's oldest and most celebrated guide to the science of aesthetic refinement (*kama shastra*), the *Kama Sutra* ("Aphorisms on Love"), is attributed to the fourth-century brahmin scholar Vatsyayana. Yasodhara's commentary, the *Jayamangala,* likely appended during the middle ages, was written to elucidate the aphorisms. A systematic representation of earlier traditions, the text is more than a compendium of sexual positions: It offers advice on the proper relationship between the genders and lays out instructions for the householder in what was known as the sixty-four arts that a cultured person was expected to master. These included categories that applied to both sexes as well as those that were gender specific. Arts such as floral arranging, dance, the proper rearing of children, cooking, embroidery, and painting were recommended for women. The socially respectable townsman was expected to be familiar with the distillation of wines and legerdemain, have knowledge of architecture, engineering, and metallurgy, and also exhibit skill in sports, such as dueling and archery. The central assumption of the text is that the appreciation and enjoyment of objects by the five senses is inextricably linked with cultural, artistic, and emotional refinement.

The *Kama Sutra* begins with the praise of the first three of the four ends of life (virtue, prosperity, and love): "Praised be the aims of life, virtue [*dharma*], prosperity [*artha*], and love [*kama*], which are the subject of this work."[10] This rather strange invocation, which seems to claim that this work on aesthetics and erotic method also covers right conduct (*dharma*) and economics (*artha*), is explained by Yasodhara's commentary that suggests that there can be no proper undertaking of the ethical or economic enterprise when the needs of love remain unfulfilled: "The advocates of eroticism consider that love, given its results, is the most important inasmuch as virtue and prosperity both depend on it and without it they would not exist. . . . Because it depends on relations with another, because it deals with men and women, love requires a know-how that is explained only in the *Kama Sutra*."[11] The text includes advice on forms of marriage, examination of one's sentiments, choice of lovers, proper conduct in amorous liaisons, as well as the particulars of preludes and conclusions to intimate encounters.

The central section of the *Kama Sutra* provides the details of erotic method—for which the text is famous—presenting the particulars of various types of positions, caresses, and embraces. There are also several sections on the "marks of love":

> When love becomes intense, pressing with nails or scratching the body with them is practiced, and it is done on the following occasions: on the first visit; at the time of setting out on a journey; on the return from a journey; at the time when an angry lover is reconciled. . . . But pressing the nails is not a usual thing except with those who are intensely passionate. . . . nothing tends to increase love so much as the effects of marking with the nails, and biting.[12]

The text explains that when the lover is "marked" in this way, it intensifies the remembrance of, and longing for, reunion. The juxtaposition of love and longing was a favorite device in Sanskrit poetry and drama.

As we have seen, the relationship between divine transcendence and immanence, the dialectic between the eternal and ever changing, is evoked through contemplation on the dance of erotic intimacy between God and Goddess, between Being and Becoming. The imagery of sensual poses and the unabashed sexual imagination found in medieval Hindu painting and sculpture indeed pay homage to this, but the play of eros (*kama*) is also celebrated in more contemporary art forms such as the Indian cinema, which puts forth enormous billboards populated with voluptuous women and amorous couples.

Yet such displays are a far cry from the highly developed erotic aesthetic of medieval India. A tension exists today between the conservative modern Hindu sensibility that initially developed during the colonial period and the more contemporary attitudes of the young, shaped by MTV and Bollywood, the Indian version of Hollywood. Both attitudes have been shaped by India's encounters with the West.

Hindu attitudes toward sexuality and gender have been influenced over time not only by colonialism and, more recently, globalization, but also by the ongoing impact of Islam. The first wave of Islam came with the Afghan raiders of Mahmud of Ghazni in 997 C.E., which led to the destruction of temples and the defacing of all erotic and unclothed sculpture. Ghazni and his followers were scandalized by the Hindus' unabashed acceptance of sexuality. The real period of Islamic conquest and expansion, however, began with the sixteenth-century defeats of Indian states at the hands of Babur, the founder of the famed Muslim Mughal empire that came to encompass much of north India. By the time that the Mughal empire became well established, the iconoclasm of the early invaders had softened, but was revived once more by Aurangzeb (r. 1658–1707). The many centuries of Muslim rule undermined the kinds of attitudes toward sexuality and the openness to women's sexual satisfaction that are evidenced by the books of the *kama shastra*. After Aurangzeb's death in 1707, the power of the Mughal empire slowly ebbed. The vacuum was filled by the British. By the middle of the nineteenth century, the British were well established in India.

The British instituted English education in India and trained young Indian intellectuals in the European classics. Exposure to British ways and the missionary culture produced a reaction that is known as the Hindu Renaissance. Centered mainly in Bengal, where the British were first established, the Hindu intelligentsia fought for social reform and were advocates of women's rights. Their goals were access to higher education for women; the abolition of *sati,* a widow's self-immolation on her husband's funeral pyre; laws against child marriage; and equal partnership of women in economic and political leadership. The Hindu reformers were far ahead of their Western counterparts in moving forward the agenda of activism on behalf of women. But as they adopted Western rhetoric to argue against the claims of European supremacy, they also adopted Victorian attitudes toward human sexuality and gender relations. The legacy of the Hindu reforms and the shaming of the Hindu sensibility by foreign cultures took a toll on the openness with which Hindus had traditionally engaged sexuality.

The Theological Uses of Eros

Bhakti

Bhakti, or devotion, is mentioned as early as 250 B.C.E. in the *Bhagavad Gita,* but *bhakti* as a popular pan-Hindu movement reached it's zenith from about 500 C.E. to 1500 C.E. It provides a path to an emotional, loving relationship to God envisioned as simultaneously universal and omnipresent *and* personal and intimate. *Bhakti* is marked by intense longing and passionate desire for communion with God, often expressed in terms of erotic mysticism. The advent of devotion was especially fortuitous for women because it did not demand the renunciation of family life and the eradication of sexual desire, which was demanded by the ascetic or monastic path. Rather, it advocated the devotional, liturgical, and ritual worship of, and intense, erotic-emotive yearning for, one's chosen vision of God (*ishta devata*).

The emergence of a populist devotional tradition provided new avenues for women's spiritual self-expression and religious authority. Many of the renowned leaders of the devotion movement were women, and devotionalism *also* altered the Hindu psychological landscape on sexuality. The devotional saints' mystical-erotic poetry reflects the transformation of eros from a harbinger of physical pleasure to a vehicle for transcendent union with God. All devotional sects accepted the doctrine of the necessity of divine grace for liberation, and ecstatic adoration and longing for God, as the surest path to grace. Although there were devotional or *bhakti* saints (*bhaktas*) by the eighteenth century whose spiritual practice was centered on the Great Goddess, most devotees throughout Hindu history have focused their love and adoration on Vishnu (or one of his major incarnations, Rama and Krishna) or on Shiva and composed devotional poetry that is sung to this day. One of the most famous *bhakti* poet-saints was the princess Mahadevi, who lived in south India. She was the wife of a king, but loved only her Lord Shiva:

> Better than meeting
> And mating all the time
> Is the pleasure of mating once
> After being far apart.
>
> When he's away
> I cannot wait
> To get a glimpse of him.
>
> Friend, when will I have it
> Both ways,
> Be with Him
> Yet not with Him,
> My Lord White as Jasmine?[13]

We see in her poetry the theme of separation and union that marks the *bhakti* sensibility.

The best-known and most enduring *bhakti* tradition has been the one that venerates Krishna as Supreme Being. The soteriology of Krishna *bhakti* schools is deeply infused with a love mysticism that is evoked by the songs of the *bhakta* poets. One of the best loved *bhakta* poets was Mirabai, the sixteenth-century wife of a Rajput prince who defied all codes of conduct for high-class women in her society. Singing songs of love and dancing in public, she associated with anyone who was devoted to Krishna regardless of gender and class and refused to consummate her marriage in fidelity to her passion for her Lord Krishna:

> Having wet me with love,
> Why did you leave?
> You abandoned your unwavering consort,
> Having ignited her lamp wick;
> She's like a pleasure boat
> Set out to drift on an ocean of craving.
> Either way Mira is dead—
>   Unless you return.[14]

The songs of Mirabai continue to be popular today and have been influential not only in a theological sense, but also in a sociological sense, for they have brought together men and women, upper and lower classes, beyond the restrictions of caste, gender, and stage of life for over five hundred years.

Mythic poetic narrative is another mode of expression for Krishna *bhakti*. Krishna's youthful adventures are rife with theological symbolism. One such narrative, memorable for its extravagant use of sexual metaphor and important for its theological significance, is the story of *Sharad Purnima* ("The Full Moon Around November"). The young Krishna goes to the moonlit forest to play his flute. Enchanted by the divine music, the young cowherdesses (*gopis*) of the surrounding villages leave their homes and husbands, drawn irresistibly to the source of the music.

Among the *gopis* is the beautiful Radha, who's yearning for Krishna and devotion to him is so great that she can only conceive of existence as part of him. In the theology of Krishna, the Lord is the divine lover who becomes accessible to those who adore him with an intensity of longing like that of the *gopis* who risk the dissolution of their familial relations, social censure, and even destitution to experience the rapture of divine love. During the course of the moonlight reverie narrated in the story of the *Sharad Purnima*, in the verdant glade, in an ecstatic burst of dance and passion, Lord Krishna unites with every one of the *gopis*; yet, he never leaves Radha's embrace.

The theology of Radha is complex; she is the feminine divine, the power and immanence of God (Lord Krishna), but she is also seen as the ideal devotee, the model of the perfect soul, liberated by love and longing. The contrast between the delight of fulfillment and the agony of separation in the relationship of Radha and Krishna is used to highlight the power and pain of love. In the twelfth century, the devotional poet Jayadeva transformed the theme of this-worldly erotic love into transcendent divine love in the celebrated poetic devotional work, the *Gitagovinda*:

> Krishna, Radhika suffers in your desertion. . . .
> She bristles with pain . . . cries, shudders, gasps. . . .
> Falls, raises herself, then faints.
> When fevers of passion rage so high, a frail girl may live [only] by your
>   charm. . . .

Divine physician of her heart,
[Radha] can only be healed with elixir from your body.[15]

Read superficially, the passage seems to be a poignant description of human love, of consummation, separation, and yearning. But Krishna and Radha are not the conventional hero and heroine of Sanskrit drama—they are God and Goddess. The *Gitagovinda* thus employs an important theme in aesthetic theory to elicit an emotive response to the quest for mystical union. The *Gitagovinda* is still sung in the temples of south India, and its composer is revered as a poet-saint.

Other poets also wrote of the amorous encounters between Radha and Krishna such as the fifteenth-century Bengali poet Chandi Das who wrote of the embraces and caresses of the lovers, which were inevitably followed by unavoidable separation, sorrow, and the rapture of reunion. The love poetry centered on Krishna and Radha also inspired Indian painting, particularly miniature paintings. The *Gitagovinda* itself has been illustrated with detailed depictions of the pair in conversation, embrace, and even union.

Another important motif that emerges from the poetic narratives of Krishna *bhakti* is the metaphor of illicit love [*parakiya prema*]. The love between spouses is considered "safe" love without the requisite risk, danger, and sacrifice required of love that is without social sanction. It is difficult for us in contemporary society, with its attendant permissiveness, pornography, and promiscuity, to understand the grave risks of passion outside marriage in a historic context. Yet, nonmarital love, historically and in the present era in certain societies, has been an endeavor fraught with the dangers of dislocation, destitution, and possible death. In *bhakti* doctrine, it is this degree of risk and surrender that the love of God demands and, like *parakiya prema,* it is marked by the pain of separation and yearning as long as the soul is embodied. Sexual desire and consummation are, thus, the metaphors for the soul's longing for an eventual union with the Divine. But it is also, seen in the relationship between Radha and Krishna, the favorite symbol for the commingling of transcendence and immanence, the masculine and the feminine and, indeed, all polarities in the Being of God.

Tantra

Sexual motives and imagery play an important role in the Hindu *tantric* traditions as well. But there is a difference in method. *Bhakti* advocates a sense of distinction between God and the human lover who seeks, and eventually experiences, union with Him. The distinction never fully dissolves as long as the body endures, for only in relationship can we savor the flavor (*rasa*) of divine love, longing, and rapture. In contrast, the *tantric* approach to Deity is that of ultimate identification rather than relationship. A body of spiritual practices (*sadhana*) that are engineered to awaken normally dormant psycho-spiritual energies is prescribed by a guru. The aim of these practices is the experiential realization of the Self as ultimately transcendent of the body-mind complex.

The *Tantras* (the texts of the *tantric* traditions), which sometimes recommend transgressive and antinomian practices, are understood by *tantric* practitioners to be written in a code that can be interpreted in a variety of ways. *Tantric* practice can be traditional or unorthodox. By far the most common, tradition-oriented *tantra,* known as right-handed *tantra,* advocates the mental perform-ance of all sexual and other unorthodox practices in order to attain liberation. The unorthodox schools of *tantra*—although rare—have garnered far more attention in the West, because of their advocacy of the literal interpretation of unorthodox methods meant to jolt the normal consciousness out of its compla-cency and catalyze a sudden awakening of enlightenment. Sexuality plays an important role in this form of *tantra* and, in the West, it has come to character-ize, inaccurately, *all* of *tantric* practice. As Paul Muller-Ortega argues:

> Recent Western nonacademic interest in the Tantra has tended to blur the important distinction between the *tantra-shastra* and the *kama-shastra.* India had a highly developed sense of erotics, the *kama-shastra,* where the goal was a cul-tured, refined love-making, a perfectly acceptable fulfillment of one of the four legitimate aims of human existence. . . . that of *kama.* The *tantra-sastra,* in using the secret ritual, did not seek to fulfill *kama,* but rather to provide a new path for the attainment of *moksha.* This statement may seem obvious, but it needs saying. When we read about those portions of the [*tantric*] ritual that include sexual terminology, we have to remember that this ritual was often only to be internally visualized.[16]

Sexuality is redefined by *tantra* in two ways. *Bhakti* encourages the transmu-tation of sexual desire geared toward physical release into an erotic longing directed toward mystical communion with God. In contrast, *tantra*—at least left-handed *tantra*—believes in the deployment of sexual union toward the psycho-physical transformation of the Self. In contradistinction to the image of *tantric* sex as a frenzy of hedonistic abandon, it was actually intended to be a disciplined and difficult experience meant to shatter habitual ways of perceiv-ing the nature of reality.

Hindu *tantra* is a style of practice that makes certain physical and metaphys-ical assumptions. The Divine is understood as One in existence but twofold in activity (most often represented by, and visualized as, Shiva and Shakti). The *one nature* but *twofold function* of the Divine is not viewed as a paradox because oppositions (symbolized by the masculine and feminine principles) such as transcendence and immanence, the One and the Many, and stasis and dynamism are seen as two poles of one reality.

This sense of the twofold nature of reality extends to the human individual who, in *tantric* cosmology, contains the cosmic polarity within himself or her-self. In *tantric* spiritual practice, the aim is the experiential unification of the life force and liberative potential (understood as the Shakti within) and the transcendent Self (identified with Shiva). Within the individual, Shakti is the path and Shiva is the goal.

This merger is often represented by sexual symbolism in iconography. The most commonly used symbol for the oneness of Shiva and Shakti is the *lingam* and *yoni*. The tubular, phallic, or dome-shaped *lingam* is a stylized representa-tion of the generative, creative force of Shiva; according to the *Skanda Purana,* the *lingam* (*linga*) denotes space in which all things come to be. The *yoni,* often depicted as an inverted triangle, the womb of Shakti, is symbolic of the univer-sal matrix in which all things arise and pass away. The sexual symbolism cannot be crudely reduced to its parts without losing a great deal of its meaning. The *lingam,* for example, is always shown as arising from the *yoni;* the *tantric* under-standing of the function of the twofold nature of God (Shiva/Shakti) is displayed through what is called the dance of Shiva and Shakti.

The meaning of the *lingam* and the *yoni* unfolds as layers are peeled away. In *tantric* thought, Shiva is the Self of God that seeks to realize and experience his own infinite potential. Shakti is the power and activity of God expressed as energy-infused matter (*prakriti-shakti*) with its capacity to give rise to life and self-awareness (*chit-shakti*) that forms the physical universe. To experience the infinite potentiality of his own Being, Shiva, the I-awareness of God, "enters" Shakti, God's dynamic, creative matrix, and the universe of infinite possibilities comes to be. In *tantra,* the fundamental truth of the universe is thus played out in the twofold nature of the individual in which the body-mind complex (the realm of Shakti) and the inner Self that transcends birth and death (Shiva) are the two aspects of one being. Through symbolism-enhanced ritual, meditation, and visualization, *tantra* seeks to move the individual toward this realization.

Tantric doctrine maintains that Shakti enfolds all aspects of life: creation and dissolution; detachment and desire; stillness and activity. Because Shakti as the ultimate power is personified as feminine, the different aspects are worshipped and meditated upon as female deities. Both fierce and gentle goddesses are revered; nevertheless, the strong, autonomous, powerful aspects of Shakti tend to dominate *tantric* ritual and meditative practice. Kali, one of the most com-plex and awe-inspiring manifestations of Shakti, has a special place in *tantric* lore. She is portrayed as dark, naked, wild haired, standing on Shiva, and wearing a garland of heads and a waistband of arms. She is, nonetheless, benevolent to the good, and holds up her hand in a gesture that signifies "do not fear"; to those who worship her, she is the fierce but loving Mother. All the elements of her portrayal offer multiple layers of meaning. For example, a devotional interpretation views her nakedness as the open, empty, uncondi-tioned space from which all phenomena emerge; the wildness of her loose, flowing hair as the uncertainty and impermanence of life; the garland of heads representing thought and wisdom and that of the arms signifying all actions.

Some Hindu feminists find in Kali an empowering and liberating model of the feminine divine. Lina Gupta writes that Mother Kali, the dark goddess, "is perpetually present in the inner and outer struggles faced by women at all times."[17] She envisions this aspect of Shakti as a potential force for reinterpret-ing the feminine:

> I believe that Hinduism does indeed contain a model and image that could be used to fit the needs of today's women, and that this model lies at the very heart of Hinduism itself. This image centers on the goddess Kali and her many

manifestations. I also believe this image must be extricated from patriarchal interpretations and understandings that have clouded its essential meaning even while tapping into—and using—the many layers of meaning that surround it.[18]

Elsewhere, I have argued for the Hindu ecofeminist implications of Kali and other powerful aspects of the divine feminine in *tantra*:

> The ubiquitous presence of Kali and other unpredictable, independent goddesses reflect Tantric conceptions of the nature of the divine feminine and its affirmation of those aspects of the creative feminine which are volatile, dynamic, imperious, and transformative. Tantra goes beyond the maternal and nurturing aspects of the nature of the feminine—whether human or divine. This perspective encourages a more reverential attitude towards nature and natural phenomena that are identified with goddesses and discourages the notion that sacred locations will nurture and sustain without adequate care and reverence. The *Tantraraja Tantra* directly identifies different cosmic geographical locations with various aspects of Shakti. This outlook can be extended to honor the needs of the earth as a whole when conceived as a living embodiment of the Divine Feminine.[19]

The nature of Kali lends itself quite easily to a struggle for a broader and more nuanced understanding of "femaleness" as it challenges all stereotypes of the creative feminine.

The body is important in *tantra* for it is seen not as an impediment to spiritual awakening, as in certain other Indian traditions, but as the vehicle for realization. The defining characteristic of tantrism is the complex of spiritual practices (*sadhana*) that is undertaken by the initiated in order to arouse, channel, and catalyze the liberative energy. As I have noted, the senses are used to initiate the liberative journey:

> The sacramentally sensuous nature of tantric rites is designed to arouse the dormant *kundalini* [liberative energy]. The passionate, emotional intensity of tantric sadhana, turned to the goal of realizing the immanence of the Divine within, aims at directing the *kundalini* through the [chakras], vivifying each [energy] center and raising it to the conclusion of its journey in the final [chakra], wherein lies unity-consciousness.[20]

Tantric practice includes chanting; fragrant scents; symbolic hand gestures (*mudras*); the creation of mystical diagrams (*yantra* or *mandala*) with flower petals, shells, and natural materials; as well as the symbolic purification and recreation of a divinized body through the use of sacred sounds (*mantras*) and detailed meditative visualization.

Tantra's somewhat undeserved reputation for hedonism and antinomian methods is rooted in a relatively rare practice known as the practice of the "ritual of the five elements" (*pancha-tattva*), which includes items forbidden in a sacred setting such as meat, fish, alcohol, and sacramental sex. The majority of *tantric* practitioners (the right-handed path) use innocuous substitutes for the five elements, whereas the rare left-handed path practices in secret and employs the forbidden elements. The ritual involves complex liturgical invocations, meditation, and worship of the woman by the man as the embodiment of Shakti. Although many *tantric* texts suggest that sacramental sex in the ritual be limited to the initiated wife of the aspirant, there were also guidelines for the involvement of women initiates other than the wife—these liaisons would be outside of the caste and class rules for sexual engagement, creating a particularly impure situation because sex between certain groups was considered transgressive. Aspirants were not permitted to undertake the practice—which was considered dangerous—without many years of rigorous yogic and meditative disciplines. I have suggested elsewhere that the value of the ritual lies in its capacity to overturn deeply held culturally rooted views about reality that stood in the way of a profound experience of the omnipresence of the Divine:

> The [*pancha-tattva*] ritual's conflation of the sacred and the profane is highly offensive to conventional Hindu sensibility and runs counter to all normative models of purity and impurity, sanctity and desecration in Hindu consciousness. It seems that the element of shock inherent in the ritual becomes itself a highly potent catalyst capable of catapulting the mind out of its familiar dualistic thought patterns. . . . By partaking of five defiling things in the [sacred and meditative] setting, the aspirant affirms their underlying purity and shatters the cognitive processes of the unenlightened mind that fractionalizes all life into myriad brittle distinctions.[21]

The ritual of the five elements cannot be isolated from its cultural context in which these elements were considered impure and defiling, especially in a ritual setting. The New Age appropriation of "Tantra" as wild sex, therefore, seems to most Hindus to be misguided at best.

Marriage

The gender relationships in the sacred stories of the *Ramayana* and the *Mahabharata* and the puranic understanding of God/dess as biune have had a deep impact on Hindu attitudes toward marriage and sexuality. Just as the relationship between the masculine and feminine principles was seen as essential for the creation and maintenance of the cosmic order, human marriage was viewed as essential for the stability of the social order. At a time when home and the place of work were one, it allowed an emotionally safe environment for the emergence of creative work, and most importantly, it provided the safe harbor necessary for the raising of *dharmic* (dutiful and righteous) children.

Traditionally, it was considered improper to take ascetic or monastic vows before having taken care of one's marital responsibilities to produce and rear offspring. A sexual relationship was the right of a wife and the responsibility of a husband. The *Dharma Sutras,* the ancient law books, are very clear on this: "When (a man's) wife is in season, he must have sexual intercourse with her as required by his vow. And if his wife wants it, he must have sex with her (at other times) as well."[22] If a man does not have sexual intercourse for three years with his wife who (is healthy), he incurs a guilt equal to that of performing an abortion.[23]

Sexual union within marriage is sanctioned not only for procreation, but for pleasure as well. That pleasure is a legitimate aim of life is expressed in the ideal of the four aims of life. But, as noted earlier, the pursuit of *kama* and *artha* are only legitimate as long as they are tempered and regulated by *dharma,* which requires that all endeavors be constrained by ritual and moral duty. Passion and pleasure in marriage, therefore, is fully warranted because of the nature of marriage as imitation of divine union. Marriage is not viewed as just a relationship between two people joined by affection; it is seen as the foundation of a stable society and idealized as the earthly version of the divine couple.

Puranic references to cosmogenesis are laced with complex sexual metaphors, thereby elevating sexuality to the symbol of divine creative momentum. To engage in sexual union within marriage is to step into the stream of celestial life, to participate in the greater continuum and partake of cosmic creativity.

Yet, although the marriage relationship was thus idealized, many practices conflicted with the ideal. Men of wealth did have mistresses and, at times, more than one wife. Polygamy and polyandry is referred to in the epics which, as I noted earlier, are important to the values and practices of Hindu society. In the *Ramayana,* the revered father of Rama (the hero of the epic and a divine incarnation) has four queens, and a heroine of the *Mahabharata,* Draupadi, is married to all five Pandava brothers—the semi-divine heroes of the narrative. Multiple spouses, however, do not seem to have been that common among ordinary Hindus. But the epics, especially the *Ramayana,* have profoundly informed Hindu society in other ways. They have been pivotal in setting the standards for the relationship between husband and wife far more than any other texts.

Whereas Western scholars have looked to texts such as the *Manu Smriti* for information about attitudes toward Hindu marriage, most Hindus—very few of whom have ever read the *Manu Smriti*—have looked to the Puranas and the *Ramayana* for guidance. Although the *Ramayana* is problematic from a Western feminist perspective, the models of human relationships that it offers have such broad and historic appeal that a reconstruction of its meaning becomes essential for any restatement of the Hindu marriage.

To be sure, there are tensions within the Hindu tradition regarding the institution of marriage and a woman's role therein. Even the injunctions of the *Manu Smriti,* often regarded as stifling for women according to the values of the contemporary West, acknowledge the importance of attending to the emotional and sexual needs of women. The text also enjoins that women be "honored and adorned" by all their male relatives if the family is to have good fortune; if the women of a family are not honored, all sacred rites are useless and misfortune will befall the family.[24]

Some women see their role as spiritual protector, as opposed to their husband's role as physical protector. Rama and Sita are venerated as incarnations of Vishnu and Goddess Lakshmi in every village in India. When women sacrifice for their families, show loyalty and fidelity, or undertake vows to fast for a period for the protection of their husbands' health and well-being (*vrats*), they are said to be like Sita. Such attitudes have made it difficult for social workers in rural India to get women to ask for help in domestic crises, but it is also true that many women continue to regard the traditional role of wife and mother as something capable of eliciting noble, and even heroic behavior, the mark of which is sacrifice.

Contemporary Issues

The issues that provoke deep controversy amongst Hindus are somewhat different from those that elicit passionate discussion among Westerners. For example, homosexuality, which is a critical issue for the contemporary West, is not a major subject of debate among Hindus. Although there are gay groups in India and a history of gay erotic poetry among Indian Muslim poets, there is relatively little formal discussion in Hinduism at present on the issue of homosexuality. Admittedly, some prohibitions against it do appear in the *Dharmasutras* and other ancient law books. Yet there is a growing gay community in India that has, as its major problem, a popular ignorance/denial about its very existence. The diaspora Indian gay community is not divided across religious lines and views its struggles through the lens of South Asian culture rather than Hindu theology. In order to provide support and services to lesbian, gay, bisexual, and transgendered people of South Asian descent, *Trikone,* a registered nonprofit organization, was founded in 1986 in the San Francisco Bay Area. It publishes a magazine and features a variety of events and claims to be the oldest organization of its kind in the world. The adoption of the "South Asian" moniker provides a sense of community that is grounded in ethnicity rather than religion, but this makes religious legitimacy all the more difficult because there is no specific organized "Hindu" gay/lesbian movement. There is, however, a Gay and Lesbian Vaishnava Association (GALVA) for Hindu Gauriya Vaishnavas. The mostly Western members of GALVA seek to reclaim what they see as a lost respect for the "third sex" that was present in Hindu culture before the Islamic and later, British, conquests. Writers on GALVA's Web site weave complex arguments about the place of the third sex in Hindu culture, noting that the *Kama Sutra* mentions persons of the third sex (*tritiya-prakriti*) as including gays, lesbians, transgenders and the intersexed. Though not a sacred text, the *Kama Sutra* is important in that it is possible to cull social understandings of forms of sexuality from it. Members of the third sex are first categorized according to whether their physical characteristics are either male or female; they are known as *napumsaka,* or gay males, and *svairini,* or lesbians. Amara Dasa, a writer on GALVA's Web site, argues that the ongoing influence of Victorian mores is to be blamed for the contemporary disinclination to acknowledge and understand the third sex in the Hindu context:

> In Vedic society, people were familiar with the third sex and could normally recognize its characteristics within their offspring. Since everyone was accommodated under the Vedic system, third-gender youths could find their place within society according to their nature and thus grow healthfully into adulthood. In modern society, however, people are afraid to even discuss third-sex issues. . . . The influence that Victorian British scholars and educators had in

creating the current homophobic environment of India cannot be underesti-
mated. Many professional and religious authorities growing up in India during
the nineteenth and twentieth centuries were heavily indoctrinated with homophobic stereotypes and views by Victorian educators . . .[25]

Methodologically, it is interesting that GALVA uses postcolonial critique to
claim cultural legitimacy for homosexuality—a very different approach than
that of Western gay and lesbian communities.

An important contemporary issue for Hindu feminists is the abortion of
female embryos. Because Hindu culture has always been profecundity, abortion is not authorized in the *dharma* traditions. Penance was also demanded
for abortion, and the *Dharmasutra* literature groups abortion with homicide as
one of the sins that makes a person an outcaste with whom social interaction
is not permitted. Yet, ironically, one of the looming social problems that India
faces today is a severe shortage of reproductive-age women because of the
large number of abortions of female fetuses. The ratio of males to females is
rising dangerously in north India. In southern India, which has a history of
matrilineal traditions, the numbers are far less alarming. Although China has a
larger number of "missing" females, it is a result of the one-child doctrine that
was enforced in past decades. In India, the problem seems to be the inability—
or unwillingness—of parents to pay dowries that can bankrupt families.
Dowries are, and have been from the outset, illegal in India, but the practice
continues even as women become scarce. Dowries are an Indian rather than
Hindu custom, and the problem of female feticide is not a "Hindu" issue:
Indians of all faiths seem to prefer male children overwhelmingly. One other
social reason for this preference may be that when a daughter marries, she is
theoretically part of her husband's family, whereas a son remains part of the
natal family and is responsible for his parents' welfare when they are old. This
holds true for other religious groups in India as well. The lack of a proper
socio-economic safety net makes old age a serious concern. Thus, the preference for boys over girls, and the resultant feticide of females, can only be
reversed, like most other social ills, through economic amelioration.

An important issue for many educated, urban, Indian Hindus and for those
in the diaspora is the concern over arranged marriages. Although arranged
marriage is still the norm for rural people in India, personal choice is becoming more of an option for the urban classes. One of the major themes of the
Indian film industry (the largest in the world and with wide international
distribution), arranged marriages have increasingly come under fire in the last
few decades by young people who want to experience the freedom of Western style romance before marriage and enjoy greater latitude in terms of
whom they choose for their mate. The issue is not merely one of "parental
controls." Endogamy, or marriage within one's social clan (*jati*), is an accepted
way of sustaining enduring community, social, and commercial networks and
shared values. Also, as we have seen, the Hindu understanding of marriage is
so intertwined with Hindu conceptions of the meaning and value of gender,
that to alter the landscape of marriage would be to irrevocably change the

religious viewpoint on sex and society. But the landscape *is* changing and that change is increasingly accompanied by transformations in Hindu gender roles, class relations, and sexual norms.

Conclusion

Like the adherents of any ancient tradition, Hindus are struggling to reinterpret their religious ethos in light of contemporary reality. The problem, however, is far more complex for Hindus in that the categories of sacred and secular are not part of the indigenous framework. In the past, there was no disjunction between religion and the rest of life and, as such, sexuality could not be pried apart from the totality of the fabric of faith. Now, it can. One can be a "Hindu" in the sense that one is born to Hindu parents, but have no investment in any aspect in the tradition, or one can be a Hindu in the sense of having a spiritual practice, a time of worship and sacred ritual, but be "an individual" quite apart from, and perhaps in opposition to, the traditional perspectives on the way one should live one's everyday life.

Because there is no founding figure, nor an ecclesiastical hierarchy, in Hinduism, no overarching authority can provide binding dogmatic support for or opposition to any given position. Thus, there really can be as many Hindu positions on a given issue as there are Hindus.

QUESTIONS FOR DISCUSSION

1. What are the shared conceptions of major Hindu theological traditions?
2. Why are Hindus uncomfortable with the term "religion" as a designation for Hinduism?
3. Explain the historic interactions that created the traditions now called Hindu.
4. Why is the body considered to be foul according to the metaphysical worldview?
5. What are the four stages of life (*ashramas*) and which is the most significant?
6. What scriptural text made the first and most important attempt to reconcile the differences between the metaphysical and organic worldviews?
7. What is the relationship between *dharma* and sexuality in the *Bhagavad Gita*?
8. How do Hindu feminists justify the ongoing veneration of Sita, the long-suffering heroine of the epic *Ramayana*?
9. What is the role of the feminine principle, Shakti, in the *Puranas*?
10. What is *kama* and what is the significance of its position as one of the four aims of life?
11. How were Hindu attitudes toward sexuality affected by the Islamic and British conquests, respectively?

12. Explain the theological use of eros in *bhakti* (devotionalism), particularly Krishna *bhakti*.

13. In both *bhakti* and *tantra,* sexual motives and imagery play an important role, but there are important differences. Explain the difference in method and approach to the use of the erotic in these two types of religious practice.

14. How does the twofold nature of reality in *tantric* cosmology, symbolized by the masculine and feminine principles, play out in *tantric* ritual and art?

15. Although the marriage relationship was idealized in Hindu tradition, many practices conflicted with the ideal. What were some of these practices?

RECOMMENDED RESOURCES

Altekar, A.S. 1995 (1962). *The Position of Women in Hindu Civilization,* 2nd ed. Delhi: Motilal Benarsidass.

Gatwood, Lynn E. 1985. *Devi and the Spouse Goddess: Women, Sexuality, and Marriage in India.* Riverdale, MD: Riverdale, Co.

Johnsen, Linda. 1994. *Daughters of the Goddess: The Women Saints of India.* St. Paul, MN: Yes International Publishers.

Khandelwal, Meena. 2003. *Women in Ochre Robes: Gendering Hindu Renunciation.* Albany: State University of New York Press.

Leslie, Julia, editor. 1991. *Roles and Rituals for Hindu Women.* Rutherford: Fairleigh Dickinson University Press.

Sovatsky, Stuart. 1999. *Eros, Consciousness, and Kundalini: Deepening Sensuality through Tantric Celibacy and Spiritual Intimacy.* Rochester, VT: Park Street Press.

Subbamma, Malladi. 1993. *Hinduism and Women.* Delhi: South Asia Books.

Vatsyayana, Mallanaga. Alain Danielou, translator. 1995. *The Complete Kama Sutra: The First Unabridged Modern Translation of the Classic Indian Text.* [UNABRIDGED]. Rochester, VT: Park Street Press.

White, David Gordon. 2003. *Kiss of the Yogini: "Tantric Sex" in Its South Asian Contexts.* Chicago: University of Chicago Press.

ENDNOTES

1. *Rig Veda* in *Hindu Scriptures,* translated and edited by R. C. Zaehner. London: J. M. Dent & Sons, 1966.

2. *Maitri Upanishad* in *The Principal Upanishads,* translated by S. Radhakrishnan. New Delhi: Indus Publishers, 1994.

3. Ibid.

4. *Yoga Sutras* in *Yoga Philosophy of Patanjali,* translated with annotations by Swami Hariharananda Aranya. Albany, NY: State University of New York Press, 1983.

5. *Bhagavad Gita* in *The Mahabharata,* translated and edited by J. A. B. van Buitenen. Chicago and London: University of Chicago Press, 1981. See also *Mahabharata,* edited by Visnu S. Suthankar, et al. 19 vols. Poona: Bhandarkar Oriental Research Institute, 1927–66.

6. *Bhagavad Gita* 7.11.

7. *Mahabharata* 12.110.11.

8. *Brahma Purana* 1.52–53.

9. Geoffrey Parrinder. *Sexual Morality in the World's Religions.* Oxford: Oneworld Publications, 1980.

10. Vatsyayana, *Kama Sutra,* translated by Alain Danielou. Rochester, VT.: Park Street Press, 1994, v. 1–2.

11. Ibid., pp. 15–16.

12. Vatsyayana, *Kama Sutra,* translated by Sir Richard F. Burton and F. F. Arbuthnot, 1883; reprint New York: Dutton, 1962, pp. 99–103.

13. From *Mahadeviyakka,* translated by A. K. Ramanujan in *Speaking of Siva.* Baltimore: Penguin, 1973, p. 141.

14. From *For Love of the Dark One,* translated by Andrew Schelling. Boston: Shambala, 1993.

15. From Barbara Stoler Miller. *Love Song of the Dark Lord: Jayadeva's Gitagovinda.* New York: Columbia University Press, 1984.

16. Paul E. Muller-Ortega. *The Triadic Heart of Shiva.* Albany: State University of New York Press, 1989, pp. 52–53.

17. Lina Gupta. "Kali the Savior" in P. Cooey, W. Eakin, and J. McDaniel, editors, *After Patriarchy: Feminist Transformations of the World's Religions.* Maryknoll, NY: Orbis Books, 1991, p. 37.

18. Ibid., p. 16.

19. Rita DasGupta Sherma. "Sacred Immanence: Reflections of Ecofeminism in Hindu Tantra" in Lance E. Nelson, editor, *Purifying the Earthly Body of God: Religion and Ecology in Hindu India.* Albany: State University of New York Press, 1998, p. 111.

20. Ibid., p. 114. See also Rita DasGupta Sherma. *"Sa Ham*—I Am She: Woman as Goddess" in Alf Hiltebeitel and Kathleen Erndl, editors, *Is the Goddess a Feminist?* New York: New York University Press, 2000.

21. Ibid., p. 118.

22. Dharmasutra of Apastamba, 2.1.18–20. In *Dharmasutras: The Law Codes of Apastamba, Gautama, Baudhayana, and Vasistha,* translated by Patrick Olivelle. Oxford: Oxford University Press, 1999.

23. Dharmasutra of Baudhayana, 4.1.17. Ibid.

24. *Manu Smrti* 3.55–57.

25. Dasa, http://www.galva108.org/Tritiya_prakriti.html.

Chapter 3

Buddhism

Alan Sponberg

The basic Buddhist attitude toward sex appears quite straightforward, indeed misleadingly so. In sharp contrast with many current views, Buddhists do not see sexual intimacy as the ultimate source of meaning in human existence. Reading the ancient Buddhist scriptures with modern eyes,[1] one might easily conclude that Buddhism seeks to suppress or even to deny human sexuality. But that would miss the key point. Our sexuality is, in the Buddhist view, perfectly natural, even if also frustratingly problematic. As a natural aspect of human existence, our sexuality is not seen as inherently sinful, nor is it something to be spiritually redeemed or consecrated through the sacrament of marriage. No form of sexual expression—marital or premarital, heterosexual or homosexual—is *in and of itself* of any spiritual significance. Our sexuality is neither inherently good or bad, nor essentially sinful or salutary. Every *expression* of our sexuality is, however, an opportunity for unskillful mental states and actions. And actions arising from unskillful and deluded mental states are of great significance in Buddhism, both ethically and spiritually.

Buddhist teachers have traditionally asserted that sexual activity (including thoughts) makes people particularly prone to expressions of greed, hatred, and delusion. And this is hardly surprising given how deeply instinctual, and thus largely unconscious, our various sexual motivations and ploys typically are. As we shall see, the goal of Buddhist practice is a radical transformation of our deepest inclinations, motivations, and aspirations. To the extent that these remain largely outside of our self-conscious purview and direction, they will indeed remain particularly problematic. Our sexuality, even if of no particular spiritual significance in itself, is nonetheless highly significant to the degree

41

that it continues to reinforce our residual unenlightened tendencies and attractions to craving and ignorance. Buddhists have thus tended to view human sexuality as part of a broader developmental process.

Acknowledging that sex and other experiences of sensual pleasure are gratifying, Buddhists also recognize the limitations of these pleasures in their quest for a more satisfying and sustainable happiness. As one progresses in this quest, Buddhists expect that sexual pleasure will eventually be left behind in favor of a more richly satisfying life of voluntary simplicity that includes sexual abstinence, just as children eventually set aside even their most cherished toys. One begins, quite naturally, having a childlike fascination with one's sexuality. And this is healthy enough, as long as that fascination does not turn into an obsession blocking the natural process of development. The "sublime life" (*brahmacarya*) that is the culmination of Buddhist practice is thus not a matter of self-denial or deprivation. Rather it is to leave behind what is limited and restrictive in favor of what is more liberating, expansive, and inclusive. The prevailing view in our contemporary culture sees sexual intimacy as perhaps the highest expression of our humanity. But for Buddhists, this would be like remaining stuck in a kind of immature "spiritual prepubescence." One would fail to grow into a spiritually mature and compassionate individual. Eventual sexual abstinence is not seen as mandatory, but rather as the natural flowering of becoming fully human. It may require lifetimes to attain, but it is clearly the goal. To explore this provocative perspective on human sexuality more deeply, however, we must first understand the Buddhist view of the basic human predicament. What, in broadest terms, is the crucial problem we all face? And how is that problem to be resolved?

The Traditional Background

According to early Buddhist sources, Siddhartha Gautama, the historical founder of Buddhism, was born around 560 B.C.E. to a family of privilege and prominence. An intense and sensitive youth, he experienced a deep personal crisis as the result of encountering four crucial "sights," or manifestations, of the human condition. First he was confronted by the threefold inevitability of old age, sickness, and death. Reflecting on what he had seen, he realized that none of the perquisites of his auspicious birth would spare him from this fate shared by all living beings. As he pondered the existential dilemma implicit in that realization, he encountered yet a fourth sight, a wandering mendicant, one who had gone forth from conventional pursuits and concerns to follow a life dedicated to insight and liberation. However bleak the magnitude of his crisis appeared to be, this fourth sight held a possible alternative. At that point, Siddhartha realized that the reality of suffering in human existence was indeed so great and so pressing that he could not simply continue his previous life of sheltered complacency. For himself, and for the sake of those he loved, including a wife and infant child according to some later sources, he vowed he would go forth in search of truth and that he would not give up his quest, however arduous and demanding it might be, until he had discovered the solution to suffering.

After a strenuous period of wandering and self-exploration, Siddhartha did succeed in his quest, realizing the nature and cause of suffering and also the path to its cessation. The culmination of his efforts came, we are told, as he sat in meditation under a large pipal tree, subsequently known as the "Tree of Awakening," or the Bodhi Tree (*Ficus religiousa*). With this realization and liberation he became a Buddha, an "awakened one"—one of many beings who have, over countless generations stretching back into primordial history, gained the same liberating understanding of the nature of reality. The central component of the Buddha's awakening is summarized in his teaching of conditionality (*pratityasamutpada*). Everything arises through a process of cause and condition. Nothing exists outside of this process of conditionality; and everything will change, conditioned by the rise and fall of its antecedents. Impermanence is thus real and unavoidable. And indeed, it is the source of human suffering to the extent that one remains stubbornly attached to any aspect of this ever-changing flux of ongoing existence. Out of ignorance with respect to the true nature of existence, all beings cling to whatever seems to offer respite, craving permanence and security where none are to be had. And out of this ignorance and craving, we respond to reality with greed, hatred, and delusion, which in turn brings a reiterative cycle of suffering upon ourselves and others.

We suffer because we do not understand, and thus resist, change. But what the Buddha realized is that this change is not random. It is not simply a matter of chance, nor is it the outcome of predetermined and inexorable fate. The Buddha saw, rather, that impermanence and change are as much an opportunity for liberation as an occasion for frustration and suffering. By understanding the nature of impermanent existence, the Buddha realized that we have the possibility of directing this process of change. Rather than simply and perpetually suffering in our resistance to change, we can choose to direct that process more consciously and more intentionally, thereby affecting a liberating change within ourselves. It is true that much of the process of impermanence remains outside our immediate influence or control, but what the Buddha asserted, based on his own realization, is that human beings have the ability to change themselves and their experience of existence in a way and to a degree that is profoundly liberating.

This process of self-transformation is the goal of all Buddhist practice. It is a transformation that entails an ethical sensibility that expresses itself as compassionate activity on behalf of the welfare of all beings. It is a heady prospect, to be sure, and certainly one not easily gained. The path to the goal, articulated by the Buddha over the forty-five years of his postenlightenment teaching career, seems misleadingly simple. It is, he said, a matter of cultivating the steps of a threefold path: ethics, meditation, and wisdom. Each step is the foundation for the next, so attention to ethical conduct—including the ways in which we express our sexuality—lies at the very foundation of the Buddhist path.

The Law of Karma in Buddhism

To understand the place of human sexuality in the broader Buddhist program of self-transformation, we must first consider the psycho-spiritual "mechanics" of the transformative process. One is able, according to Buddhist teachings, to direct the course of change in a more favorable direction to the extent that one is able to work directly with the principle of conditionality within one's own life. Change, as we have seen, is not random, but conditioned, and thus, the Buddha taught, one can direct that change to a significant degree. But how does one do this? It is done by working with the key conditioning factor in one's life, namely one's volitional actions: one's *karma*. The word *karma* simply means "act" or "action," and in the pre-Buddhist Brahmanic tradition it referred specifically to the acts of ritual sacrifice directed to the gods. These acts had spiritual significance because their proper execution secured personal prosperity and also sustained, more broadly, the whole of the cosmic order. The Buddha, however, formulated a rather different notion of *karma*.

   The distinguishing feature of the Buddhist conception of *karma* lies in the view that what determines the spiritual significance of an action is the extent to which it directly furthers (or obstructs) the quest for awakening or enlightenment. Because this process of self-transformation involves, above all else, the "reconditioning" of one's "heart-mind" (*citta*), it is the intention motivating an action that determines its spiritual value and significance. This view of *karma* is both more individualized and more ethicized than the view of *karma* advocated by many of the Buddha's predecessors and contemporaries in India. Buddhist ethics involves systematically cultivating a repertoire of spiritually skillful actions such as generosity, truthfulness, and compassion—not (just) because these actions or virtues are valuable in their own right, but because their authentic performance requires (and produces) mental states (i.e., reconditioned attitudes and dispositions) that will eventually result in a liberated heart-mind. From a Buddhist perspective, a given action is not ethical, in the sense of being spiritually efficacious, unless it arises from the proper motivation. Simply following a set of ethical prescriptions or commandments may well make the world a better place, but it will not lead one to enlightenment. The only actions that are truly *karmic,* or ethically efficacious, in the Buddhist view are those that bring about this reconditioning of the heart-mind. The underlying assumption here is a huge one, and one upon which the whole Buddhist worldview is based. It is the assertion that the nature of existence includes a universal moral order that assures that harmful acts will have harmful consequences in the future, just as beneficial acts will result in more positive results. This is the "Law of Karma," and in the Buddhist tradition it is understood as a natural law that is built into the very structure of existence just as much, say, as the law of gravity. Implicit in this assumption is the rather optimistic view that all humans (and indeed other beings) have the innate potential, and even the impetus, to act in an increasingly ethical manner as long as they actively and intentionally cultivate the insight that activates and sustains the transformation of this potential for enlightenment into an actualized capacity of awakening and liberation.

Buddhist Precepts: A Set of Moral "Action Guidelines"

We have seen that the Buddhist conception of *karma* must be understood within the context of both the principle of conditionality and the key assumption of a universal moral order governing all existence. Taken together, these basic doctrines express quite succinctly the *theory* underlying Buddhist ethics. The *practice,* however, is formulated in a set of ethical action guides known as the five precepts. Buddhists of all traditions undertake to abstain from five forms of unskillful activity: (1) causing harm to other beings, (2) taking the not given, (3) misconduct arising from sensual pleasure, (4) false speech, and (5) intoxication giving rise to heedlessness or lack of mindfulness. Two of these precepts are especially relevant to our consideration of the place of sex in Buddhist practice: the first and the third.

The first ethical precept—to abstain from harming other beings, both human and nonhuman—is actually the basis for the other four, which can be understood simply as its logical extensions or specific applications. This primary precept is frequently understood to focus specifically on taking the life of other beings, but in its relation to the subsequent precepts, we can see that all forms of intentional injury or harm are to be avoided. One can readily see that killing, stealing, and lying cause harm to others. And intoxication creates the occasion for the harming of others (and oneself) in that it undermines the mindfulness necessary to pursue one's ethical intentions. But what is the problem with sensual pleasure, including, but not limited to, sexual activity of all sorts? First, we must recognize that the problem this precept addresses is not with sensual pleasure *per se*. Rather it is with *misconduct* (i.e., unskillful, harmful actions) that arises from our desire for sensual gratification. Thus, traditional commentators specify "rape, adultery, and abduction" as the primary forms of harmful activity falling within the scope of this precept. But they also recognize that these are only the most obvious and extreme forms of unskillfulness with respect to the sexual dimension of this precept.

Actually, much more is at stake here, especially when one recalls that the point of ethical practice in Buddhism is not simply to make the world a better place, but more specifically to cultivate those virtues or dispositions that eventually will lead one to enlightenment. The deeper significance of the third precept is best revealed by considering its positive expression. Each of the five negatively formulated precepts has a positively expressed counterpart. Thus, in the case of the first precept, by abstaining from causing harm to other beings one becomes increasingly capable of actively undertaking acts of "loving kindness" (*metta*), thereby laying the foundation for the compassionate aspect of Buddhist enlightenment. In the case of the third precept, the positive goal is contentment, understood as a positive experience of emotional stillness and aesthetic simplicity. By quieting and simplifying the emotional turmoil that typically disrupts much of human life, one gains a greater openness and receptivity, not just to the welfare of other beings, but to the deeper structure of reality itself.

In the Buddhist analysis, the problem with sensual gratification is twofold: However pleasurable the gratification involved may be, it is always transitory.

And because it does not last, we are typically concerned, even obsessed, with seeking to perpetuate or repeat the pleasures we have gained, while also resisting the change that will inevitably bear them away. So characteristic of normal human behavior is this tendency, in fact, that we often fail to even actually enjoy the pleasure seized because we are already too busy grasping after its replacement. The point of the third Buddhist precept is to learn how to break this cycle in order to locate oneself more happily and more creatively within a very impermanent and often fickle world. Like Blake, the Buddha would have us recognize that "He who binds to himself a joy does the winged life destroy; but he who kisses the joy as it flies lives in eternity's sunrise."

Cultivating stillness, simplicity and contentment in our sexual relationships and activities is thus seen to be both extremely challenging yet also especially beneficial. Biologically, all living beings are deeply and often quite unconsciously conditioned by the instinct to procreate. Psychologically, we have become even further conditioned to seek security and warmth, especially in sexual intimacy and gratification. Without cultivating the mindfulness and care necessary to negotiate the complicated emotional terrain of these deeply conditioned tendencies, we are likely to be driven to harmful and even destructive extremes, all the while distancing ourselves ever more from the prospect of any true pleasure or happiness.

What then is the Buddhist attitude towards marriage? Simply put, Buddhism takes no doctrinal stance regarding marriage, seeing it as a purely secular matter having no special spiritual significance and not in need of any particular religious sanction. Because marriage is not a sacrament, as it is in some other religions, Buddhists have over the centuries happily tolerated a wide range of cultural variation that has included monogamy as well as both polygamy and polyandry. So pervasive is the lack of emphasis on marriage in Buddhism, in fact, that many Japanese Buddhists today choose to have a Christian wedding ceremony, apparently feeling that asking a Buddhist monk to simply bless their union with a brief prayer fails to do justice to the occasion.

Similarly, the procreative purpose of sex is of no special concern in Buddhist doctrine. Consequently, premarital sex, masturbation, oral sex, and contraception are not seen as especially problematic, aside from the general ethical concerns discussed earlier regarding the avoidance of causing harm and disrupting contentment through indulgence in craving. Other cultural mores and value systems may, of course, also come into play—the Confucian concern for family in China, for example. Thus, one finds different degrees of toleration and concern in this regard as one moves from one Asian culture to another.

Contemporary Buddhism

The preceding introduction presented the ancient tradition of Buddhist ethics in more contemporary terms. After some 2,500 years of historical evolution and cultural transition, Buddhism today finds itself divided into three main geographical and cultural regions. *Southern Buddhism* (as practiced in Sri Lanka, Burma, Thailand, Cambodia, and Laos) is a tradition dominated by the conservative Theravada school, which traces its historical roots back to the earliest period of historical Buddhism. Further from the Indian homeland of Buddhism, *Eastern Buddhism* (in China, Korea, Vietnam and Japan) is a more diverse tradition, both culturally and doctrinally, that reflects the teachings of the Mahayana tradition that arose originally in South Asia as a revitalization movement around the first century B.C.E. And finally, **Northern Buddhism** is practiced among the Tibetan and Mongolian peoples of Central Asia, Western China, and the Himalayan kingdoms of Bhutan, Nepal, Sikkim, and Ladakh (the latter two are now assimilated politically into India). Peter Harvey[2] estimates the world's current Buddhist population to be approximately 495 million, noting, however, that it is difficult to determine how to appropriately classify the many Chinese and Japanese with their tradition of multireligious allegiance that encompasses not just Buddhism, but also Confucianism, Taoism, indigenous animistic traditions and, more recently, Christianity as well. Many in these two populous nations would rightly identify themselves as culturally Buddhist, even while adopting forms of practice from other traditions, both indigenous and foreign.

We must recognize, moreover, that the influence of Buddhism on contemporary culture is even greater than that suggested by its current number of adherents. Although Buddhism's rate of growth has been surpassed by the recent rapid expansion of both Christianity and Islam in Asia, the contemporary influence of Buddhism remains highly significant nonetheless for two distinct reasons. Historically, Buddhism is the single cultural phenomena that has pervaded and deeply influenced every culture of both South and East Asia, two regions as culturally different and as geographically separated as either has been from the West. Also, Buddhism is currently emerging as a significant philosophical and spiritual influence in the West. The figure cited by Harvey does not include Buddhists living in the West, either Asian immigrants or recent converts. While their numbers may not seem statistically significant, Buddhists living in the West are influencing the emerging world culture in increasingly compelling ways. One has only to call to mind how the Dalai Lama's recent emergence as a world spiritual leader has come about as a result of the support of his followers in West, followers who wield considerable cultural, political, and financial clout despite their relatively small numbers. Harvey, himself, rightly points out the significance of these new Buddhist communities in the West, suggesting the impending emergence of a revitalized modern or "Western Buddhism" derived from many traditional cultural sources. The Buddhist response to modernity and globalization may also be seen in various movements of resurgent Buddhism in Asia, especially the "New Buddhism" conversion (or "reversion") movement launched by B.R. Ambedkar among the former "untouchables" of Hindu India, a movement counting as many as 25 million adherents.[3]

Given the diversity of traditions we find in Buddhism today, it is impossible to document the full range of Buddhist perspectives on sexuality in the short space of a single book chapter. We shall therefore turn to two specific case studies that reveal much about how contemporary Buddhists are adapting traditional ethical principles to current circumstances.

The Gender Politics of Buddhist Monasticism and Enlightenment

Dateline: Bangkok, the capitol city of Thailand—February 10, 2002. Ms. Varangghana Vanavichayen, age fifty-six, graduate of a business college and mother of two grown children, is ordained as the Samaneri (novice nun) Dhammarakhita. Eight fully ordained Buddhist nuns (Bhikkhuni) from Sri Lanka, Indonesia, and Taiwan conduct the ceremony, which is also witnessed by more than twenty monks and nuns from various Asian countries.[4] Although parts of modern Thailand have been Buddhist for 1,500 years, this is the first ever ordination of a female monastic in this Southeast Asian kingdom.

Auspicious—and traditional—as this event appears to be, it nonetheless unleashes a complex tangle of controversy and criticism. Why has the state-sponsored Thai monastic establishment refused to recognize this ordination? Why has Mr. Suthiwong Tantayapisalsuth, deputy director general of the Thai government's Department of Religious Affairs, challenged this development, stating, "What we don't like to see is the divisive precedent it might set for other female Buddhists?" In what way could such a traditional Buddhist act of deep commitment to the spiritual life possibly be so divisive and disruptive? The answer to these questions is complex, and by exploring that complexity we can learn much about Buddhist perceptions of the role of sexuality and gender in pursuing the spiritual path taught by the Siddhartha Gotama 2,500 years ago.

More than any other world religion, Buddhism has always valued monasticism, including sexual abstinence (but not a vow of obedience), as the epitome of the spiritual life. This is especially true of the Theravada tradition of Southern Buddhism practiced in Thailand, a tradition in which only full-time monastics are deemed true practitioners; the devotions and ethical practice of lay Buddhists are seen to have only an indirect spiritual benefit. These forms of lay practice are valued, but nonetheless seen as a pious effort to secure a more spiritually auspicious rebirth so as to become a monastic practitioner in some future life. In that context, the incident reported above might seem hardly noteworthy, and all the more so when we learn that Ms. Varangghana had been living as a *mae chi,* or nonordained nun, for nine years prior to her samaneri (novice) ordination. And yet the event was reported as a major news item across Buddhist Asia. Three aspects of this story warrant closer consideration. First, the ordination itself: Why was it so controversial and precedent breaking? Second, the fact that it took place in Thailand, a modern democratic monarchy where Theravada Buddhism is the state religion, administered by its own ecclesiastical establishment directly by the king. Third, the officiation of the ceremony by an international team of Buddhist monastics, male and female, representing all three of the main divisions of contemporary Buddhism. To unravel the full significance of these circumstances, we will need first to review the place of women and of monasticism within the Buddhist tradition. We can then return to the questions raised by each of these three key elements of the ordination.

Gender and Monasticism in Early Buddhism: In the Buddha's day, the dominant religion was Brahmanism, a tradition based on an elaborate system of ritual sacrifices, the most central of which could only be performed by male members of the Brahmin, or priestly caste. Women could gain rebirth in heaven by living virtuously, but they were barred from instruction in the sacred scriptures and rituals. A radical and highly unconventional aspect of the Buddha's teaching was that he made it equally available to both men and women, regardless of their class or caste. More radical still was his assertion that women were quite capable of achieving the same enlightenment as men, and that they could do so by following the very same spiritual path. It is thus clear that the Buddhist tradition has always recognized the spiritual potential of women, and indeed, among the Buddha's earliest followers, including those whom he recognized as fully enlightened, there were many women. Biological sex and socially conditioned gender were not seen as irrelevant conditions when it came to pursuing the spiritual path, to be sure. These often did create challenges—for men, who were constrained by obligations to family as well as ruler, as well as for women, who typically bore a disproportionate share of the responsibility for childrearing.

Nonetheless, early Buddhist women did demonstrate their ability to gain enlightenment. According to tradition, many women took to the monastic life with the same enthusiasm as their male kinsmen. This did create a problem, for in the Buddha's day women were expected to always be under the protection, at least nominally, of an appropriate male patron, whether their father, or later their husband, or later still their first-born son. The idea of a group of women independently pursuing a spiritual life outside the structures and boundaries of conventional society was virtually unthinkable, and indeed, some early scriptural sources report that the Buddha hesitated about creating a women's wing of the monastic order. When some of the Buddha's women disciples, including his aunt and step-mother, demonstrated their dedication to living the full monastic lifestyle, the Buddha gave them his blessing, pointing out, however, that great care must be taken by both monks and nuns to avoid the misunderstanding and ire of those still living within the bounds of conventional society.

The Buddha frequently characterized the ideal Buddhist community as one comprising four distinct groups of followers: male and female monastics and male and female lay followers. Reading the autobiographical stories of some of the early Buddhist nuns, it is easy to see that many found the simple monastic life far freer than the more constrained and limited conventional roles available to them within ordinary society.[5] It is thus hardly surprising that a vibrant order of Buddhist nuns emerged even during the Buddha's lifetime. What does seem surprising is that the female monastics never fared as well as their male counterparts, whether in South Asia or in East Asia. There were notable exceptions to this historical generalization, however, including a strong women's monastic tradition in East Asia even after the order of nuns completely disappeared in India as early as the tenth or eleventh century C.E. And even though formally ordained nuns disappeared or never existed in many parts of the Buddhist world, there have always been women who have taken up the Buddhist path on a full-time basis, either with or without the support of the broader society. Thus, we find in all Buddhist cultures that no longer have fully and officially ordained nuns other variant or nonstandard forms of monastic practice among women. These nonordained women monastics, numerous as they have been, have never received the same respect or support as their fully ordained Dharma brothers. Ms. Varangghana, in the news item cited earlier, was, before becoming a novice nun, part of this alternative tradition, having lived a fully monastic life for nines years as a *mae chi,* or "white-robed renunciant," a nun in every respect except for the official title. By choosing to take formal ordination as a nun, she has become part of a contemporary worldwide movement among Buddhist women of many countries to reinstitute the historical lineage of the *bhikkhuni,* the fully ordained female monastic.

Rebuilding the Order of Buddhist Nuns: The ordination of Samaneri Dhammarakhita thus marks a significant step in this major, if controversial, revival of Buddhist female monasticism in Asia, a revival that comes at a crucial juncture in Buddhist history. The fully ordained nun's wing of the traditional fourfold schema of the Buddhist community thrived for perhaps a thousand years after the death of the Buddha, but since that time it has become increasingly moribund. The full bhikkhuni ordination was transmitted from India to Sri Lanka and Burma, and subsequently to China and Korea. But none of the other Buddhist cultures of Asia ever received a lineage of fully ordained nuns — not Tibet or Mongolia, not Japan, not Laos, Cambodia, or Thailand. By the eleventh century, the bhikkhuni lineage had died out in Sri Lanka under the pressure of Hindu social values brought by invasions from South India, and the Burmese bhikkhunis disappeared soon thereafter. China and Korea have had vibrant bhikkhuni communities over the centuries, although in the twentieth century Buddhist monasticism has come under increasing pressure. In Korea, this pressure came first from the more lay-oriented Japanese Buddhists during their occupation of Korea and later from the increasing influence of Korean converts to Protestant Christianity. In mainland China, the years of Communist religious suppression decimated both male and female monasticism, damage that will take several generations to repair even after recent liberalizations. Only in Taiwan has Chinese monastic Buddhism continued to flourish, and what we see there is highly significant: All Buddhist institutions, lay and monastic, have grown exponentially with the economic boom of the last several decades, but the most striking manifestation of this Chinese Buddhist revival is the rapid increase of fully ordained nuns, who now outnumber the male monks almost two to one.[6] Not only are the nuns more numerous, they are equally well educated and administer many of the most influential Buddhist institutions — hospitals and other charities, as well as many of the larger monasteries. But China is not Thailand, and Thai Buddhism has never had full-fledged women monastics, even though it recognizes their central place in the traditional fourfold scheme of the early Buddhist community.

Introducing the Ordination of Women to Thailand: The ordination of Samaneri Dhammarakhita in Thailand attracted international attention for several reasons. As we have seen, Thailand is one of those countries where the ordination of nuns is being introduced for the first time.[7] It is easy to imagine that traditionally minded Thai Buddhists are thus ambivalent and even perplexed by a development that marks a significant departure from what is comfortable and familiar, even if this development has a venerable and historically legitimate precedent elsewhere in Buddhist Asia. But the concerns are not simply a matter of the discomfort and uncertainty that inevitably comes with change. Many conservatively minded Thai Buddhists feel a very real concern about compromising the integrity of their well-established Buddhist tradition. Can these ordinations of women be conducted in a manner consistent with proper procedure specified in the Buddhist scriptures of Thailand? If not, much more is at stake than one woman's personal spiritual practice. Unfortunately, the answer to this question is anything but straightforward, and the problems it raises are especially vexing in Thailand for several important historical reasons.

Thailand is unique in Buddhist Asia in that it is a constitutional monarchy; Buddhism is the state religion, and it is directly under the control of the crown. The Sangha Act of 1902 created a central and provincial religious administrative structure that mirrors the civil administration, thus underscoring the close relationship between religion and state. Just as the civil administration has a prime minister, so also the Buddhist establishment has a religious patriarch; and both are appointed by the crown. Historically divergent forms of Buddhist practice have existed in Thailand and are generally tolerated by the state-controlled religious establishment, but even so, the exclusively male monastic order remains, on the whole, the most conservative in Asia, both politically and culturally. Also, the state has the authority to recognize or to reject all ordinations within the country, and in this case it has refused to accept the validity of Dhammarakhita's ordination. Why? It is easy to suspect that this is a simple case of androcentric privilege and protectionism on the part of the more narrow-minded, conservative elders who currently dominate the national Sangha Council. And indeed, there is likely considerable truth to this charge, as is evident from the fact that many of the younger, less traditionally educated monks have expressed support for the effort to establish a fully ordained order of nuns. But the conservatives do have a legitimate concern. Traditionally, the spiritual authority of Buddhist monasticism has rested on the integrity of the ordination lineage. Over time, these lines of monastic affiliation became separated into distinct and mutually exclusive lineages. Although there is typically mutual respect between the different lineages, there are significant differences with respect to the number of monastic rules followed. This institutional separatism has been compounded by the increasing nationalization of different Buddhist traditions, and both of these tendencies are especially evident in Thailand's state Buddhism.

All three traditional Buddhist monastic codes specify that nuns can only be ordained by a convocation of both monks *and* nuns who have themselves been duly ordained within that lineage. Because Thai Buddhism has never had duly

ordained nuns, the conservatives argue, it is simply impossible to meet this criterion. In other Buddhist traditions, it has been possible, if still controversial,
to bring in duly ordained nuns from other Buddhist countries. This was done
in 1998, for example, when the ordination of nuns was reinaugurated in Sri
Lanka by nuns from China. Conservative factions within the monastic establishment of that country still complained, but there was no single state ecclesiastical authority that could successfully challenge the innovation. The
situation in Thailand is very different. The ordination of Dhammarakhita
actually creates a serious legal conflict. The Thai constitution prohibits both
religious and gender discrimination. But national laws regulating the Buddhist
clergy support the traditional criteria for ordination and forbid all who are
not duly ordained from wearing the monastic habit. Without recognition
from the Department of Religious Affairs, Ven. Dhammarakhita is in violation
of the law and subject to imprisonment. The Thai authorities are indicating
that they will not prosecute Samaneri Dhammarakhita, but they also feel
that they cannot acknowledge her ordination. Hence the dilemma: To the
extent that the legitimacy of Thai Buddhism remains tied to the state and its
laws, there is simply no acceptable way forward. But the historical tide favoring a revitalization of Buddhist monasticism in general and the order of nuns
in particular will not be stopped, not even if it provokes a constitutional crisis.
The force of this tide is evident from the third of the features evident in
Dhammarakhita's ordination.

The International Composition of the Ordination Team: The monks and nuns
officiating at and witnessing Dhammarakhita's ordination came to Thailand
from many different Asian countries specifically for the ceremony. Their support demonstrates solidarity for this individual woman in her quest for ordination, but it also represents a marked reversal of Buddhism's historical
tendency to become increasingly fragmented and culture bound. While this
tendency has prevailed across Buddhist Asia for the last thousand years and
more, the first 1,500 years of Buddhist history was distinguished by a very different attitude, one that was much more cosmopolitan and transnational in its
outlook. For many centuries, Buddhist monastics made their way back and
forth across political boundaries, wandering the whole breadth of Asia from
India to Korea. It is thus highly significant to see contemporary trends revers-
ing the status quo and reverting to these earlier precedents. It is all the more
significant that perhaps the most prominent issue currently uniting more
liberal-minded Buddhists across existing cultural boundaries is precisely the
issue of equal opportunity to religious practice and support for women, an
issue that the Buddha himself established as a hallmark of his teaching.

We have seen that the dramatic Buddhist revival movement underway in
Taiwan has been led to a significant degree by the reemergence of a dynamic
order of women monastics. And it is these same nuns, moreover, who are
traveling abroad to reestablish the ordination of women in other Buddhist
cultures, including Tibet, Sri Lanka, and Thailand. If these developments do
in fact represent a revitalization of Buddhist monasticism in Asia, the timing is

very opportune indeed, for in the coming century Buddhism will face its greatest challenge ever: the need to find a place in an increasingly globalized and Westernized world culture, a cultural context far more diverse and pluralistic than any traditional Buddhist society has ever been.

Contemporary Buddhism, both in Asia and in the West, is at a historical and cultural crossroad. On the one hand, most traditionally minded Buddhists feel that monasticism is the vital heart of the tradition, and that the spiritual substance of monasticism is a life of spiritual commitment lived in accord with the monastic rule—the Vinaya. On the other hand, the apparent formalism of monastic practice as it has evolved over the centuries is being increasingly challenged by less traditionally minded Buddhists. Some of these reformers, both lay and monastic, see Buddhist spirituality to lie more in individual devotion and meditation than in the communal conformity of monastic etiquette and protocol, however efficacious a discipline the latter may be. While this tension has been present throughout Buddhist history to some degree, manifesting itself, for example, in the creation of nonmonastic forms of Northern and Eastern Buddhism, it has come increasingly to the fore in the Buddhist encounter with modern Western culture. Even as we see a growing interest in Buddhism in the West, and even as traditional Buddhism may arguably be revitalized by this encounter, the place and role of monasticism within Buddhism is being questioned and challenged as never before.

Western notions of individualism and anti-institutional Protestant spirituality run counter to Buddhism's distinctive monastic tradition to a degree greater than the internal challenges to monastic dominance that have arisen sporadically from within Buddhism. The recent ordination of Ven. Dhammarakhita in Thailand is a crucial step in a monastic revival movement that may be able to bridge many of the tensions in Buddhism's encounter with modernity. A revitalized and expanded order of nuns can undoubtedly bring new energy into the tradition. But even more significant is the fact that the international and cross-cultural perspective required of this movement demonstrates precisely the shift in current Buddhist practice necessary to meet the challenge of modernity. In this sense, the recent ordination of Dhammarakhita marks not only an important shift in her own personal spiritual practice, it also reasserts early Buddhism's attitude of gender inclusivity and cosmopolitanism. In all these respects, it signals a development within Buddhism that promises to have a profound effect on the future of Buddhism throughout the world.

Homosexuality and Queer Politics in Contemporary Buddhism

Dateline: San Francisco—January, 1997. A respected and influential cleric is challenged by confused gay and lesbian congregants to clarify his seemingly contradictory statements on homosexuality. They are concerned that the ambiguity of his views might unintentionally sanction homophobic exclusion and violence—a familiar situation faced by many mainstream Christian and Jewish theologians in recent years. But in this case, the spiritual leader petitioned was His Holiness, the Dalai Lama, Nobel Laureate and spiritual exemplar for millions of Buddhists, both Asian and Western. What is the Buddhist attitude towards homosexuality? the Dalai Lama was asked. And what does the Buddha Dharma have to say about same-sex marriages? And what about the spiritual value of gay and lesbian sex? And is Buddhism willing to acknowledge the right to be a homosexual?

Homosexuality is another issue of concern and conflict for contemporary Buddhists. We again can see the Buddhist tradition struggling with the tensions of modernity, including the globalization of Western culture. During the course of his 1997 visit to the United States, the Dalai Lama found himself at the center of a maelstrom of concern, anxiety, and even anger as liberal Western homosexual Buddhists sought reassurance that their newly adopted faith did not reject them and their sexual orientation in a manner all too familiar from their experience with other traditional forms of religion. And indeed, for many a great deal was a stake given the widespread perception of Buddhism as the ultimately tolerant religion and of the Dalai Lama as its most enlightened and articulate spokesperson. Initially puzzled by the magnitude of concern regarding homosexuality, His Holiness sought valiantly to respond. In an earlier interview published in *Out* Magazine, he had asserted that gay and lesbian sexual activity was "wrong," but had then added that homosexual sexual orientation "is not improper" in itself. After some reflection, the Dalai Lama continued, allowing that "If someone comes to me and asks whether [a homosexual relationship] is OK or not, I will first ask if you have some religious vows [of sexual abstinence] to uphold. Then my next question is what is your companion's opinion? If you both agree," he laughed heartily, "then I would say, if two males or two females voluntarily agree to have mutual satisfaction without further implication of harming [the] other, then it is OK."[8]

By contemporary standards, the understanding and categorization of non-normative gender differences and sexual orientations that one finds in traditional sources, Western and Eastern, often appear inadequate, contradictory, and confused. This is true of the early Buddhist scriptures, which inevitably incorporated many prevailing cultural views, especially with regard to issues not considered to have significant spiritual relevance. From the Dalai Lama's interview and the subsequent discussions it provoked, we can begin to see that Buddhist attitudes toward homosexuality are as complex and even conflicted as they are tolerant. To understand why this is the case, we need to recognize that a number of different Buddhist principles are being brought to bear in discussing the issue. We also need to recognize that modern notions of homosexuality and homosexual spirituality have no direct counterparts in traditional Buddhist thought. Homosexual activity has been present in every Buddhist culture, to be sure, and Buddhist responses to that fact have been varied, both critical and tolerant depending on the cultural context.

First of all, we must understand that traditional Buddhism has no attitude toward "homosexuality" *per se,* because this concept is the product of a relatively recent Western cultural notion of identifying individuals in terms of their sexual orientation. The notion of homosexuality as a distinct gender identity was unknown to traditional Buddhists, just as it was to virtually all other premodern cultures. Early Buddhist texts do refer to a class (or even subcaste) of individuals known as *pandakas,* and these references are sometimes cited in discussions of homosexuality by both Asian and Western writers. Although some *pandakas* undoubtably favored homosexual activity, it is very misleading to equate them with the contemporary Western notion of "homosexual," which refers to those individuals whose sexual orientation is directed to members of the same ("homo") sex, whether gay or lesbian. The early Buddhist texts use the term *pandaka* to refer to a range of sexually dysfunctional males who have in common the psycho-physiological disorder of "lacking maleness" (*napumsaka*). This category thus would not include lesbians, nor would it include sexually healthy gay (or straight) men. Unfortunately, however, many Asian Buddhists, when asked about "homosexuality"—a concept lacking in their own traditional vocabulary—have fallen back on the specious "equation"of *pandaka* with homosexual, often going on then to point out that scriptural sources proscribed the ordination of *pandakas* along with those suffering from other medical conditions that would prevent rigorous spiritual practice. We can avoid this and other instances of cross-cultural confusion if we distinguish among homosexual activity, homosexual relationships (whether explicitly sexual or not), and the identification of oneself as a homosexual based on one's sexual orientation. We can then explore the various Buddhist attitudes to each of these aspects of "homosexuality" in turn.

Homosexual Activity: The earliest Buddhist sources, along with other Indian textual traditions, reflect an awareness of human homosexual activity, but give little indication of how widely practiced it may have been, whether as an exclusive sexual orientation or in addition to heterosexual activity. On the whole, Indian Buddhist sources either conspicuously ignore homosexual activity or, when it is addressed specifically, tend to treat it as no more (or less) problematic than comparable heterosexual acts.[9] The monastic code does devote specific attention to the varieties of both heterosexual and homosexual activity, because both constitute a transgression of the monastic vow of sexual abstinence. Cabezón (1993) cites a number of studies suggesting that homoerotic feelings and even behavior may have been viewed as less spiritually problematic than heterosexual activity in Buddhist sources from different cultures. Given that heterosexual marriage has no sacramental value in Buddhism, and also that homosexual activity has the practical advantage of leaving one freer from the worldly encumbrances of family life, including pregnancy, this attitude of benign toleration seems quite plausible.

We must not, however, conclude that homosexual activity has therefore been free of condemnation in Buddhist cultures, especially in those where conventional morals are derived from other sources. Confucian China, for example, has been explicitly critical of homosexual activity, at least to the extent that it undermines the family system, which is a pillar of Confucian ethical values. Similarly, contemporary Indian society demonstrates a notably critical attitude toward homosexual activity—at least when publically expressed. The dominant Hindu ethical value system, like Confucianism, sees more spiritual significance in the institution of the family. However, attitudes of homophobia are as likely to be a legacy of the British Raj and its Victorian sexual mores. In both China and India, these prevailing ethical values have had some influence on the thinking of many Buddhists. Japan, on the other hand, demonstrates the opposite. There we find a few indigenous Buddhist texts explicitly extolling the virtues of "male love" (*nan-shoku*), seemingly under the influence of the samurai tradition of "paedeogogical homosexuality," where an older man would mentor a younger man in a relationship that was often explicitly homoerotic.

Homosexual Relationships: The Western homosexual Buddhists who confronted the Dalai Lama were concerned about Buddhist attitudes toward homosexual activity, to be sure, but perhaps even more they wondered whether Buddhism would be any more ready than Western religions to sanction homosexual partnerships. We have seen already that homoerotic feelings and even activities were relatively acceptable, or at least tolerated, in most Buddhist traditions. And in certain Japanese Buddhist circles of the medieval period, male homosexual friendships were eulogized as specifically having spiritual value, at least to the degree that they were in accord with the basic Buddhist ethical principle of nonharm, one would assume. We must remember, however, that on the whole the Buddhist tradition has always seen the social regulation of sexual relationships as a civil rather than a spiritual matter. Thus, Buddhist practice with regard to marriage varies considerably from culture to culture, and if some segments of Western society come to accept civil marriages between same-sex partners, it seems likely that Buddhism would easily accommodate this as simply another cultural variation, even if Buddhists of certain cultural backgrounds might nonetheless find the idea personally repugnant.

This degree of toleration might not be sufficient to satisfy some homosexual couples, however, not if they are seeking in Buddhism a homosexual counterpart to the Christian notion that a sexual relationship can be spiritually consecrated and thereby become a means of spiritual practice. Remembering what we have learned about the basic Buddhist attitude regarding the problematic nature of all forms of sexual craving, it should be obvious that homosexual relationships, including those expressed in terms a marriage commitment, are still fraught with many of the same spiritual dangers as heterosexual relationships, whether religiously sanctioned as marriages or not. Thus, any expectation that the Dalai Lama might approve of, much less institutionalize, homosexual marriages would miss the point. Indeed, I suspect the Dalai Lama would have some difficulty even understanding why this would be an issue for a Buddhist.

Homosexual Identity: Another important aspect of contemporary homosexual culture and queer politics in the West is the desire to have one's identity as a homosexual accepted by society and its institutions, including its religious communities. Here again there is opportunity for much culturally based miscommunication when these expectations are conveyed to a traditionally educated Buddhist such as the Dalai Lama, as is evident in his apparent equivocation. In the interviews recounted earlier, the Dalai Lama quickly affirmed his concern that sexual orientation not be the basis for discrimination and violence. This follows readily and clearly from the first Buddhist precept to cause harm to no living being. And even though some later Indo-Tibetan Buddhist commentaries assert that oral and anal sexual activity is improper or even "unnatural," the Dalai Lama, on reflection, was quite ready to approve of consensual sexual activity as long as it did not contravene monastic vows. The issue that remains, however, is whether Buddhism would recognize one's right or even need to affirm one's identity as homosexual. From a legal point of view, there would certainly be no problem here. Many, though not all, Buddhist teachers have supported legislation barring discrimination against homosexuals. The notion the Buddhist tradition would question, however, concerns the spiritual skillfulness or value of identifying oneself with one's sexual orientation—whether gay, lesbian, or straight—just as it would question the spiritual danger of identifying oneself with one's biological sex, nationality, or profession, and so on.

The most basic point of the Buddhist spiritual path is to deconstruct all "fixed self-views," and ultimately this would have to include the view of oneself as a "homosexual" (or as a "heterosexual"). This is not to say that a homosexual orientation should not receive the same social acceptance afforded to those who are straight. It is simply to reassert that in the Buddhist tradition as a whole, whatever our sexual orientation and activity might be, it is in itself ultimately quite irrelevant to the spiritual task confronting all human beings. The ethically unskillful effects of sexual craving must be pacified, like those of all forms of craving, and this is just as true whether one is male or female, gay or straight. All other attitudes and mores regarding sexual activity and identity are derived ideally from the simple, fundamental principle of Buddhist ethics: Avoid causing harm to all beings—whatever their sex, species, or sexual orientation.

QUESTIONS FOR DISCUSSION

1. Because Buddhism sees no special spiritual significance or value in human sexuality, wouldn't it be more accurate to say that Buddhism is "anti-sex"?

2. The contemporary debate within Southern Buddhism regarding the reinstitution of full ordination for women is driven by a number of concerns, including that of ensuring a valid ordination lineage. Why is this issue so important? What broader significance does the recent ordination in Thailand have for contemporary Buddhism?

3. If we assume that homosexual activity is no less common in Asia than in the West, why would some say that Buddhism has only recently begun to address the issue of homosexuality? Is this assertion accurate?

RECOMMENDED RESOURCES

Cabezón, José Ignacio. 1992. *Buddhism, Sexuality, and Gender.* Albany, NY: State University of New York Press. Especially relevant are the chapters by Sponberg on Buddhist attitudes toward women and the feminine and by Zwilling on homosexuality in Indian Buddhist texts.

Cabezón, José Ignacio. 1993. "Homosexuality and Buddhism," in *Homosexuality and World Religions,* edited by Arlene Swidler, pp. 81–101. Valley Forge, PA: Trinity Press International.

Chöpel, Gedün. 1992. *Tibetan Arts of Love—Sex, Orgasm and Spiritual Healing.* Ithaca, NY: Snow Lion Publications. An early twentieth-century sex manual expressing nontraditional attitudes toward sexuality and women's rights written by a controversial and eccentric, yet brilliant and highly regarded, Tibetan scholar-monk.

Dresser, Marianne (ed.). 1996. *Buddhist Women on the Edge—Contemporary Perspectives from the Western Frontier.* Berkeley, CA: North Atlantic Books.

Harvey, Peter. 2000. *An Introduction to Buddhist Ethics.* Cambridge, UK: Cambridge University Press.

Leyland, Winston (ed.). 1998. *Queer Dharma—Voices of Gay Buddhists.* San Francisco: Gay Sunshine Press. See especially the contributions by Cabezón, Jackson, Hopkins, Kenpo Karthar, Zwilling, and Conkin.

Queen, Christopher S, and Sallie B. King (eds.). 1996. *Engaged Buddhism: Buddhist Liberation Movements in Asia.* Albany, NY: State University of New York Press.

Tsomo, Karma Lekshe (ed.). 1999. *Buddhist Women Across Cultures—Realizations.* Ithaca, NY: State University of New York Press.

Tsomo, Karma Lekshe. 2000. *Innovative Buddhist Women: Swimming Against the Stream.* Richmond, Surrey, UK: Curzon Press. Especially relevant are the Introduction and Epilogue and the chapters by Kusuma, Salgado and Li on full ordination for women, and the chapter by Küstermann on sexual conduct and misconduct in Western Buddhism.

ENDNOTES

1. Buddhists have no single volume of scripture comparable to the Bible. Instead, they have a three-part Canon of Scriptures, the Tripitaka, or "three baskets," comprising (1) the discourses of the Buddha and his disciples, (2) the traditional monastic code, and (3) technical treatises on Buddhist cosmology, psychology, and ethics. In sum, this amounts to more than thirty volumes in English translation. And then there is the commentarial literature collected in hundreds of volumes. For a good introduction to the earliest Buddhist scriptures, see *The Life of the Buddha* by Nanamoli (Buddhist Publication Society, 1972, with frequent reprints).

2. Peter Harvey (2000), p. 7.

3. See the chapters by Queen and Sponberg in Queen and King (1996).

4. "First female monk ordained in Thailand," *BBC News,* 11 February, 2002; "First Female Monk Ordained in Thailand, Challenging Country's All-male Buddhist Clergy," *Associated Press,* 11 February, 2002; "First Thai Woman Ordained," by Sanitsuda Ekachai, *Bangkok Post,* 11 February, 2002; "First Female Monk Raises Hackles," *Reuters,* 11 February, 2002; "Debate over Women in Monkhood," *Bangkok Post,* 16 February, 2002.

5. *Poems of Early Buddhist Nuns (Therigatha),* translated by Mrs. C. A. F. Rhys Davids and K. R. Norman (Oxford: Pali Text Society, 1989).

6. Harvey (2000: 393–394) cites current figures of 6,500 nuns and 3,500 monks, noting that in the largest monastery the ratio is even higher at 3 to 1. The shift this represents can be seen by comparing the ratio he reports for earlier periods in Chinese history when monks outnumbered nuns 1:1.5 in 729 C.E., by 1:6.5 in 1221, and by 1:2 as recently as 1930.

7. There are two other ordained nuns currently in Thailand, one of whom has taken the full bhikkhuni ordination. Both, however, received their ordinations outside of Thailand.

8. Cited by Conkin in Leyland 1998: 352.

9. Zwilling in Cabezon 1991: 209.

Chapter 4

Chinese Religion

Douglas Wile

The intersection of sex and religion in China cannot be plotted with a simple set of two dimensional coordinates. The complexities of developing general definitions of sex and religion have been outlined in the introduction to this volume, and recent scholarship on China has turned even such conventional categories as Confucianism and Daoism into moving targets. If we keep in mind that Chinese philosophy is not simply armchair speculation but the pursuit of sagehood, and that health is not merely medicine but the pursuit of immortality, then the line between religion, philosophy, and health will be seen as a seamless continuum.

China is a geographical, political, and cultural entity. Geographically, China occupies the eastern end of the Euro-Asian continent and is bounded by the Tibetan Plateau, Gobi Desert, Pacific Ocean, and Southeast Asian rain forests. Hominid remains have been dated to over a million years, and Paleolithic and Neolithic fossils from 500,000 to 50,000 B.P. have been intensively studied. The historical period begins with the Shang dynasty in the second millennium B.C.E., and China became a vast multiethnic empire in the second century B.C.E. with the unification of the First Emperor. The imperial period, lasting until the early twentieth century, was based economically on intensive settled agriculture in the Yellow River and Yangzi valleys, politically on rule by an emperor assisted by aristocratic feudal lords or a bureaucracy of scholar-officials, and culturally on patrilineal family-centered stability. Periods of openness to foreign influence have alternated with periods of isolation, and political, religious, and scientific ideas from China have continually diffused to East Asia and Europe. China's present boundaries were defined four centuries ago under the expansionist Manchu dynasty, and today it is home to 1.3 billion people, one-fifth of humanity. The modern nation state called the People's Republic of China, founded in 1949, grew out of a hundred year struggle to throw off Manchu rule; Western, Russian, and Japanese imperialism; and a civil war between Communists and Nationalists that left one government in Beijing and one in Taipei. De facto distinct governments on the mainland and Taiwan, vestigial British and Portuguese colonial presence in Hong Kong and Macao, and tens of millions of ethnic Chinese in communities all over the world has led some to speak of "Greater China."

Chinese religion, or more properly, religion in China, may be characterized as inclusive rather than exclusive in the sense that most people do not look to a single source for supernatural assistance. The anthropologist, or even casual traveler, observing the practice of religion in traditional China would find that a single family might worship their own ancestors, domestic gods, nature spirits, local or national cultural heroes, patron deities of their profession, and Buddhist or Daoist gods. They might celebrate the festival calendar; support local Confucian, Daoist, Buddhist, or popular temples; adorn idols; read scriptures or recite mantras; join quasi-religious cults or secret societies; make sacrifices; burn incense; buy charms and talismans; and avoid ghosts. They might consult shamans, spirit writers, almanacs, the *Classic of Changes,* palmists, physiognomists, astrologers, geomancers, and fate diviners of all kinds. For illness, they might call on a traditional doctor, Western doctor, or exorcist. They might find religious fulfillment in simply honoring their ancestors, continuing the family line, and achieving prosperity, or family members might feel the need to step out of the family to join Buddhist or Daoist orders to devote themselves exclusively to spiritual cultivation. Intensive Christian missionary work contributed more to the spread of Western political and scientific knowledge than to conversion to the cross, but it began the process of undermining traditional beliefs, later challenged even more during the second half of the twentieth century by the Communist government. Under Communist religious policies, monks and priests were defrocked, temples closed, and religious property nationalized. Temples, icons, and scriptures preserved as cultural relics were destroyed during the period of ultra-left fanaticism known as the Cultural Revolution (1966–1976), and all traditional observances were banned as feudal dregs.

For two generations, the theory of Marx and the thought of Mao Zedong inspired faith in dialectical materialism and scientific socialism to usher in the New China and eradicated most vestiges of traditional religious belief and observance. Both Confucianism and popular superstitions were repudiated. The waning of socialist idealism in the 1980s has been accompanied by a revival of traditional practices, and within guidelines set by the government, temples have reopened and monasteries have resumed ordination. This religious revival is focused on traditional concerns with fertility, fortune, immortality, and ethics, with little to say about sexuality. Today, the most important forces shaping contemporary attitudes toward sex in China are strictly secular: The state maintains an interest in sexuality through its one-child policy, and

Western media saturate the culture with messages about romantic love and sexual liberation. Prostitution, mistresses, and wife stealing have made spectacular comebacks, while independent literature and film expose traditional and contemporary oppression of women and explore attempts to recover natural sexuality free of both state control and the marketplace. Given religion's lack of influence on modern sexuality, this chapter will focus on sex and religion in the prehistoric and early historical periods.[1]

Sex in the Prehistoric Period and Popular Religion

From artifacts found at Neolithic sites in China, paleontologists surmise that primitive man, unable to explain sexual ecstasy, pregnancy, or childbirth, considered these to be awesome mysteries, and thus made fertility and the genitals objects of worship. Fertility was essential for success in production, warfare, and support in old age. Female fertility was worshipped in the late Stone Age through stone and ceramic rings, symbolizing the female genitalia; the double-fish motif, representing the vulva and prodigious powers of reproduction; and the frog, with its great belly and many offspring. Remnants of female fertility worship may be found in villages throughout China, where the practice of casting stones into sculptures, caves, and wells, symbolizing the vagina, accompanied by prayers for fertility continues. In the region occupied by the Yi minority in Sichuan Province, there are two mountains uncannily shaped like the male and female genitalia. Barren women keep a stone from the female mountain, Queen Mother, in their bosom or under their pillow as a therapeutic charm. Belief in the magical power of the female genitalia persisted into the nineteenth century, during which exposure of the sex organ could be used to break spells or defend against bullets and cannon. Popular iconography also uses gourds and melons, with their many seeds, to symbolize the womb; bees, shells, peaches, and flowers to represent the vulva; and the deer and sheep to depict female sexual power.

The discovery that conception does not take place without male participation may have been the origin of phallus worship. Neolithic pottery features images of exaggerated penises, and phalluses of stone and pottery have also been found in prehistoric sites. Indirect symbolism is seen in images of birds: the heads resemble (uncircumcised) penises; the eggs, testicles; and the egg whites, semen. Later, the *gui,* a jade tablet with a pointed top, served as a ritual object in worship, burials, and official ceremonies between feudal lords. To this day, among tribal minorities in China, female worshippers straddle stone phalluses to ensure fertility; worship towers, columns, and monuments as phallic symbols; or make offerings to local mountains believed to represent the phallus of a god. Worship of the sex act itself was depicted by combining fish and bird symbols, as in Neolithic images of birds holding fish in their beaks. A frequent motif on bronze, pottery, and brick combines the frog and snake, again symbolizing the union of female and male. Many Neolithic stone carvings depict paired figures in sexual congress, as well as scenes of hundreds of naked dancers with either exaggerated penises or large hips, breasts, and dripping vulvas. The *Zuozhuan* (Commentary of Mr. Zuo to the *Spring and Autumn Annals*) records a dance called *wansu* that was used for seduction, and Chinese minorities preserve fertility dances that mimic sex or incorporate staves symbolizing the phallus.

Mythology is another rich source of clues concerning prehistoric and popular beliefs about sex. One ancient creation myth tells of the goddess Nu Wa, who fashioned human beings from clay, mass producing them by flicking a vine soaked in mud, and finally teaching them to mate and reproduce themselves. In another version of creation, Nu Wa and the god Fu Xi coil their serpentine tails together, and their offspring people the earth. Jiang Yuan, the Goddess of Earth, gave birth to Ji, the God of Grain. Sowing the fields was preceded in ancient times by the ritual performance of intercourse to ensure fertility, and to this day, sowing and planting is one of the many euphemisms for sex. The myth of a solitary male god creating mankind would have seemed very strange to the ancient Chinese.

The deities of China's popular pantheon number in the thousands and represent the people's aspirations for prosperity, progeny, promotion, and, of course, love. The moon has inspired the myth of Chang E, wife of Hou Yi, the great archer whose arrows felled the nine suns scorching the earth. Although this benefited mankind, it angered the Lord of Heaven, who banished Hou Yi to earth. Later, Hou Yi obtained the elixir of immortality from the Queen Mother of the West, but his wife Chang E stole it and fled to the Moon Palace. This is the origin of lovers taking vows before the Moon Goddess and separated lovers appealing to her for help. Another deity associated with the moon and love is the Old Man under the Moon, the God of Marriage, who is in charge of tying the red thread around the ankles of predestined partners. This inspired the custom of bride and groom holding opposite ends of a red ribbon or cloth as they enter the nuptial bed chamber.

A number of myths use geographical or astronomical separation as a metaphor for the hardships of true love. The most famous is the affecting story of the Herd Boy and the Weaving Maid. Daughter of the Jade Emperor in heaven, the Weaving Maid fell in love with and married a mortal herd boy. When the Jade Emperor sent his queen to fetch the Maid back to heaven to face punishment, the Herd Boy attempted to follow them on the back of his faithful ox, but the Queen brandished a jeweled hair ornament, creating the Milky Way as a barrier between them. The Jade Emperor was moved by their plight and decreed that every year on the seventh day of the seventh lunar month they could cross the celestial Magpie Bridge and meet for one day. This story combines myth with observed astronomical phenomena.

A similar legend of love elevating mortals to the realm of the gods concerns the origins of the God of Love. As the story goes, two counties in Fujian Province were separated by a river so swift that it could not be bridged. One day an old man rowed out to the middle of the river with his beautiful daughter and promised her hand in marriage to any suitor who could hit her with a coin. So many coins accumulated on the river bed that it formed a solid foundation upon which to construct a bridge. Before the bridge was completed, however, a clever lad from Sizhou contrived a method for hitting the maiden with a coin. He was conducted to a pavilion for the marriage ceremony, but when he was seated he could not get up. This was because the old man and the beautiful maiden, who were incarnations of the God of Earth and Guan Yin, the Goddess of Mercy, had already transported his soul to the Western Paradise and made him a Buddha, leaving his physical body behind for frustrated lovers to worship. Unrequited lovers who gouge a bit of clay from his temple image and sprinkle the dust on the body of their object of desire are said to obtain their wish.

Lu Dongbin, one of the Eight Immortals of the Daoist pantheon, is the god of wine, women, and song. He is worshipped as the God of the Sword, the God of Intoxication, the God of Poetry, and the God of Womanizing. Because of his unrestrained behavior, he is the only immortal whom the Queen Mother of Heaven refuses to receive on her birthday. He has inspired many legends, short stories, and operas, and in his most famous romantic episode he transforms himself into a handsome young scholar to visit Loyang's celebrated courtesan, White Peony. They spend the night locked in the "battle of stealing essences," but she could not shake his *jing* (sexual essence). Some of the other immortals suggested a trick that allowed White Peony to catch him off guard and resulted in his losing the battle. The image of Lu Dongbin is very popular in Chinese folk religion and still evokes the yearning for romance and sexual freedom.

Polytheistic specialization has provided numerous deities for both married people and prostitutes. The carefree poet-monk Han Shan and his Sancho Panza-like sidekick Shi De were originally worshipped as gods of family harmony, but later came to be associated with marital happiness, and their congenial image is often displayed at weddings. After the wedding, geomancers may be summoned to determine the most auspicious positioning of the wedding bed, and the Old Woman of the Bed, worshipped with offerings of wine, together with the Old Man of the Bed, worshipped with offerings of tea, will be invoked to ensure conjugal bliss. For newlyweds, the object of devotion becomes the goddesses of fertility, who are so numerous that there are specialists for conception, sex determination, womb protection, parturition, nursing, grooming, walking, and so forth. As one of the strengths of polytheism is that it meets every member of society on his or her own terms, we should not be surprised to find gods of prostitution. Initially, Guan Zhong, the Zhou dynasty statesman credited with institutionalizing prostitution, was worshipped as its patron, but later the White Eyebrowed God was adopted. He is pictured with white eyebrows and red eyes, riding a horse and wielding a broadsword. Prostitutes and their clients both bow in front of the image of the god before conducting their business. Perhaps the fearsome image of the White Eyebrowed God is intended to discourage customers from leaving without paying.

Many sexual folkways with roots in the prehistoric period penetrated all levels of society, including upper-class Confucian rationalists. The earliest sexual taboos undoubtedly appeared in Neolithic hunter/gatherer bands around incest and wife stealing. Because of the clan-based organization of Chinese villages, over the centuries the incest taboo extended to any individual with the same surname, even though these now number in the tens of millions. A second primal and powerful taboo in China involved the menses. Blood, so intimately associated with birth and death, must have been considered the vital substance of life to early man. Women's bleeding without wound, clotting, or pain, and its predictable appearance at puberty and regular intervals must have been a profound mystery. Fear of the unknown led to the separation of menstruating females, which developed into the concept of ritual pollution by menstrual blood. Even the blood of childbirth requires the ritual cleansing of the birthing room, and newborn infants are shaved to cleanse the stain of passing through the bloody birth canal. The *Book of Rites* advises against intercourse during the menses, and sex manuals predict calamity for children conceived at this time. This taboo is still observed today by Chinese, although now under the scientific guise of protecting a woman's health.

Premarital sex is another taboo that is uniquely directed at women. Inspection of the hymen and displaying of the wedding night bed sheets was common in China, as in many cultures, but a kind of chemical chastity belt is described in a recently exhumed manuscript from the second century B.C.E. A lizard was raised in a cage and fed cinnabar until its whole body turned crimson. After the lizard was killed and pulverized in a mortar, the paste was daubed on a woman's arm. It was said to resist fading for a year unless the woman lost her virginity. There is also the folk belief that the appearance of the eyebrows changes after the first coition. The cult of virginity, originally intended to protect patrilineal property rights, gradually turned virginity into a commodity, and adolescent virgins became the most coveted recreational sex partners and the most potent macrobiotic supplements for sexual alchemists.

Once a woman has married and begun childbearing, a whole new set of eugenic taboos come into play. Astrological and meteorological taboos discourage couples from cohabiting during full and new moons, solar and lunar eclipses, earthquakes, storms, droughts, and floods, all of which are considered times of unstable yin-yang balance and thought to adversely affect a developing fetus. Psychological taboos for the pregnant woman include any form of sexual stimulation, anger, or violence. Similarly, fetal education calls for natural landscapes, soothing music, and high-minded thoughts.

Charms and talismans for winning lovers are many. Rat's penis suspended in a green bag from the left arm of a man or right arm of a woman enhances the powers of seduction. Burning a sanitary napkin and sprinkling the ashes on the threshold of one's house is said to attract women like flies. There are also talismans to hang on the bedstead, surreptitiously pin on a love object's clothing, or slip into the object's drink. Magical methods to rekindle love in a disinterested husband include tickling his navel with the feet, drinking the ashes of his toenail clippings in water, or drinking the ashes of fourteen hairs from one's own lower eyelashes in wine. A forlorn husband, for his part, can excite a passionless wife by taking a likeness of her fashioned from a peach branch cut from the southeastern side of the tree and placing it in the bathroom with her name on it. He can also drink the ashes of twenty strands of her hair in wine, or, if an extramarital affair is more appealing, he can write the woman's name on a piece of paper and stick it to his belly.[2]

The Confucian Influence on Sexual Culture

High-culture discourse and state-sponsored religion in China were often as far from popular culture as Church teachings were from the lives of men and women in medieval Europe. Taking their cues from Han dynasty bibliographers and historians of two thousand years ago, Western intellectual historians have often looked at Chinese religion through the convenient categories of Confucianism, Daoism, and Buddhism. As Chinese culture as a whole is often described as "Confucian," let us take this as a starting point.

China's classical age, the Shang (sixteenth to eleventh centuries B.C.E.) and Zhou (eleventh century to 221 B.C.E.) dynasties, was marked culturally and technologically by empire, dynasty, bronze, iron, the horse, the wheel, writing, class, and male dominance. From archeological evidence, oracle bone inscriptions, and the earliest classics, we see a very highly stratified feudal society with nobles, serfs, and slaves. Women were property, and vast numbers of female slaves were forced to serve as musicians, dancers, and prostitutes. Private property, inheritance, and patrilineality combined to produce an insistence on premarital virginity for brides. Women were exchanged as gifts in diplomatic and political deals, deployed as spies, or dispatched as temptresses to weaken an enemy by debauchery. Wives and concubines of the emperor and nobility were buried alive with their husbands in order to serve them in the afterlife. During the late Zhou, or Warring States Period (475–221 B.C.E.), symbolic female figures of wood, clay, or metal were substituted, but there were sporadic revivals of live interment as recent as the fourteenth century. Feminine beauty became a commodity and hence a curse. Of China's four famous beauties, Xi Shi, Diao Chan, Wang Zhaojun, and Yang Guifei, three were given away as gifts and one fell victim of political intrigue.[3]

Whether we treat Confucius as a historical person or Confucianism (Ru) as a sixth- to fifth-century B.C.E. movement, the thrust was to respond to Warring States chaos by reasserting the need for moral leadership and a return to traditional rites and roles. Steering a course between the positive law and materialism of the Legalists, the universal love and austerity of the Mohists, and the Epicureanism and nature mysticism of the Daoists, the Confucians avoided both materialism and the supernatural by sacralizing the social. Seeing no boundary between the personal or private and the political, they believed that filial piety, humaneness, and ritual decorum, the cornerstones of family harmony, are also the hallmarks of good government, which in turn is part of the larger immanent order of the world called the *dao*. We have no record of Confucius' direct comments on sex, but in discussing "The Crying Ospreys," a frank description of sexual longing from the *Classic of Odes*, he says that it expresses, "joy without lasciviousness and sorrow without trauma." The love songs of the *Odes* have traditionally been interpreted metaphorically as describing relations between the ruler and his wives, the ruler and his minister or subjects, hierogamous unions between mortals and gods, or the living and ancestors. Perhaps the polysemy of these seemingly simple poems explains their enduring quality and shows the intermingling of sex, politics, and religion in the psyche of ancient China. In contrast to later Confucian conservatives, the *Odes* themselves declare, "Men of thirty and women of twenty need not always wait for formal marriage rites," and reinforcing this notion of the claims of nature over culture, the *Record of Rites* says, "In the second month of spring, young men and women may come together without restriction." This relaxed attitude did not extend to the imperial household, where adultery and incest could threaten smooth succession, throw the sacrifices into confusion, invite censure from the ancestors, and undermine the legitimacy of the dynasty. Confucian ideologues see the political ramifications of all aspects of life, especially sexuality. When Confucius said, "There are two kinds of people who are difficult to cultivate: inferior men and women," this set the tone for the Confucian view that sexual relations can never be a meeting of equals, but it sounds positively moderate when compared with Legalist Han Fei's view that women were all "treacherous tigers." It is this basic distrust that explains the ancient practice of killing a wife's firstborn, lest it be the illegitimate offspring of a previous relationship, or killing the queen mother lest she have undue influence on the crown prince.

Mencius (fourth century B.C.E.) acknowledged Confucius as a sage and continued his legacy, deepening the antiwar sentiments and sympathy for the rights and intrinsic goodness of the common people. The "Five Classics," containing Shang and early Zhou material, were the products of Confucian editorship and have acquired almost scriptural authority. Written by and for the ruling class, and representing a Confucian reform movement rather than a radical critique of feudalism or the patriarchy, works such as the *Record of Rites* reflect a tolerant and accepting view of sexuality: "Eating and drinking, man and woman, these are man's greatest desires." Echoing this attitude and recognizing sex as a natural and legitimate human impulse, Mencius declared in separate passages, "Food and sex are our greatest desires," and, "The desire for food and sex are part of our intrinsic natures." However, his words, "There has never seen a ruler who loved righteousness as much as sex," demonstrates the Confucian emphasis on the "golden mean," or moderation in all things. When challenged by less liberal disciples, he defended legendary sage-emperor Shun's failure to consult his parents before accepting two wives from Emperor Yao by saying that Shun's parents were cruel and stupid, adding, "What transpires between man and woman in the bedroom is the greatest human relationship." Once again, weighing competing claims of parental authority and decorum against the natural right to mate, he declared that propriety could be sacrificed if there was no other way to obtain a wife. Confucian/Legalist Xunzi was even more unequivocal when he said: "Human nature is derived from heaven; feelings are the substance of human nature; and desire is the result of feelings." He taught that the desire for sex is universal in all humans regardless of their moral development, enjoyment of sex should not be a monopoly of the emperor, and abstinence should not be considered a spiritual practice.

The short-lived but revolutionary Qin (221–207 B.C.E.) dynasty reunified the empire under a Machiavellian philosophy known as Legalism. The First Emperor of the Qin carved new laws forbidding adultery and widow remarriage in stone on sacred Mount Kuaiji, thus initiating a new era of legislating sexual conduct as a form of political control. The Han (206 B.C.E. to 220 C.E.) dynasty, which followed the Qin, saw the canonization of the "Five Confucian Classics" while interpreting them according to the Yinyang School's correlative logic, the theory of omens, and Huang-Lao Daoism. The Han began on a note of liberalization, but as the dynasty declined, political rhetoric increasingly became obsessed with unchaste widowhood, incest, and licentiousness, often invoking a sterner morality in an idealized ancient past than was actually the case.

After the collapse of the Han, Confucianism had to share the stage with Daoism and Buddhism, but during the Song dynasty a major revival known as Neo-Confucianism was launched that gave it nearly another thousand years of dominance. Born partly out of a reaction to literary formalism in the examination system and partly the challenge and influence of Buddhism and Daoism, Neo-Confucianism sought to bring the truths of the classics to bear on practical contemporary problems. Integrating morality and metaphysics, it described a dualistic world of material force (*qi*) acting according to an immanent order (*li*) that could be apprehended outwardly through an understanding of nature and inwardly through meditation. Believing in a self with real moral agency, it taught that by following our "heavenly nature" and "innate wisdom," rather than succumbing to "human desires," we could rise to the level of sagehood in this lifetime. The method for "preserving heavenly principles and destroying human desires" was to purify or still the mind through meditation and to adhere to a strict code of propriety intended to express respect. Some Ming Confucians pursued these goals with religious zeal, experiencing Confucian "enlightenments," and even preaching to the masses. The negative association of "human desires" with sex and the positive association of "propriety" with separation of the sexes had far-reaching effects on the sexual culture of China.

At the apex of the social hierarchy was the emperor, checked by the keepers of the Confucian flame, his ministers and the scholar officials. Sex was no small part of the imperial institution; in fact, sex and sagacity were the twin pillars of his constructed legitimacy. Every crown prince was the product of intensive eugenic breeding, whereas the empress and his secondary wives and concubines were chosen on the basis of politics and esthetics. The hundreds, thousands, and even tens of thousands of women in his harem were not merely a symbolic display of conspicuous consumption, but sources of sexual supplementation in a regimen intended to produce a super son as his successor. Standing at the center of civilization and between heaven and earth, the emperor directed a corps of specialists who monitored astronomical, calendrical, numerological, meteorological, and geomantic data, and he was ever alert to omens of heaven's disapproval or popular discontent. He was ritually responsible for the great national and clan sacrifices and for the ceremonies

marking the seasons and agricultural calendar, and his dress, diet, and resi-
dence all reflected a ritualized rhythm. At the same time, the emperor's
monopoly of the empire's most beautiful women and the ratio of the imperial
harem to the general female population, which sometimes reached 1:600, was
recognized as engendering "bitter women and solitary men" or even causing
natural disasters, such as floods and droughts, that sometimes forced the
emperor to liberate numbers of his concubines to restore cosmic equilibrium.
A common literary conceit depicts neglected palace women sewing uniforms
for handsome young warriors at the front, who in turn fantasize about the
delicate hands that made their garments stitch by stitch.

As head of a state religion, all aspects of the emperor's life had at least theoretical ritual significance. Reinforced by the cultural obsession with fertility, yin-
yang, and the bedroom arts, the emperor's sex life was subjected to the minutest
scrutiny. The *Record of Rites* ordains 120 secondary wives for the emperor in
ranks of geometric progression: 3, 9, 27, and 81. Sexual relations with them
were regulated by the lunar cycle, such that during the waxing first to fifteenth,
he slept with ascending ranks (nine per night for nine nights, or eighty-one of
the lowest rank), culminating on the fifteenth in congress with the empress herself under a full moon, and then in descending order through the three, nine,
and twenty-seven. An alternate classical formulation called for a five-day cycle,
whereby the empress cohabited with the emperor for five days and then rested
one, which gave the next nine one chance every forty-five days. The others did
not have opportunities for solo performances, but accompanied the first nine.
The point of all this was to heighten the emperor's yang energy and to allow
him to sire a fit heir to continue the royal line and the dynasty.

Regardless of the scheme, and apart from the numerology of nines (the pen-
ultimate yang number), one function of a fixed routine was simply to avoid
wrangling among wives. The rotation system became increasingly complex,
and as the numbers swelled to the tens of thousands, officials known as "sex
scribes" were employed to oversee the details. The wives wore gold, silver,
and copper rings to signify their rank, and they were required to wear red
rouge on their cheeks during menses. Their performance and demeanor were
duly recorded to ensure the royal paternity of the offspring. During the Ming
and Qing dynasties, the concubines each had a green name plate, ten or more
of which were offered on a silver tray to the emperor at dinner by the chief
eunuch. He would turn over the names of the desired partners, who would be
delivered to his bed naked and wrapped in a feather cape to prevent conceal-
ment of a weapon. Apart from the eunuchs and sex scribes, "female officials"
served as midwives, wet nurses, and physical examiners for prospective concubines. Wet nurses to future emperors often enjoyed influence at court, as did
the opportunistic purveyors of royal aphrodisiacs.

Confucian moralizers, who are generally the authors of official histories,
often blame bad government on wine, women, and song or on the power
wielded by eunuchs and imperial favorites. Political disorder begins in the
emperor's bedroom, spreads to the court and the kingdom, and finally is read
in omens illuminated in the book of nature. Confucian historians have also

not generally been kind to the few empresses or secondary wives who actually held the reins of power after the emperor died, such as Wu Zetian of the Tang and Cixi of the Qing, who are often maligned, ironically, for their multiple lovers. One of the accusations leveled at Mao's wife Jiang Qing after the fall of the Gang of Four was that she secretly watched Western pornographic films while enforcing strict censorship on the rest of the nation.

Although teachings hostile to sexuality can be discovered in the Zhou classics, it was not until Song Neo-Confucianism that they move to the foreground. More than fifteen hundred years earlier, the *Record of Rites* had sought to regulate relations between the sexes: "In passing things between them, men and women should not make physical contact." The *Rites* goes on to spell out other conditions of separation, including not sharing the same well, bath, clothes, or bed. Men were forbidden to enter the women's quarters, and women were allowed to venture outside their walled homes only in emergencies, and then with faces veiled. Education was withheld from girls, and in a saying that all Chinese still know today, "A virtuous woman is one without talent." A good reputation rested on a nearly total blackout of information, indicating a properly sequestered existence, penetrable only by a skillful matchmaker. So strict was the isolation of women in respectable families that physicians were obliged to diagnose their female patients by having them point to the afflicted area on a small ceramic model, by interviewing them behind a screen, and by taking their pulse through a layer of gauze. When Mencius was asked whether it violated propriety to extend a hand to a sister-in-law who was drowning, he granted an exemption to the *Rites'* dictum regarding contact. In contrast, Cheng Yi, the father of Neo-Confucianism, when asked whether a starving widow could remarry, replied: "Starvation is a small matter, but violating propriety is very grave." Up until the Song Dynasty, teachings about separation of the sexes in the ancient classics had little relevance in the one-room huts of the peasantry and were probably rarely observed to the letter even in upper-class households. In the strictest sense, these prohibitions were not antisexual, but, like royal aloofness, were designed to project an aura of moral rectitude and cultural refinement in the ruling class and reinforce the dignity, authority, and charisma of the family patriarch. Additionally, they aimed to prevent the patriarch from squandering all of his energies in voluptuous pursuits to the neglect of his estates and official responsibilities. Although exceptional women were considered capable of moral development and could play an important role in the education of their sons, or even remonstrate with their husbands, the Confucian school from its inception emphasized male resistance to the temptations of the "inner rooms."[4]

The moralistic teachings of the Neo-Confucians gradually penetrated all levels of society, and once becoming orthodox, remained dominant until the very end of the dynastic period in the early twentieth century. One of their first targets was prostitution. This is illustrated in a famous story of the Cheng brothers, who were invited to a dinner party where there were prostitutes in attendance. The younger brother, Cheng Hao, offended by the prostitutes' presence, rose and excused himself, while Cheng Yi finished his meal and departed as if nothing had happened. The following morning, the younger Cheng angrily confronted his brother, who explained, "Yesterday at the party, no thought of the prostitutes entered *my* mind, but today here in your own home, *you* cannot stop thinking about them." Generally, however, Cheng Yi's state of imperturbability was thought to be unattainable without removing the temptations that inflame desire. As these philosophical teachings were translated into social action, they took the form of censorship of erotic art, literature, drama, and dance; personal ledgers of merit and demerit with point values for transgressions; and books of advice for women, advocating extreme modesty and obedience. Sexual repression was carried to great extremes, often with tragic consequences. There is a story of a gentleman named Guo Liu, who during a famine traveled to a distant village in search of food. While he was away, his wife sold her body in order to support his parents. When he returned, she found a new wife for him and committed suicide to protect his family's honor. His parents defended her actions.

The assault on human desires played out with greatest rigor in the area of female chastity. For at least a thousand years, incalculable amounts of social capital were invested in four aspects of controlling female sexuality: preserving virginity before marriage, maintaining fidelity during marriage, refusing to remarry after a husband dies, and following a husband to the grave or defending one's honor to the death. As the saying goes, "A husband is like heaven: there is only one." This ideology of absolute fidelity to one man was elevated to a cult, with widows cutting off their hair, ears, and even fingers to signify their resolve to remain in mourning for life. Stories circulated about women who cut off their arms after an accidental brush by a stranger. Married women who died fighting off rapists were honored as martyrs; women who died unsuccessfully resisting rape were considered a disgrace. Families who supported faithful widows were honored with public plaques, monuments, and official privileges, especially in cases of infant or prenatal betrothal, where marriages were not even consummated before the death of the male, but lifetime fidelity was nevertheless observed. In a short story entitled "Benediction" by China's foremost twentieth-century writer, Lu Xun, a widow is sold by her mother-in-law in order raise money to buy a wife for her younger son. Forced to remarry, and after a failed suicide attempt, she discovers that her new husband is kind and industrious. Hounded by greedy creditors, however, the new husband works himself to death, and the couple's young son is eaten by a wolf. Surviving as a servant, but treated like a pariah for being a two-time widow, she finally sees a ray of hope when a co-worker points out that she can have her stigma removed and avoid being sawed in half and divided between two husbands in the after life if she contributes a year's wages to the local Buddhist temple. The monks will install a wooden threshold at the temple entrance, and the tread of worshippers' feet will expiate her canal sins. Her Confucian employer is unmoved by this superstition and drives her out as a ritually polluting curse on his house. Eventually, she goes mad and dies in a snow drift.

The unequal price paid by women is further exemplified in a historical incident involving the Yuan Dynasty general Pan Yuanshao, who was preparing to face Zhu Yuanzhang, future founder of the Ming dynasty, on the battle-field. Fearing that in the event of defeat, his seven concubines would be defiled by the enemy, he instructed them to commit suicide, and then, having a change of heart about fighting to the death, surrendered. So rigid had cus-toms become regarding fidelity, that among the eighty Song dynasty princesses, only one remarried after the death of her husband.

Hypocrisy, however, was the order of the day, and prostitution and pornog-raphy flourished alongside official pronouncements on morality.[5] As society turned inward to focus on control of its female population, it is no coinci-dence that this period also saw the birth of footbinding, a form of body modi-fication based on esthetic idealization and eroticization of tiny feet and fetishism of embroidered silk shoes. The more than ten-year process of defor-mation, characterized as "a pair of tiny feet, a barrel of tears," was aimed at producing "three-inch golden lilies." Physiologically, the miniaturized feet were thought to create an erogenous zone more sensitive than the lips, breasts, or clitoris, and esthetically the foot became a focus of erotic interest rivaled only by the breast in American culture. It was the most important criteria for judging a woman's beauty, its charms were celebrated in poetry, and customers paid vast sums to experience the sight and smell of prostitutes unwinding their yards of bandages. For a thousand years, virtually all upper-class women had their feet bound as status symbols of privileged leisure, whereas peasants might bind a daughter's feet as a value-added feature in marketing her as a concubine or prostitute. The Manchus, who conquered and ruled China for two and half centuries, could not stamp out the practice and were hard-pressed to protect their own women from cultural contamination by the custom. Chinese men adopted Manchu dress and hairstyle in exchange for being allowed to con-tinue to bind their women's feet. The highly influential *Treatise of the Most Exalted One on Moral Retribution* says: "Sexual relations with women are what the Buddha called the root of all suffering, the root of all obstacles, the root of all killing, and the root of all cares. The enlightened stay away from it." The combination of misogyny and antisexuality, together with polygamy, prostitu-tion, and fetishism, create a set of contradictions and sexual tensions similar in their social effects, perhaps, to the Christian equation of sex and sinfulness.[6]

All forms of sexual expression had to be negotiated under the general umbrella of Confucian patriarchy. Attacks on the feudal family by Mozi's uni-versalism, Legalism's totalitarianism, Buddhism's celibacy, and religious Dao-ism's egalitarianism were successfully marginalized, leaving Confucianism squarely in possession of the center. Footbinding not only did not contradict the proper Confucian role for women, namely "indoor," it actually reinforced it. Two of the most fundamental features of the Chinese family system are polygamy, epitomized in the phrase "three wives and four concubines," and the extended family, idealized as "five generations under one roof." Polygamy was a privilege of patriarchy but also of wealth, and only financial ability defined its upper limit. Poor peasants, too, had to scrape together the bride price, and those who could not afford the privilege of reproducing also bore the guilt of what Confucius called, "the greatest failure of filial piety." Wives were not only purchased but were chosen with the help of matchmakers. Once married, a new wife entered the groom's family, often sight unseen, where she lived under the thumb of her mother-in-law and endured intense pressure to produce a male offspring. In a prosperous household, she would share her husband's bed with other women of her class as well as concubines, maids, and slave girls of a lower class. The husband–wife relationship is listed along with ruler–subject and parent–child as one of the inherently unequal "Three Bonds," but it was really the relationship with the mother-in-law that determined her quality of life. So important was this dyad that baby girls were often adopted, raised to the mother-in-law's specifications, and then married to their "brothers" after reaching puberty. The marriage ceremony itself, at which the bride and groom are feted as king and queen for a day, was presided over not by clergy, but the highest-ranking official willing to officiate, and consisted of bowing to the ancestral tablets of the groom, to heaven, and to earth. This was followed by a banquet, often representing many years of saving by the groom, after which the newlyweds were conducted to a bedroom where they were expected to produce evidence of the bride's virginity and to withstand the sometimes savagely sadistic hazing (*naofang*) that guests were allowed to visit on them while they attempted to consummate the marriage. Milder customs involving community participation in the newlyweds' sex lives include eavesdropping on the wedding bed (*tingfang*) and real-time sex education (*mingfang*), in which the couple is talked through the procedures of lovemaking. Modern Chinese wedding banquets often require the newlyweds to amuse the guests with obscene games, such as the groom eating a string of cherries draped around the bride's bosom with his hands bound or the bride nudging an apple up the trouser leg of the groom, around the crotch, and down the other side with her hands tied.[7]

Prostitution flourished alongside polygamy in China, not only as the poor man's alternative to marriage, but also as a primary cultural diversion for the polygamous rich. In the West, we are accustomed to thinking of both state and religion as enemies of prostitution, but in China, from ancient times prostitution has enjoyed state sponsorship and the tacit acquiescence of religion. Government regulation of prostitution is attributed to the statesman Guan Zhong, who while prime minister in the seventh century B.C.E. established state brothels as a means of filling the treasury, employing slave girls, rewarding soldiers, carrying out espionage and political seduction, and attracting talented men to the Qi court. Sima Qian's *Records of the Grand Historian* tells us that when the state of Qi sent eighty beautiful prostitutes to the ruler of Confucius' home state of Lu, the tactic was so successful in distracting the king that Confucius left in disgust. In succeeding dynasties, prostitution became institutionalized, and prostitutes were classed according to the circles they served: court, official, military, domestic, and private. Prostitutes were drawn from the ranks of female prisoners of war, the wives and daughters of convicted criminals and debtors, and even upper-class women trapped by circumstances or deception. A subculture of talented prostitutes and romantic scholars flourished during the Tang, and it was often in the company of courtesan poetesses and musicians that idealistic scholars found escape from domestic and political burdens, even forming intellectual and platonic relationships. Moralizers inveighed against elevating prostitutes to the status of wives or legitimizing their offspring, but it was not uncommon for men of letters to acknowledge prostitutes as their muses and to form more meaningful bonds with them than with their own wives. Although taken for granted as a social fixture, and rarely opposed by religious or progressive thinkers, prostitution was never respectable, nor did prostitutes cease to aspire to normal lives. Only religious movements that combined an egalitarian ideology with military might, such as the late Yellow Turbans, the late Qing Taiping Rebels, or twentieth-century communists have attempted to stamp out prostitution.[8]

Confucianism's chief social function was to uphold patrilineality, but several alternatives to the standard family were monastic celibacy, eunuchism, and homosexuality. Confucians never failed to point out that Buddhism was a foreign faith and that celibacy violated the sacred duty to honor one's parents by continuing the family line. Polygamy on a grand scale, such as at court, required armies of castrated harem guards, usually supplied by desperately poor parents seeking upward mobility or just a rice bowl for their sons. The Confucian critique of the peculiar institution was not usually based on the grounds of its cruelty, because the Confucian scholars accepted eunuchism as an inevitable concomitant of imperial polygamy. Rather the criticism arose from the fact that eunuchs frequently enjoyed greater influence with the emperor than the Confucian scholar-officials themselves. Castration as the severest criminal penalty short of capital punishment is attested to the fourteenth century B.C.E.. China's greatest historian, Sima Qian, wrote his magnum opus after suffering this penalty, and palace eunuch Zheng. He led several large-scale seagoing expeditions to Africa and possibly beyond more than half a century before the voyages of Columbus.[9]

Given the Confucian emphasis on patriarchal charisma, we might expect homosexuality to be strongly condemned in China. Indeed, Confucius, Mozi, and Confucian revivalist Han Yu condemned homosexuality as confounding yin and yang and weakening the family structure. He also viewed it as an ominous sign of a dynasty's imminent fall. However, like ancient Greece, Rome, and the Middle East, higher-status men often demanded sexual services of lower status and younger men as a display of power, while disesteeming women as intellectually unfit to be peers or soul mates. Demographically, too, there were large concentrations of same sex populations that had little opportunity for heterosexual life: armies, harems, monasteries, convents, prisons, corvée labor camps, and the legions of poor men who could not afford wives. Homosexuality was in some periods extremely fashionable at court, especially during the reigns of homosexual emperors, and same sex marriage was even countenanced in some locales, but so powerful was the Confucian injunction to reproduce that even confirmed homosexual men also maintained families, including plural wives and concubines. In general, the pervasiveness of polygamy made the society rather tolerant of lesbianism, which, in any event, was not thought to significantly diminish either a woman's fertility or the amount of sexual energy she could contribute to the male practitioner of the bedroom arts.[10]

The Influence of Daoism on Chinese Sexual Culture

Confucianism and Daoism run through Chinese culture like the Yellow and Yangzi rivers. As a cultural counterpoint to sober Confucian social responsibility, Daoism, in its various facets, offers a vision of utopian communitarianism and individual spiritual liberation, laissez-faire leadership, and self-cultivation. Known as "the teachings of the Yellow Emperor and Laozi" or "the teachings of Laozi and Zhuangzi" prior to the Han, the *Laozi,* or *Daode jing,* and *Zhuangzi,* dating from the late Warring States period, are its seminal classics. The *Laozi's* antifeudalism, quietism, austerity, relativism, humility, and pacifism have been variously interpreted by its admirers as precepts for the ruler, the recluse, the immortality seeker, the religious cultist, and even the military strategist. The *Laozi* frequently idealizes the soft and yielding female principle over the rigid and competitive male principle, but more to suggest that men need to cultivate these qualities than to claim that women are superior or even equal to men. The *Zhuangzi* demonstrates what the free Daoist spirit can accomplish in the philosophical and literary realms, offering a wide-angle tableau of mythological characters, fabulous beasts, craftsmen, cripples, and Confucius himself, mixed together with satire and soaring flights of imagination. In Zhuangzi's vision, every creature unselfconsciously finds fulfillment in the grand design by being true to its own nature and enjoys the consolation that life and death are part of a natural cosmic process of transformation.

In the late Warring States and early Han periods, Huang-Lao Daoism, a syncretism of Confucianism, Mohism, Legalism, Sophism, and Naturalism within a Daoist framework, gained intellectual dominance and imperial favor. According to Huang-Lao philosophy, the ruler who engages in self-cultivation becomes a kind of perfect tuning fork that brings heaven and earth into sympathetic resonance and allows society to run as smoothly as the cyclical rhythms of nature. Against this ideology of cosmic and imperial harmony, the collapse of the Han in the third century felt like the breakdown of world order and was the occasion for apocalyptic prophesy, revelations, millenarian movements, and religious rebellions that established Daoist religious communities. The *Great Peace Scripture,* the Yellow Turbans, the Way of the Five Pecks of Rice, and the Heavenly Masters all trace their spiritual authority to Laozi, who was deified as Lord Lao (Lao Jun). The Shangqing (Highest Purity) and Lingbao (Numinous Gem) revelations of the fourth and fifth centuries elaborated shamanistic ritual into meditative and visionary techniques and saw the formation of a Daoist canon and Daoist monasteries influenced by Buddhist models. During the centuries of the Tang, Song, and Yuan, Daoism often gained imperial patronage, as its boundaries expanded to embrace local shamanism, cults, alchemy, magic, exorcism, inner elixir meditation, and sexual practices.

Early Daoism may have favored primitive collectivism over feudalism, but it was clearly more interested in the individual than the family. This interest in personal salvation expresses itself very strongly in the search for immortality, whether by alchemy, inner alchemy, or sexual alchemy. Confucians attacked it as contrary to nature and the teachings of the sages; Buddhists attacked it as one more form of clinging to life. With the Han dynasty collapsing in the third century C.E. and Confucianism in crisis, popular religious and political movements arose than combined communitarian ethics, magical healing, and sexual practices. These autonomous theocracies under the leadership of Celestial Masters were eventually crushed but survive down to the present in the form of religious Daoism. What caused Confucians, Buddhists, and later religious Daoists to condemn these early movements as purveyors of "demonic doctrines" was their combination of congregational religious ritual with sexual yoga. A text has survived in the *Daoist Canon,* unnoticed until the 1970s, entitled *Salvation Ritual of the Yellow Book of Highest Purity* that describes in great detail the sexual ceremony of "uniting qi" for the purpose of "absolving sins." The solemn ritual begins with couples disrobing, bathing, burning incense, saluting the officiating priest, and invoking the gods. This is followed by meditative visualizations based on five-phase color, direction, and organ associations, petitions to the deities, mutual massage and *mudras,* and choreographed dance steps tracing the eight trigrams. After reciting a series of prayers accompanying each stage of ritualized foreplay, the ceremony builds to a crescendo described by the following text:

> Raising his head and inhaling living qi through his nose, he swallows yang according to the numbers 3, 5, 7, and 9, and recites: "May the dao of heaven be set in motion." Now she recites: "May the dao of earth be set in motion." Following this, he enters to a depth of half the head, while reciting: "Oh, celestial deities and immortals, I would shake heaven and move earth that the Five Lords might hear my plea." Now she recites: "Oh, celestial deities and Dantian Palace, I would move earth and shake heaven that the five deities of the body might each be strong." He then penetrates to the greatest depth, closes his mouth and inhales living qi through his nose and exhales through the mouth three times. Gnashing his teeth, he recites: "May nine and one be born in the midst." Now he withdraws and then returns to a depth of half a head.

This brief passage brings together all the elements of religious ritual, cosmology, inner alchemy meditation, and bedroom arts techniques and stands as one of the most remarkable documents in the annals of sexology and religious studies. We know that these sexual rituals were performed in the late Han because of contemporaneous reports by its detractors, but the *Yellow Book* appears to be of later date. It would be intriguing to know more about the folk roots of this practice and also how it survived underground in spite of centuries of persecution.[11]

The *Classic of Changes* is a work with roots in Shang and Zhou divination that is revered as foundational by all schools of thought. Though not attributed to a monotheistic god like the Old and New Testaments and the Qu'ran, its various sections are nevertheless accorded divine authorship by the god Fu Xi, the philosopher-king Wen Wang, and the sage Confucius. The classic's core is a series of sixty-four hexagrams made up of six broken (yin) or unbroken (yang) lines, or pairs of trigrams, that symbolize dynamic configurations of energy, along with their origin and future development. The *Changes* is descriptive and predictive, a work of cosmology and divination. The fundamental identification of yin and yang with male and female gives the work a cosmo-sexual cast epitomized in passages such as, "Male and female mingle their sexual essences, and all things are transformed and born," and, "If heaven and earth did not have intercourse, the ten thousand things would not prosper." These and many other passages and references confirm the general worldview that heaven and earth are simply male and female writ large, or conversely, that man and woman, including their sexual relations, are a microcosm of heaven and earth. Water vapor rises from the earth and rain pours down from the heavens in an endless cycle of fertility and renewal, hence "clouds and rain" became a poetic euphemism for sex.

In the 1920s, emboldened by the antifeudal May Fourth Movement enlightenment, scholars such as Qian Suantong, Zhou Youtong, and Guo Moro proposed that the *Classic of Changes*' unbroken yang lines represented the penis and the broken yin lines the vagina, and that the trigrams were symbols of ancient fertility cults. More recent scholars, searching for prefeudal elements in the classics, have advanced even more radical readings, suggesting that the trigrams represent various modes of congress between two partners or that the hexagrams encode secret group sexual practices. Wen Yiduo, for example, believed that the trigram *Kan* (The Abysmal), consisting of two broken lines surrounding one unbroken line, depicts typical intercourse, and the other trigrams symbolize other sexual possibilities. A number of specific hexagrams have traditionally been given sexual readings. The hexagram *Xian* (Response), for example, was interpreted by Xunzi as symbolizing the sex act, with each of the six lines describing the step-by-step stages of foreplay. Additionally, hexagrams *Tai* (Peace), *Fu* (Return), *Qian* (Humility), *Dayou* (Great Possession), *Jiji* (After Completion), with masculine trigrams under feminine trigrams and generally auspicious judgments, are often interpreted as female sexual initiative, female superior sexual postures, or even echoes of a prefeudal matriarchal past.[12]

The Buddhist Influence on Chinese Sexual Culture

Buddhism began in India in the sixth century B.C.E. as one man's search for enlightenment through the cessation of attachment and evolved into a monastic order. The finally universal religion made its way via the Silk Road into China around the beginning of the Common Era. The Mahayana Buddhism that reached China had already developed a highly sophisticated metaphysics and psychology as well as popular theistic, ritual, and magical elements, often rivaling native teachings at court and among the people. As acculturated in China, the Pure Land School, offering a practical path to paradise even in the degenerate age, and Chan Buddhism, offering nirvanic liberation in the midst of samsara through meditation and mindful living, were distinctly Chinese-flavored contributions.

Food and sex, the two areas that Confucius identified as fundamental expressions of human nature, are precisely those that many religions attempt to regulate. Historically, Christianity has been more interested in sexuality than diet, and Judaism more interested in diet than sexuality. Buddhism, however, has taken on both, advocating vegetarianism and celibacy. As Buddhism evolved, many different paths were developed to enable the faithful to progress toward enlightenment, a state that deconstructs phenomena, perception, and the self, thus ending *karma* and reincarnation. Identifying sexuality as one of the most intractable attachments, mainstream Buddhism advocated severing contact with the opposite sex, but a persistent underground believed in fighting fire with fire, breaking through conventional thinking about gender identification and even religious orthodoxy by transforming sexuality into a practice. The so-called "left-handed" Tantrism that reached China in the early eighth century attempted to collapse the dualism of samsara and nirvana by attacking the distinction of male and female. The female energy of woman, real or visualized, merges with male essence to form "translated semen" (bindu), which blazes upward along a new nerve channel to overcome all dualities and realize nirvana. In this way, the tantric adept, who is beyond good and evil, achieves the hermaphrodite state, which most closely approximates deity. Most of the Chinese tantric (*Mizong*) texts were expurgated from the Buddhist Canon and survive only in the Japanese Tachikawa literature. Robert Van Gulik has argued very convincingly that Indian tantric sexual yoga was influenced by Chinese sexual practices, a view strengthened by more recent manuscript discoveries, and tantric practices were later reintroduced into China, where they were then received as foreign.[13]

Tantric Buddhism, with its emphasis on the union of male and female energies, features an iconography of naked gods and goddesses in ecstatic embrace. Tantric art flourished during the Tang, but most was destroyed in the chaos of the dynasty's collapse and was interpreted allegorically by later commentators. In the twelfth century, Genghis and Kublai Khan conquered Tibet and brought Lamaism, or Tibetan Tantrism, back to Mongolia and eventually to China. This influence continued throughout the subsequent Ming and Qing periods, both as a popular religion and at court. Lax discipline in some monasteries led to their becoming virtual fraternity houses, and some emperors, like the licentious Ming emperor Wuzong, built temples on the palace grounds for lewd adventures with lamas and Muslim clerics. Long after knowledge of their religious significance had faded, tantric sculptures were still displayed at court as visual aids in royal sex education.[14]

Sober Confucianism could not countenance either mainstream Buddhist celibacy or tantric sexual practices. Some of their criticism was vitriolic and some gentle, as shown in the following story. An old monk raised an orphan in a remote mountain monastery. When the boy reached fifteen, the old monk took him to see the city. The boy was curious about all the new sights, and when a woman passed by, he asked, "What is that?" The old monk was afraid of awakening his lusts, and so replied, "That is a man-eating tiger." After they returned to the monastery, the monk asked the boy what was his favorite experience in the city. The boy replied, "The man-eating tiger," thus demonstrating, from the Confucian point of view, that Buddhism goes against the grain of human nature.

Bedroom Arts

The bedroom arts are the crowning achievement of Chinese culture's sexual imagination. They transformed the procreative function of sex every bit as much as foot binding transformed the power of locomotion. The extensive literature of the bedroom arts, or sexual yoga, occupied a rubric of its own in the bibliographies of *The History of the Later Han,* shared a section with medical works during the Sui and Tang, and was finally classified under Daoist works in the Song. Indeed, these texts are aimed at three different but somewhat overlapping audiences: householders, physicians, and immortality seekers. The householder texts are the most Confucian in tone, presenting techniques for the polygamous gentleman to satisfy all of his wives without destroying his health and to sire fit heirs for the family line. The medical literature emphasizes diagnosis of sexual dysfunction and the identification of sexual therapeutics, eugenics, and taboos. The school of the sexual elixir merges alchemy and meditation theory with sexual yoga to create a system for reverting to primal purity, thus achieving embodied immortality. The bedroom arts were embraced by the literati and filtered down to all classes because of their felicitous synthesis of health, pleasure, eugenics, and domestic tranquility with a vision of parlaying sexual ecstasy into spiritual transcendence. Although menses and female orgasm are what make our species unique in the realm of sexuality, the bedroom arts literature is written exclusively from a male perspective and allows the perennial fascination with fertility to be pursued in a way that perpetuates male dominance.

Most of the bedroom arts texts use two literary devices to impart a spiritual tone to the subject of sex. First, they begin with an introduction that locates sexuality in the cosmic frame of yin and yang, thus encouraging participants to experience sex as a ritual reenactment of the mating of heaven and earth. Second, the teachings are transmitted in the form of dialogues between mythological emperors, such as the Yellow Emperor, and goddess initiatresses, such as the Queen Mother of the West, or legendary physicians and immortals, which again imparts a tone of authority, mystery, and epic possibilities. Finally, Chinese sexual yoga provides a fascinating case study in how science and self-cultivation can work hand-in-hand, building on an empirical foundation of keen observation of human sexual response and interpersonal dynamics and elevating these to medical science and finally to spiritual practice.

Whether aiming simply for a more harmonious sex life in marriage or for spiritual parthenogenesis and immortality, all varieties of Chinese sexual practices are based on a shared foundation of physiological assumptions. Chinese medicine understands the body chiefly as a system of energetics; substance and structure are important only as sources of energy or to assimilate, generate, store, or transmit energy. The three primary forms of energy, or "three treasures," are sexual essence (*jing*), vital energy (*qi*), and spirit (*shen*).

In general physiology, *jing* is the material basis of life and the essence of food and water, existing either as structive potential or unattached energy derived from concentration. In terms of the reproductive system, it can refer to either semen or the sexual energy residing in the semen. In its prenatal aspect, it is pure life-giving potential; and in its postnatal aspect, it is material and subject to corruption and instability. Semen is the carrier of our prenatal endowment, the repository of reproductive potential, and the sustaining lamp of life. This lamp contains both fuel, or semen, and flame, or sexual energy, the most fundamental energy of life.

Qi is an operational term that denotes the energy entering the body through food and air, the functional activities and influences of the organs and channels, and their pathological manifestations. The last form, *shen,* takes in the functions of the heart, brain, and central nervous system, and although it relies on the material support of *jing* and *qi,* it is master of them.

The sexual essence, or *jing,* is stored in the kidney, a term covering the Western urogenital system, but is also linked to the bones, marrow, brain, teeth, and hair and opens to the outside through the ears, anus, and genitals. The kidney is responsible for controlling water, retaining the pure and eliminating the turbid, and is the seat of the fire of the "Gate of Life," or "ministerial fire," that represents the yang principle dwelling in the depths of the kidney's yin water. Forming an axis with the kidney is the heart, the seat of the "fire of the ruler," or spirit. When the heart is agitated, particularly by lust, its influence will cause the kidney to suffer seminal loss; when the kidney is deficient, the spirit will be depressed and clouded. A final function of the kidney is to absorb the *qi* taken in by the lungs, a function facilitated by deep abdominal breathing, as in meditation. The importance of sexual function in Chinese medicine can be seen in the fact that approximately half of the medicinals in Li Shizhen's monumental *Materai Medica* are for "strengthening yang and tonifying the kidneys."

Let us look at the implications of this basic medical theory for sexual cultivation. Chinese sexual science can be analyzed as the culturally constructed response to a series of perceived dilemmas based on the assumption of shared empirical experience. The first dilemma is that sexual arousal floods the entire system with positive energy, but ejaculation causes enervation and detumescence. The second dilemma is that the more we spend the essence that has the power to create new life, the more we shorten our own lives. The third dilemma is that heart and kidney, fire and water, maintain homeostasis only when the mind is calm and the semen is stable; a deficiency of water (semen) allows the fire of desire to rage unchecked, leading to loss upon loss. The fourth dilemma is that men are fire, easily aroused and easily extinguished, whereas women are water, slow to heat up but more sustainable. The fifth dilemma is that ejaculation causes depletion, but abstinence causes physiological and psychological aberrations, atrophy of sexual fitness, and obsessive fantasies. The sixth dilemma is that lovemaking creates a harmonization and bonding between partners, but ejaculation leads to loss of interest and somnolence. The seventh dilemma is that long abstinence, punctuated by occasional ejaculation, results in "violent vacuity" that is worse than consistent *reservatus* with occasional ejaculation. The eighth and final dilemma, and perhaps the granddaddy of all contradictions, is that the wives, concubines, prostitutes, slave girls and maids, who are collected as trophies of success, may end up as psychological, financial, and sexual burdens. The logical resolution to all of these dilemmas is *coitus reservatus,* which spares men the deficiency syndromes associated with semen loss, while reaping the benefits of *jing* arousal and satisfying multiple female partners. The next level of theory holds that sexual energy cannot only be conserved but also transferred. The quantum of energy lost in one partner's orgasm can be absorbed by the partner practicing *reservatus,* effectively doubling the latter's gain.

The female body could be appreciated as a landscape, the physiology of human sexual response could be studied, and the exquisite sensations of love-making poetically described, but we find little communion of souls. They remain Apollonian in their sober moderation, rather than earthy Priapic or ecstatic Dionysian, haunted by Persephone's *post coitum omne animal triste est* ("after sex every animal is sad"). Both sensation and mysticism can take us away from the ego, but Chinese sexual yoga remains scientific, impersonal, and amoral, viewing female sexual energy as a natural resource. Arrested at the "evil Eve" stage of viewing women as sexual temptresses, China never developed a Virgin Mary image of women as being less lustful than men. As for men, although the West did not come to the conclusion that semen loss was debilitating and the underlying cause of many diseases until the Victorian Age in the nineteenth century, China spent more than two thousand years under that thrall.

The details of sexual yoga and traditional sex therapy, with all their postures, prescriptions, prohibitions, and techniques, are beyond the scope of this study. More pertinent, perhaps, is the marriage of sexual yoga and inner alchemy, which gave rise to sexual alchemy, a unique system of sexual apotheosis, or using sex to become immortal. Alchemy is based on the notion that elements in nature can be transformed from baser to nobler ones, and that if herbs can cure disease, super substances can cure the ultimate disease—death. Hoping to avoid the toxicity of "outer alchemy," inner alchemists came to believe that ingesting material elements from the environment was not as refined as transmuting the elemental energies within the human body. If we let the *jing* and *qi* stand for lead and *shen* stand for mercury, they can be amalgamated in a union mythologically represented by dragon and tiger, or cosmologically by the trigrams *Kan* (Water) and *Li* (Fire). Moreover, by transmuting sexual essence into vital energy, and vital energy into spirit, we can spiral upward in a process known as "returning the sexual essence to nourish the brain." Inner alchemy is based on the further assumption that there is a prenatal etheric aspect to each of the "three treasures" that must be refined out of the gross semen, food and air, and mundane mind, a bit like the Western or Indian notion of extricating spirit from matter. The mating of these prenatal essences through microcosmic orbit mediation, circulating energy up the posterior channel and down the anterior, gestates a "holy fetus" that becomes an astral and immortal replica of oneself. By spiritual parthenogenesis, we reverse the process that normally leads to conception and birth of another human being, thus transcending nature and achieving the supernatural.

Sexual alchemy holds that *jing* loss suffered as a result of puberty and years of depletion leaves us with insufficient fuel to achieve a spiritual escape velocity. The female vagina, the gateway of new life and where so much male *jing* is lost, is the logical place to replenish our resources. Legend says that the Yellow Emperor copulated with 1,200 women and ascended into heaven. Instead of looking to the feminine essence, represented by the trigram *Kan* (The Abysmal) in our own physiology, as the "pure practices" adepts advocated, the "paired practices" school took the woman as *Kan* and made her strong middle line the highest potency of yang supplementation. The emphasis shifts to maximizing the number of partners, depersonalization and emotional distancing, and finally to a vague awareness of ovulation as an even more rarified and precious source of prenatal energy than orgasm. Some texts describe purely etheric intercourse, where the absorption of essence is accomplished without any physical contact. All of this was played out within the narrative of the "battle of essences," where women like the Queen Mother of the West, a figure who in the Chinese sexual literature combines Eve's role as sex educator and Lilith's defiance, can easily turn the tables and achieve immortality by stealing the essences of countless adolescent boys. Therefore, it was considered essential to conceal the secrets of sexual yoga from women, for whom a more socially acceptable approach to immortality via the sexual path was to "cut down the red dragon," or suspend the menses, by combining breast massage with microcosmic orbit meditation. This latter technique was especially favored by Buddhist and Daoist nuns, who believed that suspending the menses could halt the aging process. Lest the reader conclude that the foregoing is nothing but sexual vampirism, there are a number of texts that describe mutual cultivation, whereby both man and woman practice *reservatus,* both enter an ecstatic meditative state, and both potentially achieve immortality. Also, although the pathologizing of *jing* depletion permeated all levels of society, becoming a genuine phobia for many, a few skeptics condemned it on philosophical and medical grounds. It survives in China today chiefly in the pursuit of rare herbs and animal products, such as dear antlers and seal penises, to strengthen male potency.[15]

At first glance, Chinese sexual alchemy seems diametrically opposed to Christian attitudes toward sex. That is a logical conclusion if we compare Christian monasticism, celibate clergy, and the idea of sex for procreation rather than for pleasure, on the one hand, with China's multiple partners and sex as spiritual practice, on the other. However, on a deeper level, there are striking similarities. Both are based on male dominance and misogyny, and both show hostility to nature. China and Europe were strongly patriarchal and regarded women from a spiritual point of view as dangerous temptresses. That Chinese males concluded there was much profit in borrowing from the female principle or tapping the female essence should not imply a readiness to accept women as social equals. Furthermore, the harmonization with nature found in the *Laozi* and *Zhuangzi* and the equality of yin and yang found in

cosmology and medicine gives way in sexual alchemy to a rejection and reversal of nature and an equation of yin with materiality and corruption and yang
with energy and life. In this sense, Chinese sexual alchemy represents a raid
on yang resources in the female vessel. However, just as alchemy may have
been a misguided and selfish search for eternal life, it yielded valuable scientific knowledge; so, too, Chinese sexual practices had their dark side, but also
yielded the oldest and richest body of knowledge on human sexual potential.
The troubadours of the Age of Chivalry in Europe were in love with love
itself, and felt that love fulfilled was love killed, just as the Chinese were in
love with sexual energy and experienced its passage from potential to kinetic
states as tantamount to death. It would be a mistake to call these practices
"sexual mysticism," because they have little to do with the mergence of self
with other, or both with something larger, but rather with post-Lao-Zhuang
Daoism's obsession with immortality.

Philo, an Alexandrian Jew of the first century B.C.E., explicitly names sex as
Eve's sin and taught that man gave up immortality for sexual pleasure. Because
the West developed nothing comparable to China's sexual yoga, it would be
easy to claim that this is yet another example of "East is East and West is West,
and never the twain shall meet," yet on closer examination the fundamental
thinking is not so far apart. Both East and West see sex as part of "nature,"
and both see mankind in a state of "fall." In the West, our "fall" is primarily
moral; in China it is primarily physiological. Both presuppose a prefall state of
innocence: for the West it is the Garden of Eden; for China it is the womb.
Western salvation means disentangling spirit from matter, whereas in China it
is freeing yang from yin. In the matter of sexuality in the West, the weight of
the ancestors sits very heavily. Ironically, in the land of ancestor worship par
excellence, salvation can be won individually by thwarting the onset of
puberty or by supplementing what is lost in puberty by stealing sexual essence
from the opposite sex. The West could propose nothing but staying away
from women, whereas Chinese sexual practitioners propose that we go back
to the temptress and use her as a natural resource. Both China and the West
have visions of the sublime based on the sublimation of sex and rising above
our natural fate, but the Western approach is essentially mythological, whereas
the Chinese is essentially scientific. Sex is not so much sinful as wasteful.
Confucians accept that both nature and civilization are good and that procreation and worship by our descendents is sufficient; philosophical Daoists trust
nature but are skeptical of civilization; Buddhists reject both nature and civilization; and Daoist alchemists would manipulate nature to transcend the limitations of both nature and society.

Sexual Liberation

Sexual relations in China cannot be separated from the question of the
extreme differential in power between men and women. From cradle to grave,
women were under the authority of father, husband, and finally of sons. Buddhism created a space for those who wanted to opt out of the mating game,

and Daoism allowed a few privileged women to cultivate their talents and love life. Peasant rebellions were always recorded in official histories as "bandit" activity, but individual or collective acts of resistance by women were barely noted at all. One exception is an incident involving the Jiajing Emperor, who during the Ming dynasty killed over two hundred palace maids for a minor infraction of etiquette and in 1542 was the object of an assassination attempt by a group of ten maids who tried to strangle him with their bare hands.

The inferior social status of women was said to be as natural as the relative positions of heaven and earth; without education, inheritance, or the right to take the examinations or hold office, women had no political power. The first men who questioned this basic inequality often paid dearly for their heresy. One of the earliest was Li Zhi, who during the late Ming dared to accept female students and even published a book recording his dialogues with them on Buddhist doctrine. He taught that our original natures are not abstract "heavenly principles" but rather the desire for goods and sex. For daring to challenge Confucius and Neo-Confucian orthodoxy, Li's books were burned, and he was imprisoned and forced to commit suicide. Dai Zhen launched a similar attack on Neo-Confucianism, asserting that it was contrary to the liberal spirit of the sages and by insisting on what was cruel and unnatural it simply fostered perversion and hypocrisy. Yuan Mu was another prominent progressive scholar who accepted female students and published anthologies of their writings. Wang Jingqi and Ji Yun championed sexual liberation and educational opportunities for women. Li Ruzhen advocated equality and opposed matchmaking and footbinding. Another late Ming figure, Gui Youguang, dared to oppose the practice of women maintaining a lifetime of chaste widowhood for intended husbands who died before their weddings. Yu Zhengbian went a bit further, advocating remarriage for all widows and even monogamy. Chang Jiebin (1563–1640), who was a contemporary of Descartes and whose thinking should be compared with the French mathematician and philosopher, challenged the Neo-Confucians in these words: "Laozi said, 'The reason I suffer is because I have a body. Without a body, how could I suffer?' I would rather say that the reason I feel pleasure is because I have a physical form. Without a physical form, what pleasure would I know?"

In the mid-nineteenth and mid-twentieth centuries, the Taiping and Communist revolutions promoted equality of the sexes by allowing women to fight alongside men and to participate in production. Educational opportunities opened up as women were encouraged to build the "Heavenly Kingdom of Great Peace" or participate in "socialist reconstruction." Arranged marriage by parents gave way to unions based on religious or ideological compatibility. Between these two revolutions came the Reform Movement of the 1890s and the May Fourth Movement of the early 1920s. Utopian reformers of the 1890s, inspired by progressive philosophers of the past, Western models, and Buddhism, envisioned the kind of healthy sexuality that might emerge as repression and perversity faded. Reformers of the May Fourth Movement struggled with creating the kind of postfeudal relationships that would come with equality in education and employment. There was no single institution, such as the

Church in Europe, against which reformers could hurl their attacks, so they called the enemy "feudalism," "conventional morality," "hypocrisy," or "corrupt Confucians" as they did battle with the crushing weight of tradition.[16]

Conclusion

As in the West, sexuality in China has always existed in a space of tremendous tension. Ancestor worship is the religious reinforcement that translates private property, patrilineality, and the extended family into pressure on women to produce sons. Infertility has traditionally resulted in divorce, polygamy, or adoption. Whether it is Confucianism's insistence that women are intellectually inferior, Neo-Confucianism's identification of women with base "human desires," Daoism's warning to guard male essence against theft by women, Buddhism's doctrine that women are a lesser incarnation and a fatal attraction, or folk religion's equation of women with all that is polluted, devious, and disorderly, the misogynist message is consistent and inevitably colors all sexual experience.

The Oedipus complex is utterly thwarted in China, because sons have no latitude to challenge their fathers, and fathers have no incentive to dote on their daughters, although mothers compete aggressively with daughters-in-law for the affections of their sons. A firstborn daughter is said to "open the gate" for future sons, but subsequent female births might well result in infanticide. If many sons were the traditional definition of a blessed life, offering assurance of support in old age and worship in the afterlife, today's policies to control population in China have evolved from encouraging late marriage to the "one-child" policy. Withdrawal of the socialist safety net in recent years, combined with the one-child policy, has meant state intervention in couples' reproductive lives, the reemergence of female infanticide and abandonment, and the abduction and sale of women by wife brokers. Prostitution and sex slavery have made impressive gains, but divorce rates are also soaring, mostly initiated by women, and women are prosecuting wayward husbands under a new law banning mistresses. Among university students, premarital sex and cohabitation are approaching levels familiar in the West. If sexual desirability for women was formerly measured by the size of their feet, according to a standard achievable only by extreme body modification, today, standards of female beauty are dictated by Western phenotypes and fashions, once again creating ideals that can only be achieved by plastic surgery. Traditional pressure on men to save at least a year's income to purchase a wife has been as exacerbated by a lopsided ratio of 100 women to 140 men in some villages, resulting from a combination of female infanticide and medical technology that enables the selective abortion of female fetuses. For men of means, there are the age-old pressures to support and satisfy more than one woman, while guarding one's own sexual essence, and new challenges of sorting out the mixed messages of Western machismo and women's liberation.

Two and a half centuries of Manchu rule, decades of semi-colonialism, Japanese occupation, Marxist ideology, and now Western-style free-market consumerism have left China with a profound identity crisis. Part of the struggle for post-Mao cultural identity has been the search for a form of sexuality free of family or state control. Seventeenth-century Europe developed the concept of "natural man," which philosophers such as Hobbes pitted against "civilization." Confucians from Mencius to Wang Yangming spoke of "natural empathy," "the intrinsic goodness of human nature," and "a priori knowledge of the good," and the whole Daoist enterprise is based precisely on stripping away convention to find our original purity, spontaneity, and joy. In China, salvation is in moderation, not faith in a monotheistic god or his son. The spiritually ambitious aspire to become gods themselves, often consciously through the transmutation of sexual energy. In the bedroom arts, we have a model of the union of spirituality and sexuality on terms of individuality and inequality; women winners in the bedroom arts are simply those who get the better of men in the "battle of essences." In the sexual rituals of religious Daoism, we have the same union but on collective and egalitarian terms. Both, however, are transpersonal. The marriage of the spiritual, the sexual, and the personal in an egalitarian context has been as difficult to achieve in China as in the West.

Religion in the form of Neo-Confucianism took charge of controlling female sexuality, especially virginity and widowhood, whereas Daoism and medicine took over male sexuality, especially semen conservation. Control is exerted not so much by guilt or a sense of sin, but by fear of blame or loss. Today, China is looking for "natural" sex in places such as modern Western societies, their own peasant culture, or in "primitive" minority peoples within China. Chairman Mao used to insist that there was no such thing as "abstract love" outside of class consciousness, and postmodernists would say that love and sex are entirely constructed by culture. This suggests that we cannot recover what is "natural," but must evolve new cultural forms based on greater economic and gender equality if we want a healthier atmosphere for sex. The path to sexual liberation without creating new forms of exploitation of women has been fraught with great difficulty in all cultures. Is China destined to repeat our mistake of evolving from repression to recreation without combining sex and spirit? At the same time that China is looking for a new sexuality, she is also seeking a new spirituality. The sweeping away of "feudal dregs" and now the collapse of socialist humanism and the rise of consumerism have led to a resurgence of prostitution and superstition. The search has taken some back to traditional popular religions, Western religions, fundamentalism, or qigong cults, none of which are likely to play a role in initiating a rapprochement of sexuality and spirituality. It is unlikely that the religious imagination in China today will be able to positively embrace sexuality and more likely that it will exhibit a reactionary response to immodesty, premarital sex, and infidelity. In this, however, religion in China can never outshine the state, which itself will wage a losing battle to stem changes unleashed by China's opening to the global economy.

QUESTIONS FOR DISCUSSION

1. Whether we believe in a prehistoric period of group marriage or matriarchy, it is difficult to dispute the fact of patriarchy, or male dominance, during this period. What has been the effect of patriarchy on gender relations in general and sexual relations in particular?

2. China has had no religious institution comparable to the Roman Catholic Church that could speak with one voice on sexual matters. How did Chinese culture nevertheless inculcate a coherent set of beliefs and practices in the bedroom?

3. How was it possible to persuade women to cooperate in practices such as polygamy, concubinage, prostitution, chaste widowhood, and footbinding, and how is it that precept books preaching female subservience were authored by women?

4. When Western men want to demonstrate their strength, they point to their biceps, and when they want to display their sexual prowess, they boast about the number of times they can ejaculate in one night; Chinese men, however, point to the lower abdomen as the locus of strength and brag about how they can withhold ejaculation no matter how alluring their partners. Because biology cannot account for these differences, what aspects of the two cultures explain this contrast? Do you think the West's frontier mentality of unlimited resources and Chinese views on resource scarcity, moderation, and saving might play a role?

5. Is it possible to salvage anything of value from the Chinese bedroom arts, even though they were developed in a social context of gender inequality, if not sexual vampirism? Should we throw the baby out with the bathwater or attempt to adapt certain techniques if they can enhance pleasure, cure sexual dysfunction, or provide fresh inspiration in the way that we assimilate Chinese art, music, cuisine, or martial arts?

6. The Chinese saw sex as a ritual enactment of the union of yin and yang and thus part of the divine dance of the universe. Sober minds were concerned that it could become an addiction, a health hazard, or an exploitative luxury, but they never lost sight of its spiritual potential for allowing us to experience the dynamic of yin and yang, a heightened state of body-mind fusion, and a taste of ecstatic consciousness similar to shamanistic trance. Is there anything comparable in the Western tradition?

7. Do you believe that sex is simply a natural drive or that its expression is shaped by forces in the culture, such as politics, class, economics, gender roles, and religion? How has the China case influenced your views on this?

8. The Chinese incorporated both politics and sex into the realm of the religious. The Romans deified their emperors, and the European monarchs claimed "the divine right of kings," but sex was not embraced in a positive way as part of the ruling ideology. How did the Chinese include both sex and politics in their spiritual ethos?

9. Anthropologists have intensively studied the phenomenon of *koro*, or *suoyang* (shrinking penis phobia), in China and overseas Chinese communities around the world. *Koro* manifests as sudden outbreaks of Chinese men reporting fears of shrinking or disappearing penises to their physicians. This is usually associated with new social conditions of political instability, economic insecurity, or disempowerment. Why do you think the male reaction to these circumstances sometimes takes this particular medical and psychological form in Chinese culture?

10. Male aggression is sometimes explained as the need to protect the clan, tribe, or nation against invasion by outsiders or to ensure that only the genes of the strongest individuals are passed on within the group. Do you agree with Chinese theoreticians, or Western religious fundamentalists for that matter, that human survival requires men to be victors in the battle of the sexes and enforce male dominance in all spheres of life, including sex?

11. Are Chinese sexual practices predicated on *coitus reservatus* simply a pragmatic response to polygamy and the need to sexually satisfy large numbers of women or are there deeper cultural or philosophical origins?

12. We normally think of Buddhism as an Asian religion, although India is part of the Indo-European family of languages and cultures. Remembering that Buddhism entered China about the first century C.E., what Buddhist teachings on sexuality may have influenced Chinese culture?

13. Did the Chinese separate sex into distinct departments, such as procreation, recreation, self-cultivation, and love? Do we look for the same experiences in sex? Do we look for different aspects in different partners or seek all of them in one?

RECOMMENDED RESOURCES

Dikotter, Frank. *Sex, Culture, and Modernity in China: Medical Science and the Construction of Sexual Identities in the Early Republican Period.* Honolulu, HI: University of Hawaii Press, 1995.

Ebrey, Patricia Buckley. *The Inner Quarters: Marriage and the Lives of Chinese Women in the Sung Period.* Berkeley and Los Angeles: University of California Press, 1993.

Furth, Charlotte. "Androgynous Males and Deficient Females: Biology and Gender Boundaries in Sixteenth- and Seventeenth-Century China." *Late Imperial China* 9.2 (1988): 1–31.

Furth, Charlotte. "Rethinking van Gulik: Sexuality and Reproduction in Traditional Chinese Medicine." In *Engendering China: Women, Culture, and the State,* C. Gilmartin et al., editor, 125–126. Harvard Contemporary China Series 10. Cambridge: Harvard University Press, 1994.

Gilmartin, Christina K., Gail Hershatter, Lisa Rofel and Tyrene White, editors. *Engendering China: Women, Culture, and the State.* Harvard Contemporary China Series 10. Cambridge: Harvard University Press, 1994.

Goldin, Paul Rakita. *The Culture of Sex in Ancient China*. Honolulu, HI: University of Hawaii Press, 2002.

van Gulik, R. H. *Sexual Life in Ancient China: A Preliminary Survey of Chinese Sex and Society from ca. 1500 B.C. to 1644 A.D.* Leiden: E. J. Brill, 1961; repr., New York: Barnes and Noble, 1996.

Harper, Donald. "The Sexual Arts of Ancient China as Described in a Manuscript of the Second Century B.C." *Harvard Journal of Asiatic Studies* 47.2 (1987): 539–593.

Henry, Eric. "The Social Significance of Nudity in Early China." *Fashion Theory* 3.4 (1999): 475–486.

Hershatter, Gail. *Dangerous Pleasures: Prostitution and Modernity in Twentieth-century Shanghai*. Berkeley and Los Angeles: University of California Press, 1997.

Hinsch, Bret. *Passions of the Cut Sleeve: The Male Homosexual Tradition in China*. Berkeley and Los Angeles: University of California Press, 1990.

Li, Chenyang, editor. *The Sage and the Second Sex: Confucianism, Ethics, and Gender*. Chicago: Open Court, 2000.

Ling Li, and Keith McMahon. "The Contents and Terminology of the Mawangdui Texts on the Arts of the Bedchamber." *Early China* 17 (1992): 145–185.

Lu, Tonglin, editor. *Gender and Sexuality in Twentieth-century Chinese Literature and Society*. SUNY Series in Feminist Criticism and Theory. Albany, NY: State University of New York Press, 1993.

McMahon, Keith. *Misers, Shrews, and Polygamists: Sexuality and Male-Female Relations in Eighteenth-century Chinese Fiction*. Durham, NC: Duke University Press, 1995.

Ng, Vivien. "Ideology and Sexuality: Rape Laws in Qing China." *Journal of Asian Studies* 46.1 (1987): 57–70.

Overmeyer, Daniel L. "Women in Chinese Religions: Submission, Struggle, Transcendence." In *From Benares to Beijing: Essays on Buddhism and Chinese Religion in Honour of Prof. Jan Yun-hua,* edited by Shinohara, K. and Schopen, G. Oakville, Ont. Mosaic Press, 1991.

Raphals, Lisa. *Sharing the Light: Representations of Women and Virtue in Early China*. SUNY Series in Chinese Philosophy and Culture. Albany, NY: State University of New York Press, 1998.

Schipper, Kristofer. *The Taoist Body*. Karen C. Duval, trans. Berkeley and Los Angeles: University of California Press, 1993.

Sommer, Mathew H. *Sex, Law, and Society in Late Imperial China*. Palo Alto, CA: Stanford University Press, 2000.

Wawrytko, Sandra A. "Prudery and Prurience: Historical Roots of the Confucian Conundrum Concerning Women, Sexuality, and Power." In *The Sage and the Second Sex: Confucianism, Ethics, and Gender,* edited by Chenyang Li, 163–197. Chicago: Open Court, 2000.

Wile, Douglas. *Art of the Bedchamber: The Chinese Sexual Yoga Classics, Including Women's Solo Meditation Texts*. Albany, NY: State University of New York Press, 1992.

ENDNOTES

1. Recent general surveys of Chinese religion include: Jochim, Christian. *Chinese Religions: A Cultural Perspective*. Upper Saddle River, NJ: Pearson Education POD, 1985; Thompson, Laurence. *Chinese Religion*. Belmont, CA: Wadsworth, 1988; Yang, K. C. *Religion in Chinese Society*. Prospect Heights, IL: Waveland Press, 1991; Perez, Donald. *Religions of China in Practice*. Princeton: Princeton University Press, 1996; Paper, Jordan. *Chinese Way in Religion*. Belmont, CA: Wadsworth, 1997. Adler, Joseph. *Chinese Religious Traditions*. Upper Saddle River, NJ: Prentice Hall, 2002.

2. For more information on sex in Chinese folk beliefs and myth, readers may consult van Gulik, R. H. *Sexual Life in Ancient China*, Paul R. Goldin, ed. Leiden: Brill, 2003 (first ed. 1961); Ruan Fangfu. *Sex in China: Studies in Sexology in Chinese Culture*. New York: Plenum Press, 1991; Liu Dalin. *Zhongguo gudai xing wenhua* (The Sex Culture of Ancient China). Yinchuanshi: Ningxia Renmin Chubanshe, 1993.

3. Monographs on the role of women in Chinese society include: Wolf, Margery, and Roxane Witke, eds. *Women in Chinese Society*. Stanford: Stanford University Press, 1975. Schafer, Edward. *The Divine Woman: Dragon Ladies and Rain Maidens in Tang Literature*. San Francisco: North Point, 1980. Guisso, Richard, and Stanley Johannesen, eds. *Women in China: Current Directions in Historical Scholarship*. Youngstown, NY: Philo Press, 1981. Despeux, Catherine. *Immortelles de la Chine ancienne: Taoisme et alchimie féminine*. Puiseaux: Pardes, 1990. Gilmartin, Christine. *Engendering China: Women, Culture, and the State*. Cambridge: Harvard University Press, 1994. Hinch, Bret. *Women in Early Imperial China*. Lanham: Rowan and Littlefield, 2002.

4. For views of the philosophers, historians, and imperial ideologues on sex see: van Gulik, R. H. *Sexual Life in Ancient China*, Paul R. Goldin, ed. Leiden: Brill, 2003; Liu Dalin, *Zhongguo gudai xing wenhua*, Jiang Xiaoyua. *Xing zhangli xia de Zhongguo ren* (Sexual tension in Chinese society). Shanghai: Shanghai renmin chubanshe, 1995; and Goldin, Paul Rakita. *The Culture of Sex in Ancient China*. Honolulu, HI: University of Hawaii Press, 2002.

5. Sources for Chinese erotic art and literature can be sampled in translation in: van Gulik, R. H. *Erotic Color Prints of the Ming Period*. Handwritten, 1951; Beurdeley, Michel. *Chinese Erotic Art*. Secaucus, NJ: Chartwell Books, 1969; Anon. *Erotic Art of China: A Unique Collection of Chinese Prints and Poems Devoted to the Art of Love*. New York: Crown Publishers, 1977; Egerton, Clement. trans. *The Golden Lotus*. Hod Hasharon, Israel Heian International Publishing, 1979; de Smedt, Marc. *Chinese Eroticism*. New York: Crescent Books, 1981; Li Yu. Patrick Hanan, trans. *The Carnal Prayer Mat*. Honolulu, HI: University of Hawaii Press, 1996. Bertholet, L. L. C. *Dreams of Spring: Erotic Art in China*. Rutledge: Charles E. Tuttle, 1997; Norton, Bret. *The Golden Lotus: The Erotic Essence of China*. Hod Hasharon, Israel: Astrolog Publications, 2002; Wang Shih-cheng. Charles E. Stone, trans. *The Fountainhead of Chinese Erotica: The Lord of Perfect Satisfaction*. Honolulu, HI: University of Hawaii Press, 2003.

6. Some of the many monographs on the Chinese practice of footbinding include: Levy, Howard. *The Lotus Lovers: The Complete History of the Curious Erotic Costume of Footbinding in China.* Amherst, NY: Prometheus Books, 1992 (reprint); Jackson, Beverly. *Splendid Slippers: A Thousand Years of an Erotic Tradition.* Berkeley: Ten Speed Press, 1998; Ko, Dorothy. *Every Step a Lotus: Shoes for Bound Feet.* Berkeley: University of California Press, 2001; Wang Ping. *Aching for Beauty: Footbinding in China.* Peterborough, NH: Anchor Books, 2002.

7. The following are some recent works on marriage and the family in China: Chin, Ai Li. *Family and Kinship in Chinese Society.* Palo Alto, CA: Stanford University Press, 1970; Laong, Olga. *Chinese Family and Society.* New Delhi, India: Oriental Books, 1985. Jaschok, Maria. *Concubines and Bondservants: A Social History.* Oxford Univ. Press, NY: Zed Books, 1989. Ebrey, Patricia Buckley. *The Inner Quarters: Marriage and the Lives of Chinese Women in the Sung Period.* Berkeley: University of California Press, 1993; Watson, Rubie. *Confucianism and the Family.* Albany, NY: SUNY Press, 1998; Slote, Walter. *Confucianism and the Family.* Albany, NY: SUNY Press, 1998; Yan Yunxiang. *Private Life Under Socialism: Love, Intimacy, and Family Change in a Chinese Village, 1949–1999.* Palo Alto, CA: Stanford University Press, 2003.

8. For more information on prostitution in China readers may consult: Gronewald, Sue. *Beautiful Merchandise: Prostitution in China, 1860–1936.* New York: Haworth Press, 1995. Hershatter, Gail. *Dangerous Pleasures: Prostitution and Modernity in Twentieth-century China.* Berkeley: University of California Press, 1998; Henriot, Christian. *Prostitution and Sexuality in Shanghai: A Social History, 1849–1949.* Cambridge: Cambridge University Press, 2001; Jeffreys, Elaine. *China, Sex, and Prostitution.* New York: Routledge, 2004.

9. The practice of eunuchism in Chinese society is the subject of some of the following recent studies: Anderson, Mary. *Hidden Power: The Palace Eunuchs of Imperial China.* Buffalo, NY: Prometheus Books, 1990; Mitamura, Taisuke. C. A. Pomeroy, trans. *Chinese Eunuchs: The Structure of Intimate Politics.* Rutland: Charles E. Tuttle, 1992; Tsai, Shih-shan Henry. *The Eunuchs in the Ming Dynasty.* Albany, NY: SUNY Press, 1995.

10. The topic of homosexuality in China is covered in most general surveys of Chinese sexology but is also treated in several recent monographs: Hinsch, Bret. *Passions of the Cut Sleeve: The Male Homosexual Tradition in China.* Berkeley: University of California Press, 1992; Dynes, Wayne. *Asian Homosexuality.* New York: Garland Publishing, 1992; Xiaomingxiong. *Zhongguo tongxingai shi* (History of Homosexuality in China). Hong Kong: n. p., n. d.

11. Maspero, Henri. *Taoism and Chinese Religion.* Amherst: University of Massachusetts Press, 1981; Watson, Burton. *The Complete Works of Chuang-tzu.* New York: Columbia University Press, 1968; Creel, Herrlee. *What is Taoism?* Chicago: University of Chicago Press, 1970; Welch, Holmes, and Anna Seidel, eds. *Facets of Taoism.* New Haven: Yale University Press, 1979; Lao, D. C. *Chinese Classics: Tao Te Ching.* Hong Kong: Hong Kong University Press, 1982; Schipper, Kristofer. *Le corps taoiste: Corps physique, corps sociale.* Paris: Fayard, 1982; Kohn, Livia. *Taoist Meditation and Longevity Techniques.* Ann Arbor: University of Michigan Center for Chinese Studies Publications, 1989, Kohn, Livia. *The Daoist Experience: An Anthology.* Albany, NY: SUNY Press, 1993.

12. Every year sees a new crop of popular books on the *Classic of Changes,* but the number of scholarly studies in English offering significant new interpretations are

far fewer. A few of the latter are: Wilhelm, Richard. C. F. Baynes, trans. *The I Ching or Book of Changes*. Princeton: Princeton University Press, 1967; Yang Hsiung, Michael Nylan, trans. *The Elemental Changes: The Ancient Chinese Companion to the I Ching*. Albany, NY: SUNY Press, 1994; Lynn, Richard. *The Classic of Changes: A New Translation of the I Ching as Interpreted by Wang Bi*. New York: Columbia University Press, 1996; Shaughnessy, Edward. *I Ching: The Classic of Changes*. New York: Ballantine Books, 1998; Hacker, Edward. *I Ching: An Annotated Bibliography*. New York: Routledge, 2002.

13. Chen, Kenneth. *Buddhism in China*. Princeton: Princeton University Press, 1972; Wright, Arthur. *Buddhism in Chinese History*. Palo Alto, CA: Stanford University Press, 1983; Gregory, Peter, ed. *Traditions of Meditation in Chinese Buddhism*. Honolulu, HI: University of Hawaii Press, 1987; Wright, Arthur, and Robert M. Somers, eds. *Studies in Chinese Buddhism*. New Haven: Yale University Press, 1990; Gernet, Jacques. Franciscus Verellen, trans. *Buddhism in Chinese Society*. New York: Columbia University Press, 1998; Paisuku Ikedo. *The Flower of Chinese Buddhism*. New York: Weatherhill, 2000. Hodous, Lewis. *Buddhism and Buddhists in China*. Indypublish.com, 2003.

14. Doniger, Wendy. *Siva: The Erotic Ascetic*. Oxford: Oxford University Press, 1981; Shaw, Miranda. *Passionate Enlightenment: Women in Tantric Buddhism*. Princeton: Princeton University Press, 1994; Kinsley, David. *Tantric Visions of the Divine Feminine: The Ten Mahavidya*. Berkeley: University of California Press, 1997; Feuerstain, Georg. *Tantra: The Path of Ecstasy*. Boulder, CO: Shambala, 1998; Cleary, Thomas. *Twilight Goddess: Spiritual Feminism and Feminine Spirituality*. Boulder, CO: Shambala, 2002.

15. Sexual cultivation in China is explored in monographs, articles, and general studies of Chinese sexology. Van Gulik, Needham, Schipper, and Liu all devote substantial space to the art of the bedchamber. Henri Maspero's "Les procedes de 'nourrir le principe vitale'" in *Le taoisme et les religions chinoises* was a groundbreaking contribution. Wile's *Art of the Bedchamber: The Chinese Sexual Yoga Classics, Including Women's Solo Meditation*. Albany: SUNY Press, 1992, is still the only scholarly monograph on the topic; Donald Harper's article, "The Sexual Arts of Ancient China as Described in a Manuscript of the Second Century, B.C." *Harvard Journal of Asiatic Studies* 47:459–95, 1987, brought the recently discovered early Han manuscripts to light; and Isabelle Robinet's "Sexualite et taoisme" in *Sexualite et Religions,* Marcel Bernes, ed., 51–70. Paris: Editions du Cerf, 1988, is a useful short summary.

16. *Liu Dalin. Sexual Behavior in Modern China: Report on the Nationwide Survey of 20,000 Men and Women*. New York: Continuum Publishing Group, 1997; Farrer, James. *Opening Up: Youth Sex Culture and Market Reform in Shanghai*. Chicago: University of Chicago Press, 2002; Farquhar, Judith. *Appetites: Food and Sex in Postsociality China*. Durham, NC: Duke University Press, 2002; Brownell, Susan. *Chinese Femininities/Chinese Masculinities: A Reader*. Berkeley: University of California Press, 2002.

Chapter 5

Judaism

Barbara Geller

Judaism, the oldest of the Abrahamic traditions, is rooted in the religion of ancient Israel of the first millennium B.C.E.[1] Today, there are approximately 13,254,000 Jews worldwide, of whom roughly 1,582,800 reside in Europe, 4,952,000 in Israel, and 5,700,000 in the United States.[2] American Jews constitute approximately 2 percent of the population of the United States. Many identify themselves as secular Jews, whereas others are affiliated with one of the four major denominations of American Judaism: Orthodox, Conservative, Reform, and Reconstructionist Judaism. Reform and Conservative Judaism are the largest denominations, representing approximately 80 percent of religiously affiliated Jews. The Reform Movement is slightly larger. Reconstructionist Judaism is significantly smaller than the other three. However, its teachings have had a significant impact on non-Orthodox expressions of Judaism.

Although the branches of Judaism have much in common, they differ in their understanding of the nature and authority of Jewish law, and, concomitantly, in their adherence to Jewish ritual practice. This, in turn, has resulted in a diversity of practices and perspectives concerning issues of contemporary sex and sexuality. Phrased broadly, Orthodox teachings are more conservative than those of the liberal Reform and Reconstructionist movements. Conservative Judaism wrestles with the challenge of identifying a kind of middle ground. A brief overview of some key facets of Judaism in historical perspective should be helpful in better understanding the diversity of Jewish teachings and practices in this important and complex area.

At the heart of Jewish sacred story is the belief that God and Israel entered into a covenantal relationship. The vivid narratives of Exodus and Deuteronomy envision Moses returning from his encounter with God at Mount Sinai to impart to the Israelites the divinely revealed law. The Hebrew Bible draws on ancient Near Eastern political and social patterns to depict a relationship of mutual obligations.[3] God would enable Israel to thrive by blessing the land with abundant rainfall and fertile fields and by protecting her from her adversaries. Israel, in turn, was expected to obey God's commandments. Should Israel fail to adhere to the covenantal commands, divine punishment would follow.

During the tenth century B.C.E, Kings David and Solomon ruled a kingdom of the united tribes of Israel. David established a capital at Jerusalem. The city was made holy by constructing a temple to God, a project that was completed by Solomon. The Jerusalem Temple, with its male priestly establishment, became the focus of the Israelite religious system of sacrifice and atonement—a key medium both for maintaining right relationship with God and for redressing nonadherence to the divine law in order to reacquire it. In 586 B.C.E., the Temple was destroyed by the Babylonian army. However, it stood longer than the united kingdom of Israel, which following the death of Solomon was divided by civil war into two mini-states—a northern kingdom of Israel and a southern kingdom of Judah. The former was conquered by the Assyrians in 722 B.C.E. The latter, which was ruled by the descendants of David and Solomon from Jerusalem, persisted until the Babylonian conquest of the sixth century B.C.E. Within a few decades, Babylon fell to Persia, whose rulers allowed the Temple to be rebuilt. Eventually, the Second Temple would be destroyed by the Roman army in 70 C.E., bringing to an end the sacrificial system of worship. However, even during the centuries in which the Temple stood, prayer and the adherence to God's law through the study of God's Teaching, *Torah,* served as vehicles for repentance and the right relationship with God. Thus, the Book of Nehemiah depicts Ezra, a fifth-century B.C.E. Jewish priest and scribe sent to Jerusalem by the Persian king, as reading to the people from the "Book of the Torah of God" (Nehemiah 8:18) and implementing the authority and practice of God's Instructions.

Such important historical sources as the writings of Josephus, a first-century C.E. Jewish historian, describe the emergence in the late first millennium of Jewish groups whose authority was not Temple based. These included the Pharisees, the antecedents of the rabbis. The Pharisees can be thought of as part of the ancient Near Eastern scribal class, the professional literati. However, the Pharisees were students and practitioners of what ancient Judaism understood as God's Word, God's Teaching, God's Instruction—*Torah.*

The Pharisaic-Rabbinic movement and the Jesus Movement are the two Jewish groups that survived the cataclysmic Roman-Jewish War of 66–73/74 C.E. The war was the result of a constellation of factors, including the impact of the roughly one hundred years of Roman rule. For some Jews, religious and political freedom were inextricably intertwined. Many saw in Rome the mighty adversary whose vanquishing, with God's help, would usher in the end time. Although Rome was religiously tolerant, the empire did not tolerate any challenges to Roman sovereignty. Thus, Rome reacted harshly to the Jewish rebels, destroying them along with the Jerusalem Temple and much of the holy city, the location of heated battle. Pharisaic-Rabbinic Judaism and the Jesus Movement survived in large part because of shared characteristics: neither had fought as organized groups against the Romans; neither was Temple based; both were portable; both had flexible views of Torah interpretation; each claimed the identity of Israel with its worship of God and venerable history; both offered the possibility of right relationship with God and eternal life; and both took very seriously the ethical and social responsibility of caring for those in need. However, by the late first and early second centuries, the Jesus Movement, emerging Christianity, would separate itself from Judaism and engage in the complex and often painful process of creating boundaries and developing an identity apart from Judaism, from which it had emerged. Rabbinic Judaism would evolve to become nearly all of the varieties of Judaism that exist today. Indeed, the Jewish denominations noted at the beginning of the chapter are all forms of Rabbinic Judaism.

In its early centuries, rabbinic teachings were committed to writing to form the canonical documents of Rabbinic Judaism: the Mishnah, edited in the rabbinic academies of the Galilee in the early third century; the Talmuds, the Palestinian or Jerusalem Talmud, edited in Palestine ca. 400; and the Babylonian Talmud, edited in the Babylonian rabbinic academies in the sixth century. The Mishnah is arranged by topics in tractates, which are divided into six orders: Seeds (agricultural laws); Appointed Times (festivals); Women (marriage law); Damages (civil law); Holy Things (sacrifices); and Purities (sources of impurity and vehicles of purification). The Talmuds consist of mishnaic passages and commentaries, which often draw on Biblical passages to support a rabbinic ruling. Early Rabbinic Judaism would develop the belief that these core texts were not only rooted in Torah, but were themselves Torah; that is, at Mount Sinai, God had revealed two Torahs, the Written Torah and the Oral Torah, which had been passed down from generation to generation in a chain of tradition which linked the rabbis who committed the teachings to writing to the Sinai revelation itself.

In addition to the Mishnah and the Talmuds, the formative centuries of Rabbinic Judaism also saw the commitment to the writing of Biblical commentaries, collectively termed the Midrash. Each midrashic work comments on a Biblical book by chapter and verse. The Midrash is an essential source for ascertaining rabbinic values and concerns on a broad range of topics, including those of sex and gender.

However, the Babylonian Talmud, in particular, would become the foundation document of subsequent centuries of rabbinic study and teaching. Later generations of rabbis not only commented further on the Talmud, but also generated law codes and responsa to form a vast authoritative corpus that provided Jews with a frame of reference for bringing the holy into the everyday—a framework for a way of life that, in all of its dimensions, including those of sex and sexuality, was in accordance with God's law as revealed in the Dual—the Oral and the Written—Torah.

This is not to say that Jewish law, *halakhah,* is static or uniform. It is continually evolving as succeeding generations of rabbinic scholars endeavor to address both ongoing and new issues in the context of *halakhah,* drawing on a textual tradition that, often in the same document, preserves and addresses divergent legal opinions on a given topic. Thus today an Orthodox rabbi or religious court, in making a ruling, considers the many voices of centuries of religious teachings.

The European Enlightenment would serve to challenge the very theological foundations of Judaism and Christianity—that is, the divine or inspired character of their respective scriptural documents. The questioning in some Jewish circles of the nature and authority of Torah, with its mandated laws and practices, was accompanied by the opportunities and challenges posed by the emancipation of the Jews of Western Europe, a gradual process that, between 1789 and 1871, finally enabled Western European Jewry to function as citizens of their respective nations, and, in so doing, to travel freely and live where they wished, participate in a broad range of professions, and pursue studies at the great European universities. This was a monumental change from the earlier centuries of discrimination and, at times, severe persecution to which European Jews had been subject. Some Jews, especially in Germany, like their Christian counterparts, sought to embrace "modernity" through a "scientific study" of their religious traditions. If Jewish law was man-made and not divine, why should it be practiced? Shouldn't one distinguish between the timeless principles of "ethical monotheism" and the many "outdated" traditional practices? For example, as fellow citizens, would it not be more appropriate to join the majority in celebrating the Sabbath on Sunday? Gradually, such speculation as the preceding as well as reforming efforts in Jewish education and liturgical practices crystallized into a formal Reform Movement, whose adherents held synods, developed guiding principles, and established schools and congregations. Some of the early Reform leaders took very strong stances in seeking to abolish long-held ritual practices. Reform Judaism, including its more radical variety, would take root in the United States, facilitated by the migration of many German Jews in the mid-nineteenth century.

The impact of the Enlightenment, Jewish emancipation, and the Reform Movement would also stimulate reforms and reexamination within Orthodox Judaism, resulting in the emergence of Modern Orthodoxy. While maintaining a belief in the divine origin of the Dual Torah and the authority of and importance of adherence to Jewish law, with its inclusive and unified explication of what might be termed both ethical and ritual practice, Modern Orthodoxy seeks also to embrace modernity by active engagement with and participation in the larger non-Jewish environment. Other forms of Orthodox Judaism, often described as Ultra-Orthodox Judaism, differ from Modern Orthodoxy typically in their lesser degree of engagement with the larger environment and in their more stringent interpretations and practices of Jewish law. Although Orthodox Jews constitute a larger percentage of the Jewish population in Israel than they do in the United States, they are a minority there as well. However, their power is much greater than their numbers. This is due in large part to the nature of the Israeli political system in which small parties are often needed to create a government. Thus small religious parties, representing Orthodox Jewish interests, are typically part of the governing majority coalition. Also, there is no separation of church and state, as in the United States. Therefore, unlike the United States, Israel has no civil forms of marriage and divorce. Each denomination is responsible for adjudicating marriage and divorce for its adherents. However, in the case of Judaism, it is Orthodox Judaism that functions, in many ways, as the established religion of the state. Reform, Conservative, and Reconstructionist Judaism do not have legal authority in Israel as does Orthodox Judaism. Although many Israeli Jews share the beliefs and practices of Reform, Conservative, or Reconstuctionist Judaism, the movements, while growing, remain small. The intrareligious Jewish conflict in Israel is often described as secular versus religious, the resolution of this conflict remains one of the young nation's major challenges.

In the mid to late nineteenth and early twentieth centuries, Conservative Judaism emerged both in Europe and in the United States as a kind of counterpoint to both Reform and Orthodox Judaism. In the United States, it sought in part to address the religious needs of the new waves of Jewish immigrants from Eastern Europe, many of whom found neither Reform nor Orthodox Judaism to be entirely satisfactory. Conservative Judaism places greater authority on Jewish law and tradition and ritual practice than does Reform Judaism. It is rooted in *halakhah*, and, at the same time, accepts modern historical-critical scholarship, with its emphasis on halakhah's changing and varied character, both chronologically and geographically.

Reconstructionist Judaism evolved out of the Conservative movement in America, and was shaped by the writings of Mordecai Kaplan. Like the other branches of Judaism, Reconstructionism is theistic. However, whereas some Reconstructionists hold a traditional view of God, others share Kaplan's nontraditional conception of God as the "power that makes for salvation." Following Kaplan, Reconstructionism understands Judaism as an evolving religious civilization, in which religion is a central element, although not the sole element. Thus, it provides a context for Jews to embrace Judaism through other features of a culture, including, very importantly, the appropriation of its history as one's own. Ritual is highly valued as a concrete vehicle for linking an individual to a historic community, even if a person's understanding of the ritual may differ from that of another contemporary or from Jews of different times and places. Thus, for Reconstructionists, Jewish ritual practice has an important role, even if one does not believe that it is divinely mandated. Reform Judaism, too, having long since moved away from many of the views of the early radical Reformers, has increasingly and similarly affirmed the value of ritual practice in a liberal and open theological and social framework rooted in the principles of Torah.

The diverse understandings of Jewish law and ritual practice among, and within, the Jewish denominational groupings, in the context of a tradition that has neither the hierarchical structure nor the central authority of Orthodox or Roman Catholic Christianity, for example, are key factors in shaping the variety of Jewish perspectives and practices concerning issues of sex and sexuality, some of which will be discussed in the next section.

Sex and Judaism

The Ad Hoc Committee on Human Sexuality of the Central Conference of American Rabbis (CCAR), the organization of Reform rabbis, declared in its recent statement "Reform Jewish Sexual Values:"

> Jewish religious values are predicated upon the unity of God and the integrity of the world and its inhabitants as Divine creations. These values identify *shleimut* as a fundamental goal of human experience. The Hebrew root *sh-l-m* expresses the idea of wholeness, completeness, unity, and peace. Sexuality and sexual expression are integral and powerful elements in the potential wholeness of human beings. Our tradition commands us to sanctify the basic elements of the human being through values that express the Divine in every person and in every relationship. Each Jew should seek to conduct his/her sexual life in a manner that elicits the intrinsic holiness within the person and the relationship. Thus can *shleimut* be realized.[4]

The Reform statement draws on an ancient tradition that recognizes the beauty, holiness, and power of sexual intimacy in a monogamous, ongoing, and loving heterosexual marital relationship, a position that contemporary Orthodox Judaism also affirms. Many voices within liberal Judaism would extend this vision to include analogous same-sex relationships. Jewish tradition celebrates not only the procreative potential of sexual intimacy, but also its capacity to provide pleasure. It is a legitimate and important component of marriage, rooted in the goodness of God's Creation.

Historical Background: Sexual Desire

The Song of Songs, a Biblical book rooted in ancient Near Eastern love poetry, proclaims the potency and interconnectedness of love and passion: "for love is fierce as death / Passion as mighty as Sheol;/ Its darts are darts of fire,/ A blazing flame./ Vast floods cannot quench love,/ Nor rivers drown it" (8:6–7, JPS translation). This passage is memorable not only for its vivid imagery, but also because of its explicit mention of passion. The Hebrew Bible does not directly address the topic of sexual desire. However, embedded both in narrative and legal passages is a view of sex as positive and constructive, central to the fundamental institutions of marriage and the family. At the same time, when unregulated, sex could lead to chaos and the destruction of the social order. Biblical law, with its delineation of acceptable and unacceptable sexual relationships and practices, was a vehicle of regulation, the ignoring of which was a violation of Israel's covenantal responsibilities.[5]

Interestingly, as Biblical and ancient Near Eastern scholar Tikva Frymer-Kensky observes, notwithstanding the common Biblical metaphor of God as the husband of Israel, God does not behave in a sexual manner. In that sense, sex is not part of the Divine realm; nor is it part of Israel's cultic interactions with God. In the Levitical system of purities and impurities, sexual intercourse, seminal emissions, menstrual blood, and the blood of childbirth rendered a man or woman impure such that, while they remained in a ritually impure state, they could not participate in the Temple-based activities of the cult. Such rules were especially stringent for priests, the mediators of the cult. The separation of the sexual from the Divine is even present in the story of God's encounter with Israel at Sinai wherein Moses warns the people to remain pure for three days, following that with an admonition to not go near a woman (Exodus 19:14–15).[6] Moses' admonition draws attention to the highly gendered and patriarchal character of much of the Biblical text, including many Biblical laws in the cultic, economic, judicial, and sexual realms. A woman's sexuality, especially that of an unmarried daughter or wife, was subject to the control of a father or husband or, in some legal passages, was subject to established regulation enforced by the community.[7]

In the late first millennium B.C.E., Judaism developed an ascetic strain. Some Jewish groups practiced celibacy. They are described in the writings of Josephus and Philo, an Alexandrian Jewish statesman and philosopher of the first century B.C.E./C.E. A textual tradition arose with harsh views of sexuality, especially female sexuality, which was viewed as a source of chaos, even death. These elements would reemerge in some strains of early Christianity.

Rabbinic Judaism, however, rejected celibacy and generally advocated what it viewed as moderation rather than asceticism. Men were commanded to marry and to procreate. Nonetheless, talmudic culture expressed a kind of ambivalence about sexual desire, a topic which, in contrast to the Bible, the formative documents of Rabbinic Judaism discuss. These works often equate sexual desire with the *yetzer ha-ra,* the "Evil Inclination" or "Evil Desire." However, the Evil Desire is paradoxical; it is evil in its destructive potential, and, at the same time, it is "very good" in its constructive and generative qualities for in its absence "a man would not build a house, marry a woman, or have children" (Genesis Rabbah 9.9).[8] Through marriage and the study of Torah, a man could control his Evil Desire and avoid the temptation of illicit sex.

As the previous discussion suggests, Rabbinic literature is male centered. The rabbis were an elite class of male scholars and holy men. Early rabbinic literature is very self-referential; its focus is on rabbis, and then on nonrabbinic males. While it is by no means monolithic, its many voices are those of men. At the same time, women were perceived as possessing great desire that, if not regulated, would bring chaos and disorder to men. Thus, whereas classical Rabbinic literature praised and honored the mother, wife, and daughter whose behavior conformed to the dicta of Rabbinic law, the abstract female, with her unregulated sexuality, was a source of great danger. However, as was the case in the larger Greco-Roman world, men and male sexuality were regarded as active; females and female sexuality were regarded as more passive. Rabbinic commentators drew attention to the "curse" of Eve, which, even in its original Biblical context, may have reflected the seeming paradox of intense female desire in the context of the patriarchal marriage: "And your desire will be for your husband, and he will rule over you" (Genesis 3:16).

The perception of female sexual passivity is one of the Rabbinic explanations for the laws of *onah,* conjugal right, which were formulated as the husband's obligation to his wife. In its mandating of the frequency of sexual encounters, it was also a means of regulating sexual desire. It functions as a kind of counterpoint to the laws of *niddah,* the menstrual laws, which prohibit sexual relations for the period of the wife's menses and the seven days following the last day of her period. The laws of *onah* not only affirm the right of a wife to sex at regular intervals, they also prohibit a husband from having sex with her against her will, or even in her sleep, when she can neither consent nor refuse. The Mishnah links the mandatory frequency of sexual relations with the husband's profession and its demands. At one end of the spectrum is the daily obligation of a man of independent means who doesn't have to work; at the other end is a sailor whose obligation is every six months. A laborer has a twice weekly obligation, in contrast to the weekly obligation of an ass driver or the thirty-day obligation of a camel driver (m. Ketubot 5.6). A talmudic exposition on the Mishnah text posits that a scholar, unless he is away from home in study at the rabbinic academy, has an obligation to perform his marital duty every Friday night (b. Ketubot 62b). The linkage of rabbinic marital sexuality with the Sabbath is indicative of the view of marriage and marital relations as holy and good.

This view is at the heart of a number of medieval Jewish works on marriage and marital relations, of which the best known is the *Iggeret ha-Kodesh (The Holy Letter),* a thirteenth-century text. It is rooted in the mysticism of the Kabbalah, and thus views the sexual union of a husband and wife in its proper context as intimately connected with the interactions between the male and female emanations of the Divine. Husband and wife are, in a sense, both imitators of and participants in the Divine process. In discussing intercourse, the author admonishes:

> Know that the sexual intercourse of a man with his wife is holy and pure when done properly, in the proper time and with the proper intention. No one should think that sexual intercourse is ugly and loathsome. God forbid! Proper sexual intercourse is called 'knowing (Genesis 4:1) for good reason. . . . Understand, therefore, that unless it involved matters of great holiness, sexual union would not be called "knowing."[9]

Judaism regards a husband's "proper intention" as engaging in sexual intercourse not for the purpose of satisfying his own desire, but rather to provide his wife with sexual satisfaction. This is one of the obligations of a husband to his wife, and, in fact, is one of the teachings of the sixteenth-century *Shulhan Arukh,* the major authoritative law code of Rabbinic Judaism. Indeed, *halakhah* affirms the right of a barren or pregnant wife to sexual satisfaction, making emphatic its value and importance independent of procreation.

In the Rabbinic tradition, then, sex becomes holy in the context of marriage and when practiced in conformity with rabbinic teachings. The *Iggeret ha-Kodesh* continues:

> And you who have power to see and understand, is it possible there is something unseemly in that of which God is a partner? If so, the union of man with his wife, when it is proper, is the mystery of the foundation of the world and its

civilization. Through the act they become partners with God in the act of creation. This is the mystery of what the sages said, "When a man unites with his wife in holiness, the *Shekhinah*[10] is between them in the mystery of man and woman."[11]

Marriage and Divorce

The Hebrew Bible has a positive view of marriage, from its praises in the everyday wisdom of the Book of Proverbs to the law exempting a bridegroom from army service for a year so that he may "give happiness" to his wife (Deuteronomy 24:5). Its importance is emphasized in the depiction of its origins in the Garden of Eden creation story, following the creation of the woman: "Therefore a man leaves his father and his mother, and clings to his wife, and they become one flesh" (Genesis 2:24).

As discussed in the previous section, Rabbinic Judaism also has a positive view of marriage. This is not limited to its roles in providing a framework for procreation and controlling and sanctifying sexual desire. Judaism also affirms the profound importance of marriage in providing joy and love and emotional sustenance to the husband and wife. A holy institution, it offers a husband and wife an opportunity to grow in their understanding and love of God. This view of marriage is common to all forms of Judaism. In Judaism, marriage is not regarded as the lesser alternative to celibacy. The latter is not understood as a path to holiness. On the contrary, Jewish tradition is nearly always negative in its discussions of celibacy, an improper and joyless state and a violation of the commandments to marry and procreate.

In Orthodox Judaism, as part of a commitment to live a life in accordance with *halakhah,* a couple is expected to marry only halakhically acceptable individuals and to follow both the laws of *onah* and the laws of family purity. In the late nineteenth and early twentieth centuries, the latter came to refer to the *halakhah* concerning the sexual separation of a husband and wife during the period of the wife's menses and seven days thereafter followed by her immersion in a *mikveh,* a ritual pool. It is only following her immersion that she becomes again sexually available to her husband. This occurs at roughly mid-cycle when conception is most likely. The laws of family purity, or the laws of *niddah,* the menstrual laws, are rooted in the Levitical system of ritual purities and impurities (see Leviticus 15, especially 15:19). However, in the aftermath of the destruction of the Second Temple, Rabbinic Judaism shifted the focus of the laws of *niddah* from the public world of the cult to the domestic sphere of marital relations. The time of separation was increased from seven days to, as just noted, the period of menstruation followed by seven days, and the requirement of immersion in a *mikveh* was introduced.

Today, those couples who observe the laws of family purity vary in the stringency of their practices from refraining only from sexual intercourse during the required period to abstaining from any physical contact until the wife has been to the *mikveh*. She is required to remove her clothes, jewelry, cosmetics, dead skin, and hair tangles prior to her immersion so that her entire body is in contact with the water of the *mikveh*. Interestingly, in recent years the practice of immersion in a *mikveh* has been reexamined by some Jewish women, both within and outside of Orthodox Judaism. Susan Weidman Schneider writes in her book, *Jewish and Female:*

> There are two distinct schools of thought on this issue among Jewish women: those who believe that the laws of ritual purity hark back to a punitive blood taboo and reflect male fear and loathing of women; and those who believe that the laws and rituals surrounding mikveh are sensual, spiritual, expressive, allow room for women to experience a symbolic rebirth every month, and in addition, link them with a traditional Jewish woman's activity that goes back thousands of years.[12]

These women have reclaimed and reinterpreted immersion in a *mikveh* as a woman-centered practice that celebrates women in community, female autonomy, the female body, and female sexuality. In their traditional function, however, the menstrual laws, in tandem with the laws of *onah,* are, as Rachel Biale notes in her thoughtful and accessible study of women's issues and *halakhah,* an important element in the Rabbinic regulation of marriage: "Sex is a part of marital life as amenable to regulation as are property rights, mutual obligations for financial support, household chores, etc."[13]

Although the Bible depicts patriarchs and kings as having many wives, the Talmud does not describe rabbis or others as having more than one. However, polygyny was not formally banned until ca. 1000 C.E. The ban is attributed to the great German talmudist, Rabbi Gershom. It was binding on Ashkenazic Jewry, that is, the Jews of Central, Northern, and Eastern Europe, who were already living under Christian rule where polygyny was prohibited. Sephardic Jewry, that is, Spanish, Portuguese, North African, and Middle Eastern Jews, living under Islamic rule where it was permitted, had the possibility of practicing polygyny. Today, the state of Israel prohibits it for Jews.

The Jewish marriage ceremony is grounded in what, in antiquity, were two separate elements held at different times, *kiddushin,* betrothal, and *nisu'in,* marriage. The latter occurred when the bride moved into the groom's home and they began to cohabit. The earlier stage of *kiddushin* was a setting aside, a sanctification, of a woman for a man, to whom she became exclusively and legally bound. Mishnah Kiddushin states that a man acquires a woman by money, by deed, and by intercourse (m. Kiddushin 1.1). Echoes of this appear in today's traditional customs in which the bride accepts a ring from the groom, and the groom gives the bride a *ketubah,* a marriage contract. To be sure, the traditional *ketubah* is a kind of protection for the bride, with its statement of obligations of the husband, including the sum which he must pay to her should he divorce her. However, it is rooted in the Rabbinic interest in the transfer of a woman and her property from the domain of her father to that of her husband. Many liberal Jews are therefore dissatisfied with the traditional ceremony and *ketubah.* They wish to bring liturgy and ritual into greater harmony with an egalitarian view of marriage. Thus, the Reform CCAR Ad Hoc Committee on Human Sexuality states, "Since gender equality is a fundamental principle for us, our understanding of marriage requires that its obligations be mutual and reciprocal. In the traditional Jewish wedding the husband 'sanctifies' the wife; in our services, each partner 'sanctifies' the other."[14] Whereas some liberal Jews are satisfied with such practices as a double-ring ceremony and a *ketubah* of egalitarian language and mutual obligations, others, such as feminist theologian Rachel Adler, envision new rituals of marriage that reflect an understanding of marriage as an egalitarian partnership, a "covenant of lovers."[15]

Although Rabbinic Judaism regards the dissolution of a marriage as a very sorrowful event, it has always permitted divorce. However, in Jewish law divorce can only be initiated by the husband, leaving the wife in an inherently disadvantaged position. The *halakhah* is rooted, in particular, in the interpretations of Deuteronomy 24:1, which in its Biblical context is part of a larger passage that prohibits the ex-husband of a wife from remarrying her, if she had remarried in the interim: "A man takes a wife and possesses her. She fails to please him because he finds something obnoxious about her and he writes her a bill of divorcement, hands it to her and sends her away from his house" (JPS translation). In following a broad interpretation of "something obnoxious," the system of *halakhah* gave men nearly the equivalent of unilateral "no fault" divorce. At the same time, the *halakhah* developed some forms of protection for the wife, such as financial compensation in the case of divorce and a more formal and elaborate process in the writing and delivery of the *get*, the writ of divorce. In some circumstances, including a husband's affliction with "offensive" physical ailments or his failure to maintain his wife and adhere to the laws of *onah*, a woman was given the opportunity to petition a rabbinical court to compel a husband to grant her a divorce by giving her a *get*. Some rabbinic authorities argued that sexual incompatibility and wife beating were also grounds for divorce. However, even if a court granted the wife's petition, it was not necessarily able to impose its ruling on a recalcitrant husband.

Some of the imbalance in divorce would be redressed by a decree in ca. 1000, also attributed to Rabbi Geshom. It prohibited a husband from divorcing his wife without her consent. This was a major innovation in divorce law. However, it was only partially effective because of the social and economic vulnerability of women and the problems of enforcement in a system where a woman remains married according to Jewish law until she receives a *get*. This has resulted in tragic situations in which a woman is rendered an *agunah*, a "chained" wife. Her husband has left. However, because she was not given a *get*, she cannot remarry. The disappearance of a husband because of desertion or death, which, in the case of the latter remains unverified, such as that of a soldier presumed to be dead but legally missing in action, leaves a woman in this limbo state. A recalcitrant husband who refuses to give his wife a *get* can keep her "chained." In the pain and anger of divorce, the halachic gender imbalance can become a tool of vengeance and extortion for recalcitrant husbands.

Orthodox and Conservative halachic authorities have endeavored to find solutions to the plight of the *agunah* in the context of Jewish law. In the case of the latter, this has included a modification in the traditional *ketubah* and an increased focus on the rabbinic authority to annul marriages in some situations. Many Orthodox authorities have offered halakhic solutions, although none have been entirely successful. Some have turned to civil authorities to aid in enforcing the decree of the rabbinical court. This raises questions of not only *halakhah*, but outside of Israel, also of issues of separation of church and state. However, it is encouraging that redressing the plight of the *agunah* has become the focus of serious and substantive ongoing campaigns, conferences, and studies in which a large and growing number of Orthodox women are engaged as leaders and active participants. These women are learned in Jewish law, the traditional domain of men, and are indicative of the impact of feminism and the women's movement on Orthodox Judaism as well.

Reform and Reconstructionist Judaism, whose commitments to gender egalitarianism are a key interpretive lens in their responses to *halakhah*, have come up with different solutions. Reform Judaism does not require a *get*. The documents of a civil divorce are sufficient to declare that a marriage has been dissolved. The Reconstructionist Movement offers an egalitarian *get* that can be issued by either a man or a woman. A woman can issue a *get* in response to a recalcitrant husband. Although the use of a traditional *get*, given by a husband to his wife, is encouraged, it can also be supplemented by the granting of the egalitarian *get* by the wife to create a mutual exchange of documents of divorce.[16]

The different means of divorce among the branches of Judaism are again grounded in the various understandings of the nature and authority of *halakhah*. They are both a reminder of diversity within Judaism and a source of significant fragmentation in that the Orthodox position is that non-Orthodox marriages and divorces in Judaism are not valid.

Nonmarital Sex

In today's culture in which nonmarital and casual sex are commonplace, Judaism affirms the holiness of marriage and sexual intimacy in marriage as part of a loving, committed, and exclusive relationship. Violent and coercive sex, incest, and pedophilia are, of course, prohibited and regarded as abhorrent. Promiscuity and adultery are also condemned. In Orthodox Judaism, sex is unacceptable outside of marriage. However, the Reform and Reconstructionist branches of Judaism in recent years have acknowledged the potential for holiness in nonmarital relationships of love, commitment, and exclusivity. Thus, the 1998 CCAR statement of "Reform Jewish Sexual Values" declared, "In a Reform context, a relationship may attain a measure of *qedushah* [holiness] when both partners voluntarily set themselves apart exclusively for each other, thereby finding unique emotional, sexual, and spiritual intimacy."[17]

The sexual practices and attitudes of Jews, as distinct from the positions of Judaism, are difficult to assess or quantify with certainty. However, survey data suggest that when grouped by religious affiliation, Jews and the unaffiliated have the most liberal views on a broad range of social issues, including some issues of sexual behavior.[18] As in the larger society, premarital sex, multiple sexual partners in the course of a lifetime, and cohabitation outside of marriage have become increasingly common. This is the case not only for American

Jews, but also for Israeli Jews, especially among the 70 percent who identify themselves as "secular Jews."[19]

Contemporary Issues

Having discussed Jewish views of sexual relations, and relatedly, marriage, divorce, and nonmarital sex, let us now turn our attention to three issues of sexuality—abortion, birth control, and homosexuality—all of which today elicit a broad range of religious and moral stances, as well as varied positions concerning the appropriate role of government in regulating behavior. Our focus will be on contemporary perspectives.

Abortion: In the context of perspectives on abortion, Judaism occupies a kind of middle ground. It neither prohibits abortion under any circumstance nor sanctions it on demand. Orthodox Judaism, rooted in *halakhah,* is most stringent. However, it allows abortion when there is a physical threat to the mother's life. Contemporary halakhic argumentation is often rooted in the teachings of the medievalists, Rashi and Maimonides, whose interpretations of earlier Jewish legal writings are regarded as highly authoritative. They disagree in their understanding of the halakhic basis for abortion. Rashi follows a number of talmudic texts in greatly valuing a fetus as a potential life, but in not viewing it as a full life. It becomes a full life when its head, or most of its body, has emerged outside of the mother. The mother's life has priority until this point. Maimonides, on the other hand, likens the fetus in a life-threatening pregnancy to a "pursuer" who will destroy the mother's life unless it is destroyed. Maimonides' position has been interpreted by some to absolutely limit abortion to only when the mother's life is in mortal danger. In contrast to this very restrictive view, others, often drawing on Rashi's perspective, have broadened the scope of permissible abortions to include very serious, although non-life threatening, physical danger to the mother. A few have extended this further to include grave issues of mental health.

Conservative Judaism roots its understanding of the halakhic basis for abortion in its interpretations of Rashi. Conservative authorities are more permissive than their Orthodox counterparts in permitting therapeutic abortions for the sake of the mother's well-being. Conservative Judaism allows abortion when there is risk, even when it is nonlife threatening, to the physical or mental health of the mother. The latter can serve as a basis for permitting the destruction of a severely deformed fetus.

Reform Jewish voices are generally emphatic in advocating a woman's right to make her own decision concerning abortion, without government interference. Some maintain that in addition to the factors just noted, socioeconomic factors are also a valid determinant if another child would threaten the welfare of the family's children. However, 1985 Reform responsum stated, "We do not encourage abortion, nor favor it for trivial reasons, or sanction it 'on demand.'"[20]

Like the Reform Movement, the Reconstructionist and Conservative Movements oppose the governmental regulation of abortion, a position shared by the great majority of American Jews. As a group, American Jews are pro-choice and liberal in their views on abortion. For example, in survey data from 1982 to 1985, 82 percent of American Jews, in contrast to 39 percent of white Protestants and 37 percent of Catholics, thought that abortion should be available if a woman did not want additional children.[21]

The position of the Israeli Government on abortion is indicative of a kind of compromise between the nation's secular and religious communities. Legislation enacted in 1980 mandated the establishment of hospital committees before which women could seek a legal abortion. Women who were under seventeen or over forty years of age or who were carrying a fetus with a significant medical defect were viewed as eligible to receive an abortion, as were women who were unmarried or whose pregnancies were the result of rape, incest, or adulterous relationships. The jeopardizing of the physical or mental health of the mother, as well as issues of economic and social hardship, were also acceptable grounds. However, in 1980, as the result of the demands of the nation's religious parties, economic or social hardship was eliminated as a legal criterion for an abortion.[22] Today, more than 90 percent of applications to receive an abortion are approved. Thus, in 1999, 19,674 of 20,581 applications were approved.[23] A significant number of abortions are also performed illegally by physicians.[24]

Birth Control: Orthodox Judaism is grounded in a halakhic tradition that, consistent with a harshly prohibitive view of male masturbation, forbids the "spilling" of male seed and interprets the Biblical injunction "to be fruitful and to multiply" as directed at men. Therefore, the use of birth control by men is forbidden. However, women are not bound by this prohibition. Indeed, the Talmud describes the use of a *mokh,* a kind of cotton tampon, as a form of birth control for minor, pregnant, and lactating women (Yevamot 12b). Later commentators disagreed as to whether the device was inserted precoitally or postcoitally. However, the textual tradition was clear in providing a basis for the use of birth control by women, at least under certain circumstances. Generally, Orthodox halakhic authorities allow it only if pregnancy would pose a serious health risk to the woman. Today, there is also much discussion among halakhic authorities concerning which forms of birth control are acceptable. In Israel, however, as in the United States, contraception for both men and women is readily available.

In contrast to Orthodox Judaism, Reform Judaism permits the use of birth control by both men and women. It encourages responsible family planning that considers not only the health of the mother, but also the welfare of the family and any future child. It also takes note of the importance of birth control and family planning as a means of alleviating the conditions of severe impoverishment in which so many children are raised and as a response to the challenges of global population growth. More than forty years ago, the Commission on Justice and Peace of the Central Conference of American Rabbis stated:

> As Jews, we take pride in our historic emphasis upon the values of family life. We believe that it is the sacred duty of married couples to "be fruitful and multiply" unless child-bearing is likely to impair the health of the mother or offspring. This

is the position which we took in 1929 and which has support in traditional sources. We believe, moreover, that a righteous God does not require the unlimited birth of children who may, by unfavorable social and economic circumstances, be denied a chance for a decent and wholesome life. Therefore, we declare that parents have the right to determine the number, and to space the births of their children in accordance to what they believe to be the best interests of their families. We hold, moreover, that apart from its procreation function, the sex relation in marriage serves positive spiritual values. Contraceptive information and devices should be legally and inexpensively available to married persons.

They argue that overpopulation has taken on worldwide significance and urgency. A number of nations are suffering from what has been termed "explosive population growth" whereby the birthrate is outrunning their resources and living space, making it difficult for citizens to attain decent living standards. Means should be placed at the disposal of the United Nations, through the World Health Organization, to enable it, where requested, to provide birth control education techniques and materials. The effort to solve this problem should not be delayed, for the penalties will be famine, increased poverty, and unrest that leads to conflicts.[25]

Homosexuality: Perhaps more than any contemporary issue of sex and sexuality, the topic of homosexuality has evoked a very broad range of positions among and, at times, within the Jewish denominational branches. In recent years, discussions and debates within non-Orthodox Judaism have focused on social and communal issues, including the ordination of homosexuals to the rabbinate, their acceptability as community leaders, the nature and legitimacy of same-sex relationships, the appropriateness of same-sex marriage or commitment ceremonies and the presiding of rabbis at such events, the legalization of same-sex marriage, and the role of government in guaranteeing the civil rights of homosexuals.

In contrast, Orthodox Judaism, drawing on a long halakhic tradition rooted in the Hebrew Bible (Leviticus 18:22; 20:13), views male homosexuality as unacceptable. It opposes a morally neutral or positive stance concerning homosexual relationships even as it joins other Jewish movements in vehemently opposing the persecution of homosexuals and, of course, acts of violence and hatred directed against homosexuals. Thus, Modern Orthodox rabbinic authorities Norman Lamm and David Bleich have condemned homosexual activity. However, in likening homosexuality to illness, they have sought the healing of the homosexual and his treatment by the community with care and compassion. Rabbi Bleich has written, "There is indeed strong reason to believe that Judaism regards homosexuality as pathological. . . . While Judaism regards the homosexual act with repugnance, it has the greatest sympathy for the homosexual as a person . . . [but] society has a definite obligation not to bestow a seal of legitimacy on homosexual activity."[26]

Interestingly, the halakhic tradition views lesbianism as a relatively minor offense, a form of licentiousness, but not at all akin to the grave sexual offense of male homosexuality. The relative lack of rabbinic concern with lesbianism reflects both its absence of mention in the Hebrew Bible as well as the male norms of *halakhah* on issues of sexuality. Rachel Biale aptly comments, "Sexual acts between women are not considered a violation of the law because no act of intercourse takes place. The male sexual experience of heterosexual intercourse is the standard for defining what is a sexual act, and thus what is a sexual transgression."[27]

In contrast to Orthodox Judaism, the Conservative Movement has had to formulate policies on issues of homosexuality in the face of significantly divergent Conservative voices, balancing a generally more tolerant view of homosexuality with a concern for the halakhic tradition. At present, the Conservative rabbinical schools do not accept openly gay and lesbian students nor does the movement knowingly ordain gay and lesbian rabbis. Conservative rabbis are not permitted to preside at same-sex commitment ceremonies. The individual congregational rabbi, in consultation with the lay leadership, can determine the acceptability of gay and lesbian congregants for positions of leadership. At the same time, as a 1990 resolution of the Conservative Rabbinical Assembly stated, the movement supports equal rights for homosexuals, welcomes them as members of congregations and "[c]all[s] upon our synagogues and the arms of our movement to increase our awareness, understanding and concern for our fellow Jews who are gay and lesbian."[28]

Today, both the Reform and Reconstructionist movements have policies of full equality for gays and lesbians. Consistent with the preceding, they can attend the movements' rabbinical schools and be ordained as rabbis. Same-sex unions are accepted, and rabbis can preside at commitment ceremonies. The Reconstructionist Movement has played an important pioneering role in the movement toward full equality in liberal Judaism. Thus, the 1992 report of the Reconstructionist Commission on Homosexuality stated:

> We affirm the importance of loving, caring, intimate relationships as a primary source of companionship and comfort. Jewish tradition accords committed relationships which are invested by Jewish ritual with the value of *kedushah*, holiness. We affirm the qualities of mutual respect, trust, care, and love in committed relationships regardless of sexual orientation. Same-gender partnerships have the same potential for embodying these qualities as do heterosexual marriages. As we support the long-term commitment of heterosexual couples and acknowledge the *kedushah* of their marriages, so do we support long-term partnerships between gays or lesbians and affirm that *kedushah* resides in committed relationships between same-gender Jewish couples.[29]

In the 1990s, Israel enacted state laws and military regulations to prohibit discrimination against homosexuals in employment and in the army. This followed by a few years the formal decriminalization of the sodomy statute in the penal code, a statute, which to be sure, had not been enforced in decades.[30] Today the Israeli courts are discussing and ruling on the legal rights of same-sex couples. These cases are emerging out of a changing dominant culture which is both increasingly accepting of homosexuals and lesbians and which wishes to accord them equal protection under the law.

Circumcision: Our discussion would not be complete without a mention of male circumcision. Indeed, for centuries the circumcised penis was the quintessential marker of Jewishness. Today, for many, male circumcision is the ritual most closely associated with Judaism, although paradoxically, it is not unique to Judaism in a religious context (see the chapter on Islam), and, in North America, it is widely practiced in a medical context. The Jewish circumcision ceremony, the *berit milah,* is practiced by all of the Jewish denominations and by many secular Jews as well. It is rooted in Jewish sacred story, a "sign" of the covenant (*berit*) between God and Abraham, to be carried out through the generations on males at the age of eight days (Genesis 17:11–12). It continues to be carried out on the eighth day after birth unless medical reasons preclude it. This caveat is consistent with the life-affirming character of the *halakhah,* with its overarching concern with the health and well-being of the individual, and, concomitantly, the subordination of halakhic practices to serious issues of health. Although the circumcision of the child was traditionally the responsibility of the father, it is usually performed by a *mohel,* a specialist, traditionally male, in the rituals and in the procedure of circumcision. It can be carried out in a synagogue, home, or hospital. Today, a growing number of physicians are trained in the rituals of circumcision. Thus, the Reform Movement has instituted a Berit Milah Board, through which physicians and nurse midwives can receive training to become certified ritual circumcisers, with the intent of bringing together medical, religious, and ritual expertise. To date, more than 200 men and 25 women have been certified.[31]

As is the case in the larger society, some voices within liberal Judaism are questioning the appropriateness of circumcision. Many of the concerns are rooted in the growing body of evidence that there is no medical basis for circumcision and in the beliefs that the procedure is painful to the child, a form of genital mutilation, inherently sexist, and a man-made archaic and "primitive" institution—the last, a view held privately by some of the nineteenth-century Jewish reformers who did not dare to voice it publicly for fear of the reaction within the Jewish community, given the centrality of circumcision to Jewish identity.[32] Although some have sought to modify the rituals and procedures of circumcision, others have endeavored to create new rituals of birth and entry into the community for Jewish male infants, similar to the naming ceremonies for infant girls.

Gender and Judaism

Our examination of issues of sexuality in Judaism has inevitably addressed issues of sex and gender. As feminist theory reminds us, the former is rooted in biology whereas the latter is socially constructed. Although it is beyond the scope of this chapter to examine the complex topic of gender and Judaism, it is important to reiterate that the formative literature of Rabbinic Judaism reflects the interests and concerns of the male rabbinic class. Women were generally exempted, and indeed excluded, from the rabbinic hierarchies of achievement and holiness-producing activities—the study of Torah and the performance of *mitzvot,* for which women were generally responsible only for those commandments that were negative (thou shalt not. . . .) and not time bound. The arena of the good wife, in Rabbinic literature, was the domestic realm, where her responsibilities focused on her husband and on the household, including the rearing of children. The good wife, who is envisioned as conforming to the dicta of rabbinic law, was also a nurturer whose activities encouraged and enabled her husband and sons to study Torah. Although women were not physically confined to the home, those women who were out in the marketplace were generally envisioned as acting on behalf of their husbands. Notwithstanding the greater freedoms and protections offered to women in rabbinic *halakhah,* relative to Biblical law, the former was also highly gendered, rendering unequal treatment to women in the intertwined judicial, religious, sexual, and economic realms, including the rights to inherit, control, and dispose of property. This was especially true for the nonautonomous male-dependent categories of the wife and the unmarried minor daughter. At the same time, rabbinic law created the possibility that some women could amass and control personal wealth. Nonrabbinic sources, especially inscriptional data, confirm the existence of such women during the formative centuries of Rabbinic Judaism. These women, perhaps more so in the Diaspora than in Roman Palestine, served in leadership positions in the ancient synagogue and, like their pagan and Christian counterparts. participated in the Greco-Roman practice of civic benefactions, serving as donors to religious and civic institutions. To be sure, they were part of a small socioeconomic elite. However, they are a reminder of the importance of distinguishing between the images of women that the rabbis created in their literature, and the realities of the lives of the flesh and blood Jewish women of antiquity.[33] At the same time, it was primarily the former that would shape the normative images, roles, and expectations concerning women in succeeding centuries.

Not unexpectedly, today gender distinctions, especially in the religious realm, are more pronounced in Orthodox Judaism, given the authoritative role of *halakhah* and tradition. For example, Orthodox Jewish women are not ordained to the rabbinate; they do not count as a member of a minyan, the quorum of ten required for formal communal worship, nor can they be called to read from the Torah at worship services. In Ultra-Orthodox contexts, women are more likely to be in family arrangements with clear distinctions between the domestic and public realms, focusing their responsibilities on the raising of children and the running of the household. On average, their families are larger. Some women work outside of the home out of economic necessity, sometimes to enable their husbands to devote their time to Torah study. In Modern Orthodox Judaism, with its goal of bridging the halakhic and secular arenas, women, in their non-religious activities, are likely to lead lives very similar to those of their non-Orthodox counterparts. In some Modern Orthodox congregations, while a woman cannot serve as a rabbi, she might serve as the congregational president. A growing number of Orthodox women, as noted above, are also engaging in Torah studies, a domain formerly limited to men.

The Conservative, Reform, and Reconstructionist Movements ordain women to the rabbinate and allow full participation in synagogue worship.

The ordination of women is a recent phenomenon, inaugurated with the ordination of Rabbi Sally Priesand to the Reform rabbinate thirty years ago. The growing number of women in the rabbinate and in lay leadership positions is a vital step in the path towards gender egalitarianism, one of the goals of Reform and Reconstructionist Judaism. However, as Jewish feminists have noted, gender egalitarianism requires also the transformation of the gendered institutions, images, laws, liturgy, and rituals which are embedded in Judaism, and the creation of new institutions, images, and so on rooted in gender equality. Notwithstanding the remarkable strides of the past few decades on the road to full gender equality, the process of transformation is ongoing and far from complete.[34]

Conclusion

Our discussion of issues of sex and sexuality in Judaism has examined a broad range of Jewish teachings on a number of key topics in this important area.[35] The range of views is illustrative of the very profound and dynamic role that religion continues to play in shaping human experience, even as it is shaped by human experience. The events of the new millennium, like those of the past, are also a reminder of the power of religion to inspire what is best and what is worst in humankind.

At the heart of Jewish teachings on sex and sexuality is the principle of the sanctity, value, and holiness of the individual. In its 1992 position paper, the Reconstructionist Commission on Homosexuality drew on this principle as part of its endeavor to promulgate, in a religious context, a transformation of attitudes concerning homosexuality, stating:

> We regard the Jewish values that affirm the inherent dignity, integrity, and equality of human beings as having primacy over historically conditioned attitudes based on the biblical, rabbinic, and medieval texts that condemn homosexuality as an abomination. It as our duty to correct the misunderstandings and resulting injustices of the past and to fulfill the Jewish obligation to seek justice.[36]

Analagously, in a world plagued by poverty, violence, hatred, and the degradation of the environment, we need to collectively affirm this principle, with its all-embracing affirmation of humankind, overcome the "historically conditioned attitudes" that generate the sorrows of our time, and work together in the process of *tikkun olam,* the repair and healing of the world, to better the lot of all of humankind, of all creatures, and of all creation.

QUESTIONS FOR DISCUSSION

This chapter has presented data, addressed issues, and raised questions that are specific to the study of sex and Judaism and relevant to the larger topic of sex and religion, and, indeed, to the academic study of religion. You may wish to consider and apply the data, issues, and ideas presented in this chapter as you answer the following questions.

1. How can one consider the teachings on issues of sex and sexuality in Judaism given the diversity of beliefs and perspectives within that tradition?

2. What are the principles or beliefs that are shared throughout the tradition? Which ones generate diverse perspectives?

3. How does the question of scriptural authority unite and divide Judaism and shape teachings in the areas of sex and sexuality?

4. What is the distinction between the beliefs and practices of Judaism and those of its adherents?

5. Are there teachings and practices that can be regarded both as "oppressive" and as "liberating"? Are such categories valid?

6. In analyzing and evaluating Jewish teachings on sex and sexuality what are the cautions if one is an adherent of that tradition? If one is outside of the tradition?

7. What are the similarities and differences in the teachings on a given topic of sex and sexuality between historically related traditions? Historically unrelated traditions?

RECOMMENDED RESOURCES

Books

Biale, David. *Eros and the Jews: From Biblical Israel to Contemporary America.* Berkeley: University of California Press, 1997.

Biale, Rachel. *Women and Jewish Law: An Exploration of Women's Issues in Halakhic Sources.* New York: Schocken Books, 1984.

Boyarin, Daniel. *Carnal Israel: Reading Sex in Talmudic Culture.* Berkeley: University of California Press, 1993.

Central Conference of American Rabbis. "Symposium: Human Sexuality." CCAR Journal: A Reform Quarterly. Fall 2001.

Feldman, David M. *Marital Relations, Birth Control, and Abortion in Jewish Law.* New York: Schocken Books, 1974.

Goldman, Alex J. *Judaism Confronts Contemporary Issues.* New York: Shengold Publishers, 1978.

Greenberg, Blu. *On Women and Judaism: A View from Tradition.* Philadelphia: The Jewish Publication Society, 1981.

Hauptman, Judith. *Rereading the Rabbis: A Woman's Voice.* Boulder: Westview Press, 1998.

Magonet, Jonathan, ed. *Jewish Explorations of Sexuality.* Providence, RI: Berghahn Books, 1995.

Solomon, Lewis D. *The Jewish Tradition, Sexuality, and Procreation.* Lanham, Maryland: University Press of America, 2002.

Wasserfall, Rahel R., ed. *Women and Water: Menstruation in Jewish Life and Law.* Hanover, NH: Brandeis University Press, 1999.

Web Sites

International Council of Jewish Women at http://www.icjw.org.uk/ijwhrw/index.htm and www.lesbian.com/jewish/jewish-intro.html

ENDNOTES

1. Jewish sacred story shares with Christianity and Islam the belief in their common ancestry in Abraham, depicted in the Hebrew Bible, the New Testament, and in the Qur'an as the quintessential person of faith in and right relationship with God.

2. Sergio DellaPergola, "World Jewish Population, 2001," *American Jewish Year Book, 2001,* Volume 101 (New York: The American Jewish Committee, 2001), pp. 540–541. Demographers must address the different understandings of who is a Jew among the Jewish denominations. Whereas Reform and Reconstructionist Judaism may regard the child of a Jewish mother or father as a Jew, Orthodox and Conservative Judaism regard only the child of a Jewish mother as Jewish. This is significant in the United States, for example, where, since the mid-1980s, more than half of those Jews who have married are married to non-Jews. Demographic studies of recent trends in United States Jewry draw heavily on the highly regarded *National Jewish Population Survey of 1990.*

3. The Hebrew Bible is the academic designation for what Christianity designates as the Old Testament. In Jewish contexts, it is often called the *Tanakh,* a Hebrew acronym for *Torah, Nevi'im, Ketuvim*—Pentateuch, Prophets, and Writings—a tripartite division of the Hebrew Bible. The term Torah is both central to Judaism and is laden with ambiguity. It is sometimes translated as "law," but is better understood as teaching or instruction. In its narrowest sense, it refers to the Pentateuch, the first five books of the Hebrew Bible. In a broader sense, it designates the Hebrew Bible in its entirety. However, as will be discussed later, in a still broader framework, it refers both to the Hebrew Bible and to the formative later documents of Rabbinic Judaism, the Mishnah and Talmud. In its broadest sense, Torah refers to the received tradition of authoritative rabbinic teachings.

4. Central Conference of American Rabbis Ad Hoc Committee on Human Sexuality, "Reform Jewish Sexual Values," *CCAR Journal* (Fall 2001), p. 9.

5. See similarly, Tikva Frymer-Kensky's chapter "Law and Philosophy: The Case of the Bible" in Jonathan Magonet, ed., *Jewish Explorations of Sexuality* (Providence, RI: Berghahn Books, 1995), pp. 3–16.

6. Ibid., pp. 4–6.

7. Such differences reflect the different sources of Biblical law. From a historical-critical perspective, the Hebrew Bible is a composite work. It consists of Israelite sources from the first millennium B.C.E., spanning a broad period of time and associated with different regions and institutions in ancient Israel. These sources

were edited at various points to eventually take shape as the Hebrew Bible. For a helpful introduction to the complex topic of biblical authorship, see Richard Elliott Friedman, *Who Wrote the Bible?* (San Francisco: Harper, 1997).

8. On sex in talmudic culture, see the thoughtful studies by David Biale and Daniel Boyarin: David Biale, *Eros and the Jews: From Biblical Israel to Contemporary America* (Berkeley: University of California Press, 1997), especially Chapter 2, pp. 33–59; Daniel Boyarin, *Carnal Israel: Reading Sex in Talmudic Culture* (Berkeley: University of California Press, 1993).

9. *The Holy Letter: A Study in Jewish Sexual Morality.* Edited and with an introduction by Seymour J. Cohen (Northvale, NJ: Jason Aronson Inc., 1993), Chapter 2, p. 72.

10. The *Shekhinah* is the Divine Presence.

11. *The Holy Letter: A Study in Jewish Morality,* Chapter 2, p. 92.

12. Susan Weidman Schneider, *Jewish and Female: Choices and Changes in Our Lives Today* (New York: Simon & Schuster, 1984), p. 207.

13. Rachel Biale, *Women and Jewish Law: An Exploration of Women's Issues in Halakhic Sources* (New York: Schocken Books, 1984), p. 173. Customs associated with the separation of the menstruant have varied not only in time, but also according to place and community and cultural contexts. See, for example, the ethnographic studies in Rachel R. Wasserfall, ed., *Women and Water: Menstruation in Jewish Life and Law* (Hanover, NH: Brandeis University Press, 1999).

14. Central Conference of American Rabbis Ad Hoc Committee on Human Sexuality, "Reform Jewish Values," *CCAR Journal* (Fall 2001), p. 21.

15. Peter S. Knobel, *Is Reform Jewish Marriage Kiddushin?* retrieved June 30, 2002, from *http://www.bethemet.org/knobel/pk-marriage.html.* See also Rachel Adler, *Engendering Judaism: An Inclusive Theology and Ethics* (Philadelphia: Jewish Publication Society, 1998).

16. *Reconstructionist Egalitarian Get,* retrieved June 30, 2002, from *http://members.aol.com/Agunah/egalitar.htm.*

17. Central Conference of American Rabbis, "Reform Jewish Values" *CCAR Journal* (Fall 2001), p. 13.

18. John P. Hoffmann and Alan S. Miller, "Social and Political Attitudes among Religious Groups: Convergence and Divergence over Time," *Journal for the Scientific Study of Religion* 36:1 (1997): 52–70.

19. Ronny Shtarkshall and Minah Zemach comment on the complexities of this designation in their study of issues of sexuality in Israel, "The term 'secular Jew' embodies the problematics and the uniqueness of the Israeli situation. One part of it—Jew—defines the national sociocultural and historical identity. The second part—secular—defines a relationship to Judaism as a religion and religious lifestyle, and the choice of humanistic or secular democratic frame of reference over a religious one." However, as they also note, "The influence of Judaism on family, gender, and sexual issues is exerted not only through the subtler cultural and indirect sociocultural forces, but also through the political, social, and economic power of the religious minority of the population." In Ronny Shtarkshall and Minah Zemach, "Israel *(Medinat Yisrael)*" *The International Encyclopedia of Sexuality,* Volume II. Edited by Robert T. Francoeur (New York: Continuum, 1998), pp. 678, 690.

20. "CCAR Responsum No. 16, 'When is Abortion Permitted? (1985)'" in Walter Jacob, *Contemporary American Reform Responsa* (New York: CCAR, 1987), p. 27, as quoted in Lewis D. Solomon, *The Jewish Tradition, Sexuality and Procreation* (Lanham, MD: University Press of America, 2002), p.191.

21. Andrew Greeley, *Religious Change in America* (Cambridge, MA: Harvard University Press, 1989), p. 91.

22. Shtarkshall and Zemach, p. 724.

23. "Abortions in Israel," retrieved February 18, 2003, from *http:// www.us-israel.org/ jsource/Health/abort.html.*

24. Shtarkshall and Zemach, p. 725.

25. CCAR, *Yearbook,* Vol, LXX, 1960, p. 71, as quoted in Alex J. Goldman, *Judaism Confronts Contemporary Issues* (New York: Shengold Publishers, 1978), pp. 129–130.

26. David Bleich, *Judaism and Healing: Halakhic Perspectives* (New York: Ktav, 1981), pp. 70–72. See also Norman Lamm, "Judaism and the Modern Attitude to Homosexuality" in *Encyclopedia Judaica 1974 Year Book* Jerusalem Encyclopedia Judaica pp. 194–205.

27. Biale, p. 197; see the discussion of lesbianism in halakhic sources on pp. 192–197. See also the superb study by Bernadette J. Brooten, *Love Between Women: Early Christian Responses to Female Homoeroticism* (Chicago and London: The University of Chicago Press, 1996), pp. 61–71.

28. Homosexuality and Conservative Judaism: A Resolution of the Rabbinical Assembly," retrieved February 16, 2002, from http://www.members.tripod.com/djs28/conservative/.html.

29. *Homosexuality and Judaism: The Reconstructionist Position. The Report of the Reconstructionist Commission on Homosexuality, January 1992,* Revised edition. (Wyncote, PA: Federation of Reconstructionist Congregations and Havurot, Reconstructionist Rabbinical Association, 1993), p. 37. See also Saul M. Olyan, "Introduction: Contemporary Jewish Perspectives on Homosexuality" in Saul M. Olyan and Martha C. Nussbaum, eds., *Sexual Orientation and Human Rights in American Religious Discourse* (New York and Oxford: Oxford University Press, 1998), pp. 5–10.

30. Shtarkshall and Zemack, p. 708.

31. "200th Reform Mohel Certified: Jewish Ritual Practitioners Celebrate Milestone," retrieved June 29, 2002, from *http://www.huc.edu/news/berit/html.* Traditional *halakhah* requires also that male converts to Judaism be circumcised.

32. See similarly, Lawrence A. Hoffman, *Covenant of Blood: Circumcision and Gender in Rabbinic Judaism* (Chicago and London: The University of Chicago Press, 1996), p. 213; see also the discussion on pp. 209–220.

33. See, for example, the overview in Barbara H. Geller Nathanson, "Toward a Multicultural Ecumenical History of Women in the First Century/ies C.E." in Elisabeth Schussler Fiorenza, ed., *Searching the Scriptures: Volume One: A Feminist Introduction* (New York: Crossroad, 1993), pp. 272–289. On marriage in Judaism in the ancient world, see the recent study by Michael Satlow, *Jewish Marriage in Antiquity* (Princeton and Oxford: Princeton University Press, 2001).

34. See the pioneering studies by Susannah Heschel and Judith Plaskow: Susannah Heschel, ed., *On Being A Jewish Feminist* (New York: Schocken, 1983); Judith

Plaskow, *Standing Again at Sinai: Judaism from a Feminist Perspective* (San Francisco: Harper & Row, 1990). Our brief discussion has focused on gender and Judaism, and not on gender and Jews. The latter is an even more complicated topic if one endeavors to ascertain the role of Judaism in shaping views of gender by women who identify themselves as Jewish. That identification can have a broad range of meaning and significance. For example, is it significant that many of the pioneering and leadership figures of the feminist movement in the United States of the last forty years have been Jewish women?

35. Jewish teachings on issues of sex and sexuality are not limited to these topics. Recent and new topics include, for example, addressing the issues raised by assisted reproductive techniques.

36. "Homosexuality and Judaism: The Reconstructionist Position," p. 36.

Chapter 6

Christianity

Anthony F. LoPresti

In Christian circles, few subjects spark as much passion and controversy as those related to sex and gender. Whether it be an assembly of Baptists or Presbyterians, Catholics or Episcopalians, issues such as abortion, homosexuality, or the relationship between the sexes are sure to generate spirited—if not heated—discussion. Pluralism is no doubt alive and well in large numbers of Christian denominations. Moreover, the differences one finds in particular congregations are only magnified when one church community is brought into dialogue with another. While there likely would be considerable agreement on basic premises, there no doubt would be notable divergence in a number of specific conclusions. Differing emphases and particular points of controversy will also appear as one cultural manifestation of Christianity is compared with another. This chapter will survey several of those areas of controversy after first offering some general background information on Christianity that will provide the reader with important touchstones and perspective.

Though initially a small Jewish splinter group originating in first-century Palestine, Christians today are found in abundance on every continent, with particularly high concentrations in Europe and Latin America. Collectively representing nearly one-third of the world's population, Christians nevertheless are as diverse in their beliefs as they are plentiful. Although clear areas of commonality exist, there are often sharp and divisive differences on such major issues as church structure and authority, appropriate forms of worship, proper interpretation of scripture, and appropriate norms for sexual ethics. The three largest branches of Christianity are Roman Catholicism, which is centrally organized around the pope, Protestantism, which is widely diverse in its varieties, and Orthodoxy, which is largely organized along national lines. The first major break in the Christian Church began in the latter half of the eleventh century when Christians of the east (today's Orthodox) and of the west (today's Catholics) clashed over a variety of issues touching on theology, church authority, and culture. For more than a century the two sides quarreled, with all hopes for reunification ending when Western crusaders seized and ransacked Constantinople (today's Istanbul, Turkey) in 1203. A further splintering of Christianity would occur roughly 300 years later when sixteenth-century Protestant reformers, fed up with the endless scandals and abuses that plagued the Western medieval church, broke away from Rome and sought to restore the integrity of the faith. Prominent groups of Christians that trace their origins to this period include the Lutherans, Baptists, Presbyterians, and Congregationalists. And in a dispute that was as much political as it was religious, Catholicism suffered another major fissure in 1534 when King Henry VIII established the Church of England, a church that today is affiliated with millions of other Christians who jointly constitute the worldwide Anglican Communion. The American branch of this Communion is the Episcopal Church; Methodists, though independent, also have their roots in the Anglican tradition. Pentecostal churches—presently the fastest-growing form of Christianity in the world—began to appear in the early twentieth century as an outgrowth of Holiness churches, which, in turn, sprang from a religious revival in Methodism. Today, there are more than 25,000 Christian churches, most of which are small and unaffiliated local communities. Roman Catholicism remains the largest Christian denomination, claiming slightly more than 1 billion adherents.

Yet despite the considerable diversity, all Christian communities take as their inspiration the life of Jesus of Nazareth, an itinerant Jewish preacher and teacher whom Christians proclaim to be the "Son of God." Known for his ability to speak with great spiritual insight and touch the hearts of his listeners, Jesus called for repentance and conversion in anticipation of the coming reign of God. True to his Hebrew roots, Jesus taught from the paradigm that Adam and Eve's sinfulness had disrupted God's original intention for creation. Instead of harmonious relationships governed by love, the world after the Fall was filled with conflict, alienation, and estrangement from its creator God. Now, as the appointed time was drawing near, God would break into human history with power and judgment, calling all to reform their ways and recognize the God of Israel as the one true God and Lord of creation. Following in the footsteps of the Hebrew prophets, Jesus called for a radical commitment to justice, compassion, forgiveness, nonviolence, and an unflinching advocacy for the poor. Notably, he had very little to say about sexual morality, and he himself led a celibate life—a highly unusual choice for a Jewish man of the first century. Over time, he developed a reputation as a healer and wonderworker, a man of great vitality whose embrace included even women and children—two groups considered to be near the bottom of the social order. His ability to see beyond differences in gender, age, or social and economic status was remarkable for its time. As a champion of human dignity, he no doubt took to heart the biblical lesson that all people are created "in the image and likeness of God" (Genesis 1:27), thereby according to each an intrinsic goodness and value.

Remarkably, Jesus referred to God as his "Father"—sometimes the word is translated as "Daddy"—and taught his followers to pray to their God and Father with the words, "Thy kingdom come, thy will be done on earth as it is in heaven." At a time when the Romans were the dominant, and often brutal, power controlling Israel, such a prayer bordered on political subversion. Were God's kingdom to take hold, the social implications for all parties involved— Jews and Romans, families and individuals, the powerful and the marginalized, men and women—would be far-reaching. Increasingly, Jesus was perceived as a religious and political threat by the ruling authorities, and one might have expected his ideas to have quickly been forgotten after the Romans executed him, a deed that prompted his followers to flee, fearing for their lives.

Instead, inspired by powerful religious experiences, the disciples went on to preach that God had raised Jesus from the dead and now offered eternal life to all who professed faith in Jesus as the "Christ," or God's "anointed one." For Christians, Jesus is the person who most clearly reveals God. He is the bearer of God, the symbol of God, the Son of God. Through his life, death, and resurrection, Jesus discloses that what is found at the heart of the universe is *love,* that the character of ultimate reality (i.e., what religions tend to name "God") is self-communicating goodness. In particular, the Christian belief in the resurrection signals that in the end good will triumph over evil, that forgiveness will prevail over sin, and that love will overcome death. Furthermore, the description of Jesus as God's Son, and the subsequent experience of the Spirit of God dwelling in their midst, began for Christians a process of reenvisioning the traditional God of Israel as a being whose nature is essentially *relational,* a "trinity" consisting of Father, Son, and their (holy) Spirit. Put another way, Christians have come to understand the nature of God as *being-in-relation-to-another,* a communion of "persons"—Father, Son and Spirit—who dwell together as one in love. As Catholic theologian Catherine LaCugna explains:

> the point of trinitarian theology is to convey that it is the essence or heart of God to be in relationship to other persons; that the mystery of divine life is characterized by self-giving and self-receiving; that divine life is dynamic and fecund, not static or barren. . . . Further, the goal of Christian life is to participate in divine life and to become holy, living in conformity to Jesus Christ by the power of the Holy Spirit.[1]

In the ensuing decades, Christianity slowly spread across the Roman empire, aided enormously by the missionary work of Paul of Tarsus, a one-time persecutor whose evangelical zeal and theological acumen has left a permanent mark on the Christian faith. Particularly influential have been Paul's letters to the Christian communities he founded, works that had no small impact on Christian notions about the proper exercise of human sexuality. Emerging from the heart of Judaism, Christians continue to hold sacred all the books of the Hebrew scriptures as well as their own collection of inspired writings: four "gospels" (each of which is a distinctive retelling of Jesus' life, death, and resurrection); one account of the growth of the early church; several epistles or letters, many of which were penned by Paul; and the Book of Revelation, a highly symbolic account of visions pertaining to the final days of history. In total, references to sex in the Christian scriptures are relatively few, with Paul's admonitions, limited though they are, far outnumbering those from Jesus.

Even before the composition of their scriptures, however, Christians began gathering together on Sundays to mark the day of their Lord's resurrection with prayer, the proclamation of scripture, and the "breaking of the bread." The latter is a ritualized remembrance of Jesus' final meal with his disciples, variously known today as the Divine Liturgy, the celebration of the Eucharist, the Lord's Supper, or Holy Communion. Although liturgical practice is one of the areas in which contemporary Christians have significant differences, there is general agreement that Jesus' Last Supper was a culminating event that crystallized his life of service and love in the enduring symbols of bread broken and wine poured out. For many Christian communities, the celebration of the Eucharist is a ritual pregnant with meaning. It is a recalling of God's total self-giving in Jesus, a joyful celebration of thanksgiving, a sign of unity and commitment, and a life-giving feast of love that foreshadows the fullness of God's reign. As we shall see, many of today's Christians would use similar expressions to describe the values inherent in human sexuality. Yet because Christianity is fractured into thousands of different denominations, articulating *the* Christian position on contemporary issues of human sexuality is extremely difficult, if not impossible. Complicating matters is the fact that there are many millions who answer to the name "Christian," but who do not concur with the official teaching of the church to which they belong. Consequently, the next section will present not only the common strands of thought on sexuality within Christianity, but also those areas of divergence, paying particular attention to the pivotal issues on which differences in sexual thought and practice hinge.

Sex and Christianity

The Christian Vision

Since its founding nearly twenty centuries ago, Christianity has looked upon human sexuality with a mixture of both wonder and suspicion. Awed by its power and attraction, yet leery of its destabilizing effect on the mind, Christian thinkers have embraced sex cautiously, seeing it as a part of God's good creation that is nevertheless tinged by the ravages of human sin. Much like a fire that can bring both warmth and destruction, so can sex deliver both life and death. Through much of its history, Christianity has valued sex chiefly for its procreative potential. Other positive qualities of sex—such as the feelings of intimacy it can foster or the physical pleasure it can deliver—were largely overlooked or disparaged. In the twentieth century, however, Christian theologians began to offer a more positive assessment of the interpersonal aspects of sex, moderating their apprehensions towards sexual pleasure and deepening their appreciation of sexual intercourse as a profound expression of human love.

Today, Christians across the denominations are much more likely to regard their sexuality as a good and powerful gift, a "sacred energy given us by God and experienced in every cell of our being as an irrepressible urge to overcome our incompleteness, to move toward unity and consummation with that which is beyond us."[2] Sexual energy is a life force that is with us from birth. Although by puberty this force usually gravitates around the desire for sex, Christians would maintain that one's sexuality permeates virtually every facet of life. Our inborn sexual energy manifests itself whenever we move beyond our own little worlds and engage in what might be described as a creative transcendence or a transcendent creativity. What sorts of activities might be included under such a heading? Certainly any interpersonal relationship that deepens our capacity to love, stretches our ideas about friendship, engages our deepest emotions, or draws us to a new level of intimacy. But also whenever we reach deep into the well of personal creativity and participate in some form of artistic expression, allow our imaginations to run free, experience some form of religious transformation, or otherwise live in communion with nature. Thus, speaking broadly from a Christian perspective, one can be acting sexually without necessarily being involved in a physical sexual relationship. Contrary to the prevalent popular view that equates sex with intercourse and insists that one must be having sex to be living a whole or complete life, Christianity teaches that all people, regardless of their involvement in sex acts, can lead full and sexually satisfying lives so long as "sexuality" is not reduced to genitality.

Obviously, genital sexual expression is important; at times even sublime. In such intimate sexual encounters, we experience a profound unity of body, mind, and spirit while also recognizing that our partner is nevertheless "that which is beyond us." Sex at its best, Christians would say, involves submersing ourselves into the mystery of the other in a pleasurable and exciting act of self-giving and receiving that simultaneously draws us closer to the divine, trinitarian life. In other words, Christians would maintain that tender and dynamic lovemaking—particularly in the context of marriage—is not only a richly satisfying human experience, but also one of the premiere ways of encountering the mystery we name God, the God Christians equate with love (cf. 1 Jn 4:16). As the Radio Bible College puts it, "Being captured by our lover will give us a taste of being caught up in Christ's love in a way that we feel deeply enjoyed without shame. In essence, sexual intimacy within marriage should draw us to deeper worship of God who initiated sexuality [both] for His glory [as well as] our delight."[3] Like the Eucharistic feast many Christians celebrate on Sundays, genital sexual intimacy is a celebration of love, both human and divine.

By the same token, Christianity also recognizes that sexual energy can be misdirected, perverted, or corrupted, becoming an instrument of alienation and dissolution rather than of unity and transcendence. If we are not careful, our urges for sexual consummation can run out of control, clouding our minds and potentially propelling us into abusive and exploitative relationships. Any relationship that fails to respect the inherent dignity of the people involved runs counter to Christian thinking, which is grounded in the belief that all people are sacred, having been created in the image and likeness of God. St. Augustine, a fifth-century bishop whose influence has been enormous in Christian ethical thought, was particularly sensitive to the alluring and corrupting capacity of disordered sexual desire. "Lust is a usurper," he wrote, "defying the power of the will and playing the tyrant with man's sexual organs."[4] One-night stands, child sexual abuse, Internet porn, date rape, compulsive masturbation, raunchy bachelor parties, adults-only strip clubs, or any sexual encounter in which one person is left feeling used and abused would all be instances of what Augustine (and most Christian churches today) would call a hideous corruption of the God-given gift of human sexuality.

Historical Background

Historically, Christianity seems to have been much more conscious of the dangers of sexual expression than of its more positive, life-affirming aspects. While Jesus himself had very little to say about the matter, Paul recommended marriage only for those who, due to the force of their sexual passions, are unable to remain virgins. (It should be noted that Paul believed that the end of the world and the fullness of God's reign was near. Starting or expanding a family, at this point, would be an unhelpful distraction.) Sexual sinners, according to Paul, will not be among those who inherit the kingdom of God (cf. 1 Cor 6:9–10). Permanent celibacy became the ideal, due in part to the cultural influence of Stoic philosophers who advocated subordinating—if not suppressing—the emotional life to rational ends. Such a position fit together nicely with the example of Jesus' own celibate life, and hence the notion of celibacy as a "higher calling" came into vogue.

   Through the centuries, many Christians have also venerated Jesus' mother, Mary, honoring her as a lifelong, spotless virgin (her conception of Jesus was understood to have occurred through the power of the Holy Spirit). Thus, the model often presented to Christian families was that of the "Holy Family," composed of two perpetually continent parents, Mary and Joseph, and their celibate son, Jesus.[5] Although this threesome undoubtedly encouraged virtue of many varieties, they were less than completely helpful to the vast majority of Christians for whom sexual relations were an inescapable, and largely welcome, part of life. Insofar as twenty-first-century Christianity frequently speaks on behalf of families and the procreative activity that this usually implies, it is somewhat ironic that traditional Christianity has often held up what most would perceive as an asexual ideal.[6] Acting in a manner consistent with this heritage, Pope John Paul II in 2001 beatified Luigi and Maria Quattrocchi, a twentieth-century Italian couple who, on the advice of a spiritual director, spent the last twenty-five years of their marriage in separate beds.

Interpreting the unwilled and uncontrollable movements of lust as painful reminders of Adam and Eve's fall from grace, St. Augustine was one of the early and influential Fathers of the Church who believed that continent marriages were the best marriages. "The better [the husband and wife] are," he wrote, "the earlier they have begun by mutual consent to refrain from sexual intercourse with each other."[7] Yet somewhat paradoxically, this sinner-turned-saint was also one of the many theologians who, recalling God's command to the first couple to "be fruitful and multiply" (Gen 1:28), considered procreation to be something good—often the only sinless justification for marital sexual activity. As the centuries passed, however, even marital intercourse came under increasingly negative scrutiny. (Nonmarital sex was always unhesitatingly condemned.) In the East, "Orthodox clerics regulated when and how the [married] couple had conjugal relations. The list of prohibited activities was extensive. Ultimately, a couple escaped all censure only if they produced a child through marital relations restricted to vaginal genital contact in the 'missionary' position, on a day not set aside for religious observance or bodily purification."[8] Bishops and priests in the medieval West seemed to be obsessed with sexual sins, revealing a particular distrust of sexual pleasure. According to Theresa Gross-Diaz:

> Anything that was not strictly necessary for procreation was forbidden: thus foreplay was condemned, as was any position taken merely for enhancement of sensation or variety; a man who made love to his wife exuberantly, "in the manner of an adulterer," sinned gravely. . . . There are few, if any, glimmerings of the notion that sexual relations might actually strengthen the tie between husband and wife and bring them closer to God.[9]

Though not as scrupulous as the medieval confessors, the Protestant reformers showed a considerable ambivalence towards sexuality. Holding that no human achievement could merit God's favor, they frowned upon celibacy and affirmed Christian marriage. Yet believing that the human will was corrupted by sin, they were distrustful of the ways fallen people expressed their sexual desires and prescribed instead modesty and self-control. Having abolished self-governing religious orders for women—which in Catholicism served to provide a measure of independence from men—the reformers gave their blessing to the housewifely ideal, thereby embracing a societal ethos that stationed women as their husband's subordinate and helpmate. Such a role found resonance in the Bible which, from the story of the Fall onwards, is more or less permeated by a patriarchal view of the world. Whether the subordination of women to men after the Fall should be considered *prescriptive,* a divinely-imposed punishment in accord with God's desires, or *descriptive,* a tragic consequence of sin's entry into the world, is a question that contemporary Christians continue to debate. Virtually all Christian communities, however, emerge from a history in which women were associated with sinful sensuality yet paradoxically valued for their reproductive and nurturing capabilities. What has rarely been appreciated in the Christian tradition is a woman's ability to fully image Jesus; consequently, women have had limited opportunities

for ordained ministry, formal teaching roles, or other church leadership positions that are otherwise open to men. Instead, the model offered for emulation has been the Virgin Mary, a woman of few (if any) recorded words who
is revered for her sexual abstinence, motherly qualities, and receptivity to the
will of God the Father and the Son.

Pivotal Theological Issues

As already noted, although Christians may share centuries of history and
many common ideas about sexuality, the specific conclusions they draw on
controversial contemporary questions are often quite disparate. Behind these
disagreements lie some fundamental theological differences, particularly with
regard to the most common sources of Christian moral guidance, namely
scripture, Church teaching and tradition, reasoned generalizations about the
meaning of human experience, and concrete human experiences themselves.
What authority each of these sources carries and the precise relation that does
or should exist among them are the issues that underlie most disagreements.
A brief word on each is in order.

First, Christian ethics, sexual or otherwise, always begins with the biblical
witness; however, there is considerable disagreement over how the Bible
should be interpreted and whether its authority is always paramount. Some
Christians—primarily evangelical or fundamentalist Protestants—regard the
Bible as the timeless and errorless word of God, whereas others—Catholics,
Orthodox, and mainline Protestants (Episcopalians, Methodists, Presbyterians,
United Church of Christ, etc.)—tend to see it as an inspired, yet historically
and culturally conditioned source of wisdom. The first group tends to read
scripture literally, deriving therein divine commands and prohibitions that
carry universal force. The second group, utilizing modern methods of critical
scholarship, is more inclined to seek out biblical patterns of behavior that can
inform and guide (analogically) present-day morality. Aware of that broad distinction, one should also keep in mind that there is also a great deal of overlap
in the conclusions Christians draw from scripture, even with their significant
methodological differences.

Second, Christians who are not inclined to derive their morality entirely
from biblical sources often turn to the writings of the early church fathers or
other authoritative declarations issued by the community's leadership over the
course of time. As might be expected, churches that trace their roots back to
apostolic times, namely, the Orthodox and Catholic churches, are more likely
to draw from their extensive theological heritages than those communities
whose histories are not as far-reaching. Moreover, Roman Catholicism, with
its highly centralized and hierarchical power structure, maintains that its ecclesiastical leaders enjoy a special form of guidance from God's holy Spirit,
allowing its bishops and pope to teach morality definitively and, in some cases,
infallibly. Among all the Christian churches, Roman Catholicism stands out
for its leadership's willingness to assert its authority in the name of preserving
traditional (Catholic) Christian sexual prohibitions. Many Christians,

however, including large numbers of the Catholic faithful, find elements of that tradition suspect (not to mention sexist), and the moral arguments of the Catholic hierarchy unpersuasive.

Third, because of their relatively optimistic views regarding man's (sic) ability to ascertain the divine moral order, Catholic theologians have a long history of utilizing a natural law ethics, a form of reasoning that seeks to draw generalizations about the meaning and value of human experience through a careful and nuanced analysis. Natural law theory holds that there is an objective moral order to the universe, laid down by God, that is independent from but accessible to human beings. Through the powers of observation and reason, exercised within a wider community of critical discernment, one can appropriate God's eternal law regardless of one's religious stance. Experience reveals what is most fulfilling for human beings, and reason interprets that experience so as to distinguish what is "natural" (morally appropriate) human conduct, "as differentiated from behavior that humans may often exhibit, but which is not in conformity with their true nature or highest ideals."[10] One advantage of natural law thinking is that it is theoretically open to anyone who has reason and intelligence, thereby facilitating a moral conversation among people of various religious traditions. Following this approach, even an atheist could agree with a Christian that procreation is essentially a good thing (it engenders an awesome wonder over the marvel of new life, it initiates the joys and satisfactions that are part of parenthood, it makes possible the continuation of the human species, etc.), and that promiscuity is essentially a bad thing (it deadens the capacity for intimacy, it exposes people to sexually transmitted diseases, it runs the risk of children being born into less-than-ideal living conditions, etc.). Among the disadvantages some Christians find with the natural law approach is that it has a tendency to make God (and the Bible) superfluous to the moral enterprise while pinning its ethical judgments on a human reason that is historically conditioned and always susceptible to error. Nevertheless, reasoned generalizations will always play some role in Christian moral analysis, more so, perhaps, in the Catholic world where the hierarchy is apparently committed to retaining many of its traditional natural law arguments, even in the absence of a responsive audience.

Fourth, how the insights gleaned from concrete human experiences should inform Christian ethics is another major issue that divides Christian communities. All of us derive a certain amount of moral guidance from our own life experiences: We become committed to wearing seat belts when we are touched by an accident involving someone who was not; we learn that flaming someone on the Internet is wrong when we are victimized ourselves or when we become aware of the hurt our own harsh words have caused. The same is generally true with experiences in the sexual realm. The problem arises, however, when concrete experiences suggest a moral evaluation that differs from what the traditional sources of morality (scripture, tradition, reasoned generalizations) have said. For example, whereas traditional norms of morality have condemned same-sex unions in no uncertain terms, more recent experience has indicated that same-sex couples may indeed participate in loving and life-giving relationships that are comparable to heterosexual marriages. Historically conscious Christians who believe that moral norms evolve (and are therefore inclined to trust the moral wisdom derived from experience) will be apt to approve such relationships—and that is precisely what we are beginning to see among some Lutheran, Episcopal, and Presbyterian congregations. Christians with more of a classical consciousness who tend to lean on any of the three other sources for eternally valid moral guidance will likely oppose same-sex relationships (e.g., Evangelical Christians, Orthodox, Catholics). For those who are uncommitted to favoring any of the four sources, the difficulty will lie in deciding how to arbitrate between the conflicting values and claims that the different sources present. Lacking precise rules of discernment, American Christians are often inclined to listen to the perceived wisdom of their own experiences rather than the moral judgments of an external source, be that scripture, church teaching, or the authority of human reason. In this they are like most Americans (and Westerners) who accord a certain primacy to personal freedom and autonomy.

Given the plurality of moral methodologies operative within the many branches of Christianity, it is not difficult to see how there might be substantial disagreement on controversial sexual topics. The remainder of this chapter will offer a brief survey of current issues of interest, indicating the Christian position or positions and the ethical warrants that support them.

Marriage and Divorce: Christianity has long been affirming of monogamous, heterosexual marriage, seeing it as a divinely ordained institution that provides a framework for sexual intimacy, social and domestic partnership, and the propagation of the species (cf. Gen 2:18–24). Less often noted, though always implied, is that marriage provides the context through which the vast majority of adult Christians learn to grow in holiness and work out their salvation. Many Christians—Anglicans, Catholics, and Orthodox prominent among them—refer to marriage as a "sacrament," meaning a privileged place for encountering and communicating with God. Holding unto the ideal of lifelong fidelity in marriage, Christianity has traditionally frowned upon divorce, believing it to be, in the words of C. S. Lewis, "more like having both your legs cut off than it is like dissolving a business partnership."[11] Noting the trauma and disorder that divorce often inflicts on children, many Christian communities have strengthened their marriage preparation programs and some have spoken out against the no-fault divorce laws prevalent in many states. It is a reluctant realism that hangs over Christianity, recognizing that when marriages ultimately do fail, divorce may be a necessary, although always lamentable, option.

Remarriage after divorce has been especially problematic for Christians in light of Jesus' declaration that "anyone who divorces his wife, except on the ground of unchastity, causes her to commit adultery; and whoever marries a divorced woman commits adultery" (Mt 5:32). Because of varying interpretations of this and other pertinent passages, Christian churches have adopted different policies with regard to accepting second or third marriages. Roman

Catholicism, emphasizing the irreversible quality of the marriage vows ("till death do us part"), teaches that it is impossible for validly contracted Christian marriages to be dissolved. Therefore, the church does not allow remarriage after a civil divorce unless the previous marriage is annulled by a church marriage tribunal (i.e., determined to have never existed from a spiritual standpoint). Because annulments are far from automatic, many divorced and remarried Catholics find themselves alienated from, and often bitter towards, their church. In recent years, the Vatican has encouraged priests to withhold Holy Communion from those known to be in "irregular marital situations," but the policy is normally not enforced.

In the Orthodox Churches, "divorced persons who remarry do so not as their right but as recipients of a special gift of God's mercy to be accepted with repentance, gratitude and the firm intention faithfully to fulfill all that belongs to married life." Unlike first marriage ceremonies that are festive and celebratory, Orthodox liturgies for second marriages have a penitential character. Third marriages are even more reluctantly accepted in Orthodoxy, but three is as far as it will go; fourth marriages are never an option. With a particular sensitivity to the tragic consequences of human sinfulness in the world, Protestant churches tend to look upon failed marriages with resignation and regret. Some churches will countenance remarriage only in cases of sexual infidelity, faithful to a literal interpretation of Jesus' words. Other mainline communities, less concerned with fulfilling precise biblical criteria, hope that a second marriage will be "an opportunity to use wisdom gained from the past to create a new relationship of loving commitment and joy."[12] On the whole, the divorce rate among Christians does not appear to be appreciably different from that of society at large. On the other hand, there is some evidence that couples who pray together and attend church regularly together are less likely to divorce.[13]

Relations between the Sexes: Like the issue of sex itself, Christianity has had a decidedly mixed reputation when it comes to promoting the full equality of the sexes. As previously noted, most biblical authors worked out of a patriarchal paradigm. Although there are notable glimpses of female agency scattered throughout the Hebrew and Christian scriptures (e.g., Queen Esther in the Book of Esther, the bride in the Song of Songs, Mary Magdalene in the four gospels), in general biblical women derive their identity through males and are most often prized for their childbearing potential. No doubt the most revered woman in the Christian scriptures is Mary, mother of Jesus, about whom very little is actually known. Yet through the centuries, the figure of Mary has been socially and sexually constructed (primarily by men) in such a way that her traditional titles of handmaid of the Lord, virgin, and mother have come to be controlling images in the Christian feminine ideal. Given the patriarchal bias of history, many observers today would argue that the symbolism itself is complicit in the subordination and suppression of women. As theologian Elizabeth Johnson puts it:

> Being responsive to the inspiration of the Spirit, being virginal, and caring for the needs of one's children are not bad things—in fact they are quite excellent

values in themselves. But when in the tradition about Mary they are set within an androcentric framework, so that the ideal of woman becomes the passively obedient handmaiden, the asexual virgin, and the domestically all-absorbed mother, then the tradition implicitly and explicitly supports the truncation of woman's fulfillment.[14]

Jesus, in contrast, was notably progressive in his interactions with women, welcoming them into his circle of disciples and treating them with an unusually high degree of respect. When a voice from the crowd called out "Blessed is the womb that carried you and the breasts at which you nursed," highlighting maternal biological features, Jesus is said to have replied, "Rather, blessed are those who hear the word of God and observe it," a universal call to holiness to which women and men could equally aspire (cf. Lk 11:27–28). His approach was precedent setting—but its staying power proved to be limited. While scholarly research shows that women indeed occupied important leadership positions in the early days of the church, later generations of Christians would capitulate to the norms of a patriarchal society, calling on women to be submissive to their husbands who, in turn, were to love their wives as the Lord loved the church. This paradigm would be enshrined in the Christian scriptures (cf. Eph 5:21–28; Col 3:18–19; Titus 2:3–5) and recalled from generation to generation. Through the centuries, Christianity's treatment of women was little better than what women received from society at large. It has only been in the latter part of the twentieth century, prodded on by the feminist movement, that the church has more or less recognized women as equals with men, though the majority of Christian women are still excluded from ordained ministry within their respective churches. As might be expected, churches that strongly adhere to a biblically based morality are more likely to subscribe to a traditional place for women in church and society, whereas churches that more clearly hear God's voice in the signs of the times are apt to take a more liberal view of feminist causes.

In June of 2000, the Southern Baptist Convention stirred considerable controversy when it decided to insert the following paragraph into its statement of the Baptist Faith and Message:

> The husband and wife are of equal worth before God, since both are created in God's image. The marriage relationship models the way God relates to His people. A husband is to love his wife as Christ loved the church. He has the God-given responsibility to provide for, to protect, and to lead his family. A wife is to submit herself graciously to the servant leadership of her husband even as the church willingly submits to the headship of Christ. She, being in the image of God as is her husband and thus equal to him, has the God-given responsibility to respect her husband and to serve as his helper in managing the household and nurturing the next generation.[15]

Some Christians find in this excerpt a beautiful articulation of the divine vision for a happy and faith-filled family life. Others would call the alleged equality of the sexes illusory, insofar as the man is placed over his wife as the "servant leader," while she is to "submit herself" as his "helper." Looking at the historical record, one cannot gloss over the fact that Christian husbands have not always loved their wives "as Christ loved the church"; some, in fact, have been physically and emotionally abusive. Tragically, too many times in the past abused women were advised by their Christian pastors to remain submissive to their tormentors, in supposed fidelity to the Bible's commands. In recent years, such counseling practices have become relatively rare, with many Christian churches now joining forces in the fight against domestic violence. Notably, Pope John Paul II, who tends to strike relatively privileged Westerners as socially conservative, has been a strong voice internationally in speaking out against the degradation, subordination, and violence that women suffer in many parts of the world. In the United States, many Christian denominations have spoken approvingly of a woman's right to pursue a career outside of the home, to receive equal pay for equal work and, in general, to fully develop her talents and gifts. Yet it must be added that some Christian churches continue to glorify the motherly role—to an extent that dwarfs what is said about fathers—whereas others are rather spotty in their support for welfare, food stamps, quality child care and prenatal care—all issues that touch women much more deeply than men.

An often taken-for-granted Christian doctrine that many western feminists would applaud is that of monogamy, rather than polygyny, in marriage. Generally not a hot-button issue in the West, it has been a major point of controversy in Africa where tribal customs often permit, if not encourage, a man to take multiple wives. Clearly, this is not only an issue of religion, but also one of culture. Hence, Christian missionaries in Africa have been subject to the charge of cultural imperialism (i.e., favoring and imposing their own cultural practices while denigrating and forbidding indigenous ones). In defense, Christians have argued that not all cultural customs equally do justice to the universal truth that all human beings are of equal dignity and value, and that only a custom of monogamy within marriage can support a woman's proper claim of equality. In this regard, Christianity and Western feminism see very much eye to eye.

Nonmarital Sex: Nearly every Christian church would hold that marriage provides the *best* environment for the full, genital expression of human sexuality. The majority would argue, on biblical, traditional, and experiential grounds, that marriage is the *only* acceptable environment for full sexual expression. When human beings rebel from God's design for sex, tragic consequences follows. The Assemblies of God, one of the larger Pentecostal churches, describes the danger as follows:

> Today the human devastation of immoral sexual activity is well documented. Even society recognizes that sex outside of marriage exacts a great penalty. Each day the broken hearts of abandoned spouses, the children born out of wedlock, the families torn by divorce, the emotionally scarred children, the injuries to extended family, the scores of people dying from sexually-transmitted diseases,

and the thousands of aborted babies who are denied life, all cry out to us that sexual expression outside of God's plan is a tragic mistake. The price is far too great.[16]

Millions of Christians would agree with this assessment. Yet judging by the reported levels of sexual activity, there is every indication that vast numbers of individual Christians have few moral qualms with sex outside of marriage, so long as it is safe, monogamous, and consensual.[17] What many theologians and pastors find missing from that equation is any reference to lifetime commitments, the absence of which leaves the door open to many of the social problems cited earlier. Christians, especially those from the religious right, have been strong advocates of abstinence-only programs of sex education in public schools and have not supported the distribution of condoms in junior and senior high schools. Whether this course of action is likely to reduce sexual activity (and pregnancy) among teenagers remains an unresolved question. One does not have to be a conservative Christian, however, to be alarmed at the level of sex among teenagers, many of whom are caught in a whirlwind of hormones and peer pressure, have yet to attain the emotional maturity that only comes with age, and are often neither willing nor able to take on the serious responsibilities that would arise should pregnancy unexpectedly occur.

On the other hand, some of the more liberal Protestant churches have begun to embrace the idea that not all sex outside of marriage is the same. They would agree with more traditional Christians that there is no basis in Christianity for justifying rape, incest, prostitution, promiscuity, adultery, or any sexual practice that exposes people to sexually transmitted diseases. They likewise would be extremely hesitant to endorse genital sex in a steady loving relationship when those involved are teenagers. However, there is some openness to the idea that for a responsible single adult in a committed loving relationship, the choice to be fully expressive sexually, when there is little to no risk of pregnancy or disease, is not necessarily incompatible with an authentic Christian witness. While continence is still the general recommendation, some Christian churches believe it is best to leave the final decision on the degree of sexual involvement to the discretion of the individual believer. Following a societal trend, cohabitation is also common among Christians, even though the statistics indicate that couples who live together before marrying have a considerably higher incidence of divorce than those who do not.[18]

Abortion: In the political arena, conflict over abortion often whittles down to whether one is pro-life or pro-choice. In the realm of Christian ethics, the moral analysis is considerably more complex. Several elements come into play in any Christian analysis of abortion: (1) the status, value, and rights of an unborn human life; (2) the well-being of a pregnant woman, including both her physical and mental health as well as her ability to exercise some control over her body's reproductive capacity; and (3) the interests of third parties—fathers, families, and religious and civil communities—in the outcomes of pregnancies. Disputes arise when concerned parties fail to agree on the relative weight each of these values should carry when one comes in conflict with another.

Although there are no direct references in the Bible to abortion *per se,* there are a number of texts (Job 31:15, Is 44:24, 49:1; Jer 1:4–5; Lk 1:41,44) that suggest a positive evaluation to unborn life in the womb. Many indicate that the developing fetus is already in close relationship with God, among them this passage from Psalm 139:

> For it was you who formed my inward parts;
>   you knit me together in my mother's womb.
> My frame was not hidden from you, when I was being made in secret,
>   intricately woven in the depths of the earth.
> Your eyes beheld my unformed substance.
> In your book were written all the days that were formed for me,
>   when none of them as yet existed. (verses 13, 15–16)

Churches that rely solely or principally on the Bible for direction in ethical matters find in quotations such as this sufficient warrant for condemning abortion outright. Reading this passage, they clearly see God's hand at work in the creation of a new human life. Intervening in this process, in this view, would be a sin against God and a sin against the newly conceived child. Consideration of the mother's desires and well-being, while not insignificant matters, do not alter the fundamental presumption in favor of preserving the life of the developing new child. The clash of values is aptly captured in this quotation from the Lutheran Church-Missouri Synod's 1984 document, *Abortion in Perspective:*

> We have emphasized as strongly as possible the protection to which the unborn child is entitled. We do not overlook, however, the fact that in the gestation and birth of children mothers bear by far the greatest burdens. The child's life is dependent upon his mother in a unique manner, a manner which calls for an act of self-spending on her part. Indeed, we may even say that in the manner of human gestation and birth we see a deeper truth than our attachment to independence and individualism can reach. The life-giving burden carried by mothers, and only by mothers, must be kept clearly in view throughout our ethical reflection. This fact alone gives the mother's claims a certain preeminence in those cases where the life of the unborn child and the equal life of the mother come into conflict. . . . In the rare situations of conflict we must recognize the permissibility of abortion. Despite the progress of medical science, there are still unusual circumstances in which a mother will die if an abortion is not performed. . . . Even in such circumstances a mother may choose to risk her own life as an act of love, but such an act of self-giving cannot be required. It must be freely given, not imposed.[19]

Christian teaching through the ages is similarly disapproving of abortion, though speculative distinctions were often made in the past concerning when God infused a fetus with a "soul." (Abortions performed after ensoulment were considered far more serious than those performed before.) Exactly when a fertilized ovum can be called a "person" (and is thus due the rights and protections afforded any human being) is a medical, biological, philosophical, and theological question that eludes easy answers. Modern-day Roman Catholicism has been uncompromising in its view that new life is to be treated as a person from the first moment of conception. Believing that it is never permissible to voluntarily kill innocent human life, the church teaches that "direct abortion, that is, abortion willed as an end or as a means, *always* constitutes a grave moral disorder."[20] There are no exceptions. Similarly, "the Orthodox Church brands abortion as murder; that is, as a premeditated termination of the life of a human being. . . . The only time the Orthodox Church will reluctantly acquiesce to abortion is when the preponderance of medical opinion determines that unless the embryo or fetus is aborted, the mother will die."[21]

One might justifiably speculate that Jesus, whose concern for the vulnerable is well documented, would want to protect a defenseless life *in utero*. Yet there is also reason to believe that this same Jesus, an intimate friend and defender of women, would be sympathetic to the plight of women caught in an unwanted or unintended pregnancy. Authentic Christianity, as demonstrated in Jesus' life and ministry, is concerned with enhancing the quality of *all* human life, not just preserving unborn human life. Given women's historic experience of oppression and exclusion from power, the argument is often made that women must be given the freedom to decide whether or not to continue a problem pregnancy if they are to achieve the autonomy necessary to fully actualize their humanity. Some Christian communions, such as the United Church of Christ, weigh in strongly in favor of allowing the woman to make her own decision. In so doing, she actualizes her moral agency. Other mainline Protestant denominations, recognizing the moral ambiguity of the issue, hold that abortion is always a tragic choice but one that may be ethically warranted in individual cases, particularly those involving rape, incest, life-threatening situations, or severe fetal abnormalities. How severe these abnormalities have to be and how much risk a mother can be expected to bear before an abortion might be justified are questions that are left unanswered and hence continually debated. No conscientious Christian ever chooses an abortion without being deeply disturbed on some level. Likewise, no Christian of good faith can remain unmoved by the plight of a pregnant woman who feels she has no other viable choice. Commitment to following Jesus would suggest that one of the strongest Christian imperatives would be to work toward a society in which the causes of problem pregnancies—irresponsible sexual conduct, poor contraceptive practice, male sexual aggression, and insufficient support systems—are directly and effectively addressed.

Contraception: Until 1930, when the Anglican Communion modified its teaching, Christians around the world had been unanimous in their condemnation of artificial means of birth control. For centuries, the procreation of children had been defined as the primary purpose of marriage, with love and personal fulfillment only rising in importance over the last hundred years. The twentieth-century advent of reliable means of birth control brought with it a consciousness that was now able to think about sex as a loving and pleasurable activity independent of the generation of children. "In God's design," as the Seventh-Day Adventists recently put it, "sexual intimacy is not only for the purpose of conception. Scripture does not prohibit married couples from enjoying the delights of conjugal relations while taking measures to prevent pregnancy."[22] Today, virtually every Christian community accepts the use of contraception within marriage for the purpose of exercising responsible parenthood, enhancing the expression of marital love, and protecting the health of the woman.[23] Whereas most churches continue to look favorably on couples who generously bring new life into the world, they also maintain that "respect and sensitivity should also be shown toward couples who do not feel called to conceive and/or rear children, or who are unable to do so."[24]

The one notable exception to what has just been stated is the Roman Catholic Church, which, grounding its position in a traditional natural law argument, continues to hold that each and every act of intercourse must remain open to the transmission of new life.[25] The teaching is largely ignored by the majority of Catholic couples, though it is generally regarded to be a litmus test for Catholic priests who aspire to be bishops. The mainstream of Catholic theologians vigorously debated the issue in the 1960s and 1970s, with the vast majority breaking from the hierarchy's published pronouncements. Today the topic is widely considered passé. Rarely is the issue even mentioned in the theological journals, other than to note how the official stand undermines the church's credibility in matters of sexual ethics. Nevertheless, the larger idea that lies behind the teaching is one with strong Christian roots, namely that children are a good outcome of marital intercourse, to be welcomed and cherished as God's gift and blessing. They are not living trophies to be added to the household only when the time is deemed right nor cute little instruments of parental fulfillment who round out a life in suburbia. Other Christian churches would no doubt share these views, but they would not concur with the Catholic hierarchy that it is God's will that the unitive and procreative meanings of sexual intercourse never be separated. The Catholic stand has met with particularly strong condemnation when the venue is that of an overpopulated country with limited resources or a developing nation in the midst of an AIDS epidemic. In these contexts, whatever good is achieved by holding together the unitive and procreative meanings seems vastly outweighed by the likely spread of disease or the introduction of a new life that cannot be sufficiently supported.

Masturbation: Like contraception, masturbation has a long history of condemnation coming from Christian quarters. Although there is no direct biblical teaching on the subject, the Hebrew scriptures generally speak favorably of procreative sex, as does the Christian tradition. For a long time, faulty knowledge of human biology contributed to the common belief that all vital material necessary for human life was contained in the male's sperm. Hence to spill the seed was to waste a potential life. Masturbation, therefore, was thought to involve the deliberate destruction of innocent human life.

Today, when medical and biological knowledge is clearly far superior, many Christian communities nevertheless remain uneasy with the practice of masturbation, widespread though it may be. Drawing once again from its natural

law heritage, Roman Catholicism maintains that masturbation is "an intrinsically and gravely disordered action, [since] the use of the sexual faculty, for
whatever reason, outside of marriage is essentially contrary to its purpose."[26]
Whereas most other Christian communions would take exception to the
characterization of masturbation as "intrinsically and gravely disordered," the
implicit point many would agree on is that our sexuality is essentially a *relational* power, an "irrepressible urge to overcome our incompleteness." Insofar
as masturbation is a solitary activity aimed at self-pleasuring, it fails to achieve
the full potential of our God-given sexual power. As Orthodox theologian
William Basil Zion explains:

> masturbation is indeed a speaking to oneself of the sexual language. . . . What is
> morally problematic is whether this form of speaking to ourselves is a refusal of
> the language of love or a preparation for the language of love. . . . Masturbation
> speaks of our lack of the other. The moral question is not a matter of the waste of
> seed (as the reality of female masturbation shows us) or even the falling into the
> libidinous for those whose vocation lies in marriage. It is, rather, the question as
> to why one masturbates in place of loving, or, for that matter, in place of praying.
> To make the evil simply a matter of releasing sexual passions is far to simplistic.[27]

Thus the Christian moral evaluation of masturbation will generally hinge on
the particular motives, fantasies, and circumstances surrounding the masturbatory activity. Of the main branches of Christianity, mainline Protestant
churches are the least likely to be exercised by masturbation, unless it
becomes an obsessive, self-centered practice. Some Protestants will go so far as
to endorse certain manifestations of masturbation, particularly those involving
sexual self-exploration or self-affirmation, and in cases where injury, age, or
disability make interpersonal sexual encounters difficult, if not impossible.
A major challenge for most Christian churches is in encouraging members to
realize their sexual potential in a morally responsible way, without provoking
disabling guilt when efforts fall short of the mark. Anecdotal information
would suggest that feelings of guilt have been quite common in the past, turning masturbation into one of those topics that Christians rarely discuss yet,
ironically, regularly practice.

Homosexuality: At present and for the foreseeable future, no other issue roils
Christian communities such as those having to do with gay and lesbian sexuality. Just as society is in the midst of a major social, cultural, and moral
reevaluation of homosexuality, so are many of the Christian churches. The
two most prominent questions being debated in the mainline Protestant
churches are whether same-sex unions should be blessed and whether practicing homosexuals can be ordained to the ministry. The answers to both of
these questions, naturally, are dependent on the moral evaluation given to
homosexual acts in the first place. It is to that issue that we now turn.

As with contraception and masturbation, Christianity has a long history of
condemning homosexual acts.[28] In both the Hebrew and Christian scriptures,
those who engage in same-sex acts are judged rather harshly. The Book of

Leviticus, for example, bluntly states that "if a man lies with a male as with a woman, both of them have committed an abomination; they shall be put to death" (Lev 20:13). Paul includes "sodomites"[29] on a list of those who will not inherit the kingdom of God (cf. 1 Cor 6:9–10) and in his letter to the Christians in Rome speaks of the "shameless acts" men commit with other men (cf. Rom 1:18–32). On the surface at least, the scriptural testimony against homosexuals appears to be devastating. Conservative and some mainline Protestant churches find in scripture an eternal and definitive condemnation of homosexuality. To that strong testimony one can add the Catholic natural law objection that homosexual acts are "intrinsically disordered" because they are closed to the gift of life and do not proceed "from a genuine affective and sexual complementarity."[30] The Orthodox also object on the grounds that homosexual acts "do not symbolize the unity between Christ and His Church as sacramental marriage does."[31]

Large parts of the mainline Protestant churches, as well the preponderance of Catholic theologians, read the landscape quite differently.[32] First, it is pointed out that the biblical authors were unaware that some individuals are homosexually oriented; their operative assumption was that those engaging in homoerotic acts were heterosexuals acting "unnaturally." Had they known what we know today, so the argument goes, their moral evaluation might have been different. Second, it is noted that the prohibition of homosexual acts found in Leviticus is part of a "Holiness Code" that similarly imposes the death penalty for adultery (20:10), cursing one's parents (20:9), and for various forms of incest (20:11,14). The code also stipulates that if a man and a woman have sex during the woman's menstrual period, they "shall be cut off from their people" (20:18). Essentially, the code is designed to maintain cultic and ritual purity, distinguishing the Israelites from neighboring pagan tribes. Such concerns, gay and lesbian supporters argue, are worlds apart from contemporary pastoral issues. What the author of Leviticus was trying to prevent is entirely different from what gays and lesbians are trying to achieve by entering into permanent, loving, monogamous unions. Third, it is argued that one of the characteristic marks of Jesus' ministry was not a slavish adherence to the law, but rather a call to compassion and solidarity with those who are oppressed. Homosexuals in today's society are victimized by hate and prejudice, denied legal protections heterosexuals take for granted, and told that their experiences of finding love and acceptance and even God through their lovers' embrace are invalid and intrinsically disordered. It would certainly seem, the argument concludes, that disciples of Jesus must listen carefully to what their gay brothers and sisters are saying, and make the homosexual struggle their own.

Obviously, in a short space we can only scratch the surface of a very involved and deeply felt debate. What should be plainly apparent is the difference made by diverging interpretations of scripture and the role that experience plays (or does not play) in forming moral evaluations of homosexual conduct. As made clear in the discussion of other sexual issues, and perhaps even more so in this case, Christians are a long way from reconciling their conflicting theological stands. Currently, there is a significant (but not overwhelming) trend among theologians and ordinary "people in the pews" to reexamine traditional viewpoints on homosexuality, with an eye to becoming more accepting. Catholic, Orthodox, and Evangelical leaders, however, are generally pulling the other way. From the perspective of the sexually active homosexual who would like to remain a part of the church, there are nonetheless some encouraging signs. Roman Catholicism teaches that homosexuals "must be accepted with respect, compassion, and sensitivity," and without "unjust discrimination."[33] In 2003, the Episcopal Church, though not without controversy, ordained a man who lives in an openly gay relationship as bishop of the New Hampshire diocese. The more liberal leaning United Church of Christ continues to welcome sexually active gay men and women into the ministry as part of a long-standing (since 1985) initiative to be "open and affirming."[34] And some Lutheran synods and Episcopal congregations have approved the blessing of same-sex, marriage-like unions.

Still, it is hard to deny that the way Christian teaching has been expressed in the past has contributed to the hatred and homophobia that remain in the air today. Much as the churches have begun to own up to their role in fostering anti-Semitism, so too they may one day have to come to terms with the way Christian teaching has encouraged hateful attitudes and physical violence towards homosexually oriented persons. Less visible, but no doubt more prevalent, are the emotional scars many carry in secret. Due to both content and presentation of teaching, a large number of gay and lesbian Christians continue to feel guilty and ashamed for wanting to act on their deeply felt sexual attractions. To them, their feelings are analogous to heterosexual love. Some church teaching, however, especially that of Roman Catholicism, seems to classify such desires together with other "disorders" such as bestiality and pedophilia. To most gays and lesbians, the comparisons are inappropriate and hurtful. The fact that Catholic priests who were known to be pedophiles were once allowed to preside at sacramental rites from which gay and lesbian couples were simultaneously excluded strikes many as warped and hypocritical. Ironically, estimates of gay men in the Catholic priesthood typically range from one-third to one-half, several multiples higher than the general population; the incidence of clerical pedophilia is generally considered to be more in line with societal trends.

Many others would find troubling the Web site of the Assemblies of God, which speaks approvingly of ministers and psychologists successfully "treating" homosexuality, ostensibly to reverse the patient's orientation.[35] Besides the fact that such claims have been dismissed as scientifically unfounded by the Surgeon General of the United States,[36] they foster the impression that homosexuality is a sickness that needs to be cured, a freakish disorder that somehow escaped the good hand of the Creator God. It is perhaps not surprising that many gays and lesbians no longer practice Christianity.

Conclusion

As this survey comes to a conclusion, it should be clear that in the panoply of Christian denominations, one can find representatives from either end of the theological spectrum, and several in between. If one were shopping for a religion based on a set of preestablished positions on sex and gender issues, the

Christian Department Store would be certain to carry something that fit your tastes. Laying nuances momentarily aside, one can ascertain two major schools of thought within the broad Christian tradition. The first, ably represented by Roman Catholicism, adheres to traditional sexual morality that is easily caricatured as a series of negative responses to anything that deviates from procreative heterosexual intercourse within a stable marital relationship. The second, embodied in a variety of mainline Protestant communities (the Lutherans, Episcopalians, Presbyterians, etc.) struggles to remain faithful to the Christian tradition while taking seriously the insights to be found in society's evolving sexual mores. Ironically, the more countercultural Christian denominations have been growing in recent years, whereas the more accommodating have been losing members.

Can anything be said in summary that all Christians, or at least most, could bring themselves to accept? Perhaps. It would seem that despite the prohibitions and condemnations, the heart of the Christian vision is positive and affirming of sexual beings. Created in the image and likeness of God, women and men are "fearfully and wonderfully made" (Ps 139:14), designed to live in intimate relationship with one another and their God. Through the gift of their sexuality, they are driven beyond the confines of their bodies into a transcendent creativity, epitomized in the union of two lovers clasped together in an erotic, almost mystical, embrace.

Against the backdrop of a culture that packages, sells, and glorifies a carefree attitude toward sex, Christianity wants to maintain that by holding together the enduring values of intimacy, pleasure, and parenthood, our sexuality will not only be physically and emotionally rewarding, but also socially and spiritually uplifting. God is self-communicating love, Christianity proclaims, and one of the best ways to encounter God is to be a part of a loving, committed, mutually giving and receiving sexual relationship.

Despite the good news about sex, Christianity has often gone to great lengths to warn the world of its dangers. One is left to wonder how different the world might have been had the churches expended as much capital purifying the social order as they did seeking to circumscribe people's sexual pleasure. If Jesus' life is to be the measure of all things Christian, then attention to sexual issues must be subordinated to larger social concerns involving the alleviation of human suffering. Freed from the daily threat of premature death, men and women can then experience more abundant life through the richly satisfying, God-given gift of human sexuality.

QUESTIONS FOR DISCUSSION

1. How would you characterize the Christian vision of human sexuality, as relatively positive and affirming or more cautious and restrictive?

2. The chapter describes the Christian vision of sexuality as a "sacred energy" or "life force" that propels human beings into "transcendent creativity." Is this expecting too much from the sexual drive or is it a helpful expansion of common presuppositions?

3. Can Christianity make an important contribution to the public debate over sexual values and practices, or does the diversity in the Christian witness effectively undermine whatever position is taken?

4. Christian churches have traditionally placed strong emphasis on the procreative good of sexual intercourse. What role should that value play in contemporary discussions of sexual morality?

5. Many Christian churches would maintain that there exists an *objective* sexual morality, that is, one that is either given universally by God or can be adduced through the use of human reason. How does this position challenge Western and American ideals of personal autonomy and freedom of expression?

6. Moral difficulties over abortion are often worked out when one group of values is given precedence over another. How would you evaluate the Christian configuration of these values, and how is that configuration similar to, or different from, your own?

7. Is it possible to personally affirm a homosexually oriented person yet condemn his or her deeply felt sexual feelings? How does this case differ from that of an adult with sexual feelings toward children?

8. In an age when sexual mores can evolve rather rapidly, can the Christian reliance on "holy tradition" serve as a helpful caution against changes in sexual morality that may ultimately prove to be short-lived trends growing out of a particular historical, social, or cultural location? Or do some Christian churches just need to "get with the times"?

RECOMMENDED RESOURCES

Books

Cahill, Lisa Sowle. *Sex, Gender and Christian Ethics*. Cambridge: Cambridge University Press, 1996.

Genovesi, Vincent J. *In Pursuit of Love: Catholic Morality and Human Sexuality*. Collegeville, MN: The Liturgical Press, 1996.

Nelson, James B. *Between Two Gardens: Reflections on Sexuality and Religious Experience*. New York: The Pilgrim Press, 1983.

Stuart, Elizabeth, and Thatcher, Adrian. *People of Passion: What the Churches Teach About Sex*. London: Mowbray, 1997.

United States Catholic Conference. *Human Sexuality: A Catholic Perspective for Education and Lifelong Learning*. Washington: USCC, 1991.

Zion, William Basil. *Eros and Transformation. Sexuality and Marriage: An Eastern Orthodox Perspective*. Lanham, MD: University Press of America, 1992.

Video

The Good Book of Love: Sex in the Bible. New York: A&E Home Video, 1999.

Web Sites

Assemblies of God USA. *Relationships, Conduct, and Sexuality.* http://ag.org/top/beliefs/relationships/relations_00_list.cfm.

Evangelical Lutheran Church in America. *A Message on Sexuality: Some Common Convictions.* http://www.elca.org/dcs/sexuality.html.

Greek Orthodox Diocese of North and South America. *The Stand of the Orthodox Church on Controversial Issues.* http://www.goarch.org/en/ourfaith/articles/article7101.asp.

Lutheran Church–Missouri Synod. *Human Sexuality: A Theological Perspective.* http://www.lcms.org/ctcr/docs/sxty-01.html.

Orthodox Church in America. *On Marriage, Family, Sexuality, and the Sanctity of Life.* http://www.oca.org/pages/ocaadmin/documents/All-American-Council/10-Miami-1992/Synodal-Affirmations.html.

(Roman Catholic) Sacred Congregation for the Doctrine of the Faith. *Declaration on Certain Questions Concerning Sexual Ethics.* http://www.ewtn.com/library/CURIA/CDFCERTN.HTM. *N.B.* This url is case sensitive.

ENDNOTES

1. Catherine LaCugna, "God in Communion with Us," in *Freeing Theology: The Essentials of Theology in Feminist Perspective,* ed. Catherine Mowry LaCugna (San Francisco: Harper San Francisco, 1993), 106.

2. Ronald Rolheiser, *The Holy Longing: The Search for a Christian Spirituality* (New York: Doubleday, 1999), 196.

3. Radio Bible Class, "What's the Purpose of Sex?" retrieved November 13, 2001, from the RBC Ministries Web site: http://www.gospelcom.net/rbc/questions/answer.php?catagory=ethics&folder=sex&topic=Sex&file=purpose.xml.

4. St. Augustine, *City of God* (New York: Doubleday, 1958), Book 14, Chapter 20.

5. Most Protestants came to reject traditional Catholic teaching about the Virgin Mary, holding that biblical references to Jesus' "brothers" clearly implied that Mary and Joseph were sexually active. Catholic and Orthodox officials, on the other hand, argue that in Semitic usage, the term "brother," is applied not only to children of the same parents, but to nephews, cousins, and half-brothers as well.

6. It should be emphasized that those who remain celibate either by circumstance or choice do not, by that fact, become "asexual" beings. As previously noted, one's sexuality is a dynamic and creative life force that does not necessarily have to be channeled towards genitality. Jesus, a celibate renown for the intensity of his love, could not have been anything but a man charged with sexual energy. Such a characterization, however, has not traditionally been included in either religious or secular portraits of Jesus.

7. St. Augustine, "On the Good of Marriage," Chapter 3 from the *Select Library of Nicene and Post-Nicene Fathers,* Volume 3, retrieved November 13, 2003, from the Christian Classics Ethereal Library Web site: http://www.ccel.org/fathers2/NPNF1-03/npnf1-03-32.htm#P3736_1760974.

8. Eve Levin, *Sex and Society in the World of Orthodox Slavs, 900–1700* (Ithaca, NY: Cornell University Press, 1989), 162–63.

9. Theresa Gross-Diaz, "Sexuality and Spirituality in the European Middle Ages," *Chicago Studies* 32 (April 1993), 38.

10. Lisa Sowle Cahill, "Sexuality, Marriage, and Parenthood: The Catholic Tradition," in *Religion and Artificial Reproduction,* ed. Lisa Sowle Cahill and Thomas Shannon (New York: Crossroad, 1988), 37.

11. C. S. Lewis, *Mere Christianity* (New York: The Macmillan Company, 1960), 82.

12. Evangelical Lutheran Church in America, *A Message on Sexuality: Some Common Convictions,* retrieved November 13, 2003, from the ELCA Web site: http://www.elca.org/dcs/sexuality.pf.html.

13. Cf. Andrew M. Greeley, *Faithful Attraction: Discovering Intimacy, Love, and Fidelity in American Marriage* (New York: Tom Doherty Associates, 1991), esp. Chapter 4. It should be noted that the data do not indicate that shared prayer and worship *cause* couples to stay together, but rather shows a *correlation* between religiosity and lower rates of divorce.

14. Elizabeth A. Johnson, "The Marian Tradition and the Reality of Women," in *Horizons on Catholic Feminist Theology,* ed. Joann Wolski Conn and Walter E. Conn (Washington, D.C.: Georgetown University Press, 1992), 98.

15. *Baptist Faith and Message,* section XVIII, "The Family," retrieved November 13, 2003, from http://sbc.net/bfm/bfm2000.asp.

16. "Why Does the Assemblies of God Believe People Are to Participate in Sexual Relations Only in a Monogamous Heterosexual Marriage Relationship?" retrieved November 13, 2002, from the Assemblies of God USA Web site: http://www.ag.org/top/beliefs/relationships/relations_03_sexual.cfm.

17. In Hispanic cultures where *machismo* is alive and well, males are often given tacit approval to exercise their sexual prowess without even a hint of monogamy. Christianity naturally condemns such customs, even as many Hispanic Christians are frequently inclined to be more tolerant.

18. Cf. David Popenoe and Barbara Dafoe Whitehead, "Should We Live Together? Second Edition. What Young Adults Need to Know about Cohabitation before Marriage: A Comprehensive Review of Recent Research," retrieved November 13, 2003, from the National Marriage Project Web site sponsored by Rutgers University: http://marriage.rutgers.edu/Publications.

19. Lutheran Church—Missouri Synod, *Abortion in Perspective,* retrieved November 13, 2003, from the Lutheran Church—Missouri Synod Web site: http://www.lcms.org/cic/abort2.html.

20. Pope John Paul II, *Evangelium Vitae* (New York: Random House, 1995), paragraph 62 (emphasis added).

21. Stanley Harakas, "The Stand of the Orthodox Church on Controversial Issues," retrieved November 13, 2003, from the Greek Orthodox Diocese of North and South America Web site: http://goarch.org/en/ourfaith/articles/article7101.asp.

22. General Conference of Seventh-day Adventists, "Christianity and Contraception: Seventh-day Adventist Ethical Guidelines," published by the Loma Linda University Center for Christian Bioethics in *Update* 15:3 (September 1999): 2.

23. Churches that stand in strong opposition to abortion also object to any means of contraception that acts after, rather than before, an egg has been fertilized.

24. Evangelical Lutheran Church in America, *A Message on Sexuality*.

25. Cf. Pope Paul VI, *Humanae Vitae* (Washington, D.C.: U.S. Catholic Conference, 1968), paragraphs 11–12.

26. *Catechism of the Catholic Church* (Vatican City: Libreria Editrice Vaticana, 1994), paragraph 2352.

27. William Basil Zion, *Eros and Transformation. Sexuality and Marriage: An Eastern Orthodox Perspective* (Lanham, MD: University Press of America, 1992), 283.

28. More recently distinctions have been made that encourage respect and love for homosexually oriented persons, while still disapproving of their sexual activities.

29. The terms "sodomy" and "sodomite" actually derive from the biblical city of Sodom, which, according to some Christian interpretations, was destroyed by God because of the prevalence of same-sex intercourse. More recent Biblical scholarship has called into question traditional assumptions about Sodom's sin, pointing out that the Bible itself offers conflicting testimony (cf. Jeremiah 23:14, Ezekiel 16:49-50, Sirach 16:8, 2 Peter 2:4–10, Jude 7), often suggesting that the primary vice of Sodom was its inhabitants' lack of hospitality.

30. *Catechism of the Catholic Church,* paragraph 2357.

31. Zion, *Eros and Transformation,* 309.

32. Readers unfamiliar with dynamics of internal church debates should keep in mind that the views of theologians in a particular Christian denomination will not necessarily correspond with the official teaching of that denomination. The same might be said of ordinary believers vis-à-vis their positions in comparison to the official teachings of their church. Pluralism and polarization are quite common in Christian sexual ethics, even if unity is often the stated goal.

33. *Catechism of the Catholic Church,* paragraph 2358.

34. See the United Church of Christ Coalition for LGBT Concerns Web site: http://www.ucccoalition.org/programs/ona.htm.

35. Cf. Assemblies of God USA Web site: http://ag.org/top/beliefs/relationships/relations_11_homosexual.cfm.

36. *The Surgeon General's Call to Action to Promote Sexual Health and Responsible Sexual Behavior,* Section III, "The Public Health Problem," retrieved November 13, 2003, from The Virtual Office of the Surgeon General: http://www.surgeongeneral.gov/library/sexualhealth/call.htm.

Chapter 7

Mormonism

Klaus J. Hansen

The Historical Context

The birth of Mormonism, ca. 1820–1844, coincided with the birth of modern America. This was an age of fundamental and dramatic change. Though it could of course be argued that change is characteristic of the entire history of America, many scholars are in agreement that it was in the first half of the nineteenth century that material, intellectual, and psychological change accelerated to a degree unknown to previous generations. This was the age of the "market revolution," with farmers shifting from subsistence agriculture to the growing of cash crops (such as wheat in the North and cotton in the South); the rapid growth of manufacturing; and the gradual shift of society from rural to urban. Although for many Americans this rapid transformation was a cause for optimism, for a growing number it was a source of anxiety. Numerous religious movements attempted to address this anxiety, seeing in this age of instability and uncertainty opportunities for returning society to an even keel—even as they themselves were perceived by many to be contributing to the upheavals of the age. Among the prominent religious movements of this period were the Shakers, the Oneida Perfectionists, and the Mormons—each seeking in its own way to create order out of chaos. Differing radically among themselves about how the problems brought by these changes should be addressed, they were in agreement that one of the most fundamental symptoms of the turbulence of the age was the weakening of the traditional family. They were also in agreement that given the changed circumstances under which families had to cope, a reinstitution of the "good old days" was not a solution.

However, although each group had its own ideas about how the family should be reconstituted, they were in agreement that a reordering of relations between the sexes was essential to their respective agendas for religious and social change. The Shakers, under the leadership of "Mother" Ann Lee, regarded sexual relations as a major source of society's ills and instituted celibacy as a remedy. John Humphrey Noyes, founder of the Oneida community of religious "perfectionists" in western New York, agreed with the Shakers that sexual relations were indeed a source of major social and familial conflict, but saw the solution in the institution of "complex marriage"—a kind of holy family in which the perfected believers shared sexual relations with many partners under the guidance of their leader Noyes, who firmly rejected accusations that he had in fact instituted a form of sexual license. The Mormons, likewise, vigorously defended themselves against charges of sexual libertinism leveled at them for their practice of plural marriage, popularly called polygamy. Although perhaps not the most radical experiment in sexual reform, it certainly involved a far larger number of adherents than any other antebellum American reform movement.[1]

Mormonism had its origins in the "Burned-over District" of western New York in the 1820s at a time when farms, villages, and towns were consumed by the fires of religious revivals. As a boy of fourteen, Joseph Smith, confused by the conflicting claims of various revivalists, asked God in prayer which one taught the truth. In a vision of two divine personages (who he identified as God the Father and Jesus Christ), he was told that he should join none of the competing sects, but prepare himself for a future mission on behalf of mankind. Some years later, following the instructions of a divine messenger who called himself the Angel Moroni, young Joseph (by now in his mid-twenties) published a sacred record titled The Book of Mormon. The record was intended as a companion to the Bible and was purported to be an account of the religious history of early Americans known to Smith and his contemporaries as Indians. Shortly after, in April 1830, Smith founded or rather, as he put it, "restored" the Church of Christ, which was soon nicknamed the "Mormon" church after one of its major sacred texts. Mormons prefer the official name, which was coined in 1837—Church of Jesus Christ of Latter-day Saints.[2]

The newly founded church quickly gained adherents who, in a series of migrations, moved from western New York to Ohio, to western Missouri, and then back to western Illinois where they founded the city-state Nauvoo on the banks of the Mississippi River. It was here, in 1844, that Smith (now called the Mormon Prophet) was murdered by a mob. In order to escape from persecution, Smith's successor, Brigham Young, led the "Saints" in an epic trek to the shores of the Great Salt Lake, where they established their Rocky Mountain kingdom of God under the protection of the "everlasting hills."[3]

Joseph Smith had secretly introduced plural marriage in Nauvoo shortly before his death. It was left to Brigham Young to establish the practice in the

Rocky Mountains, announcing it to an astonished and outraged world in 1852. Plural marriage remained a major source of conflict with evangelical Protestants and the United States government until it was officially outlawed by the church in 1890, in direct response to enormous pressure from the federal government. Although the majority of Mormons accepted this edict, if reluctantly, a vocal minority of die-hard believers have persisted in the practice to this day to the consternation of church leaders, who exact the ultimate penalty of excommunication for such disobedience.[4] Another minority of Smith's followers never accepted the principle of plural marriage in Nauvoo (his wife Emma among them), refused to follow Brigham Young on his Western trek, and established what they regarded as the authentic church founded by Joseph Smith, naming it The Reorganized Church of Jesus Christ of Latter Day Saints with headquarters in Independence, Missouri (recently renamed The Community of Christ).[5]

Although the so-called "Utah Mormons" no longer practice plural marriage, the heirs of Joseph Smith and Brigham Young continue to adhere to the underlying beliefs and principles that justified polygamy in the nineteenth century. Although these beliefs and principles were not in evidence in the very early years of Mormonism (allowing dissenters to disavow polygamy), they did evolve in the founding period, reaching their doctrinal apex in the last years of Smith's life—especially in the revelation of the "New and Everlasting Covenant." This covenant held out the promise of eternal family relationships to faithful Mormon men and women who were "sealed" in marriage for "time and eternity" by those with the proper authority (i.e., those holding the Mormon priesthood) in sacred edifices called temples. The "celestial family" was the culmination of an evolutionary process that had its beginnings in the preexistence, where humans had lived as spirits—the offspring of divine parents (a heavenly father and a heavenly mother) who are gender-differentiated physical beings. In Mormon cosmology, spirit is matter, but far more refined than the matter of this world. As part of a divine plan, these spirit children are required to take up earthly bodies in preparation for a future state of immortality and "eternal life." Life on earth is a school in which all will be rewarded with immortality (because of the redeeming sacrifice of Christ) in one of three "degrees of glory." However, only those most diligent in obeying the laws of God will achieve eternal life—a reunion with their heavenly parents, a reunion denied to those who were less than valiant in resisting the many temptations of this world. Those who have entered into the New and Everlasting Covenant are among the most "exalted," having earned the privilege of becoming heads of eternal families in emulation of their heavenly parents. Their spirit children, resulting from a union of gender-differentiated premortal beings, will likewise be required to experience mortality on a planet not unlike this earth. Thus, those having achieved exaltation are gods in embryo, as expressed in a famous (some critics might say blasphemous) phrase: "As man is God once was: as God is man may become." To faithful Mormons, however, this is far from an invitation to spiritual pride. On the contrary, confronted with such awesome prospects most of them respond with a spirit of humility.[6]

Because sexuality is one of the most exalted of the divine attributes, discretion in matters sexual is of special concern to Latter-day Saints. Not surprisingly, many of their rules for sexual conduct are derived from their biblically rooted New England heritage, with strong echoes in the Book of Mormon, which condemns fornication and adultery as well as "unnatural acts" and "perversions" as heinous sins. Sexual relations are permitted in heterosexual marriage only. Although sex in marriage is permitted as the natural expression of love between husband and wife, its primary purpose is procreation. Prolonged celibacy among healthy adults is seen as unnatural and as against the will of God—as is sexual transgression. In either case, humans are wilfully rejecting the laws of God.

Because of the immense number of spirits eager to come into this world, it is necessary for mortals to have large families. However, the fact that far more women than men met the rigorous requirements regarding sexual morality (a typical nineteenth-century bias) for entry into the New and Everlasting Covenant created a problem. The solution was the principle of plural marriage, which enabled one worthy male to have many offspring with several worthy wives, facilitating the peopling of this planet with spirits from the pre-existence under optimal conditions. This was one of the reasons why Joseph Smith secretly initiated a group of trusted followers into the practice of plural marriage in Nauvoo shortly before his death in 1844.

In theory, Mormon teachings regarding sex are timeless, but they are of course practiced in a historical context and are thus subject to varying cultural manifestations. Joseph Smith was attempting to establish a communal society at a time when in American society at large such values were giving way to the strivings for individualism. By the 1820s and 1830s, American culture had moved a long way from the relatively stable social order of colonial times to the increasingly atomistic society of capitalism—from the traditional Calvinism, which saw God as the center of the world, to an individualistic ethos, which saw humans at the center, and from a society in which behavior was largely controlled by the norms of the community to a society in which moral standards were internalized. Teetotalism (abstinence from alcohol) and sexual restraint became two of the most important means of expressing this modern attitude, at times leading to purity crusades that had a tendency to erupt into antisexual hysteria. It is not surprising, then, that Mormons, after they had established their kingdom of God in Utah, became the object of such crusades, even though their sexual morality was essentially "puritanical" (one commentator has called it "Puritan Polygamy").[7]

Contemporary Mormonism

As long as Mormons were separated from the world in their religious, social, economic, and political Rocky Mountain kingdom they did not share the kinds of sexual anxieties manifested in the modernizing United States. However, with the demise of polygamy, Mormons, too, could no longer avoid the tensions of the modern world. Within the kingdom, polygamy especially, but political and economic communitarianism as well, had served to maintain boundaries that facilitated social control. With the advent of the twentieth century, as Mormons likewise began to experience the centrifugal forces of individualism, new mechanisms of boundary maintenance had to be devised. The most notable of these was a stricter enforcement of the "Word of Wisdom"— dietary rules that admonished Mormons to avoid alcohol, tobacco, and caffeine. Rather than leaving adherence to the discretion of individual members, the "Word of Wisdom" was redefined as a commandment, and obedience was mandatory for good standing in the church. Although the rules regarding sexual conduct did not change, adherence was monitored more closely, and excommunications for transgressions became more frequent. As Mormons, in American public opinion, were transformed "from satyr to saint" (in the words of a prominent commentator),[8] their newly won respectability was bought at the cost of an internal backlash against their polygamous past. Mormon historians from the 1920s to the 1940s downplayed the historical importance of polygamy—if they mentioned it at all. So did church publications. It has been estimated that 20 to 40 percent of Mormon families were polygamous in the second half of the nineteenth century. In an attempt to minimize the importance of polygamy after it was outlawed, some Mormon publications reduced its incidence to 3 or 4 percent. In the first half of the twentieth century, Mormons, by and large, accepted the middle-class values of their erstwhile (largely Protestant) antagonists, including attitudes toward sex and marriage.[9]

These values were promulgated by church leaders through organizational channels. The Mormon Church is essentially a hierarchically structured lay organization. At the top of the pyramid stands the prophet, addressed as president, who is assisted by two counselors and a quorum of twelve apostles. Below these, several dozen members in middle-level positions carry out many of the church's administrative duties. These are all full-time positions collectively designated as "General Authorities." Ecclesiastically, the church is organized into "stakes" (equivalent to dioceses) and "wards" (equivalent to parishes), which are administered by a lay-priesthood of males. In addition, auxiliary organizations for women and young people may include women in their leadership. Church policy is formulated by the president, with the aid of the counselors and the apostles. Twice a year, church members are instructed by the president and other general authorities who hold conferences in Salt Lake City. Messages from these conferences are transmitted by television, radio, and print media worldwide. More often than not, these messages include advice on sexual matters—primarily general admonitions on chastity, sexual purity, and clean living, though from time to time also on more specific issues, such as birth control, abortion, or homosexuality.

The monitoring and enforcement of such advice is largely the responsibility of authorities at the stake and ward level, and highly gendered. Priesthood authorities are all male and are the only ones authorized to interview church members. Lacking the institution of the confessional, all members are not monitored equally. By and large, interviews are part of the ladder of advancement in the male lay priesthood, which begins at age twelve, when young men are normally ordained to the rank of Deacon, the first office in the Aaronic (or lower) priesthood. As they grow into their teens, candidates are more frequently queried about their sexual history, with masturbation becoming a major concern as males mature sexually while advancing through the ranks of Teacher and Priest. A more daunting hurdle is advancement to the Melchizedek (or higher) priesthood, usually at age eighteen, with ordination to the office of Elder.

Some psychologists and psychiatrists have reported a significant degree of anxiety regarding sexual matters among Mormon adolescents. Although the sexual behavior of women is not monitored to the same extent as that of men (in part because they are not eligible to hold the priesthood), therapists have also reported a considerable degree of sexual anxiety among young women. Mormon women are more likely to engage in premarital sex than men. Admonitions from the pulpit enjoining women to modesty of dress suggests belief in their potential role as temptress. In recent years, female sexuality has become a matter of growing concern as an increasing number of young women are being called to serve as missionaries and as church authorities are acquiring a more sophisticated understanding of female sexuality. Nevertheless, concerns regarding matters sexual continue to be highly gendered, with most of the exhortations directed toward young males. For example, even today vestiges of the belief in the "spermatic economy" can still be encountered in popular mythology: Male sperm is a precious fluid that wastes a man's energy if expended casually and promiscuously. A man's sexuality is "active," a woman's "passive."[10]

For males, the most pervasive institutional monitoring of their sexual behavior is in their teenage years, with the most searching interviews occurring on their threshold to adulthood in preparation for missionary service. For those not serving as missionaries, such an interview most likely occurs in preparation for temple marriage. It is at this juncture that the sexual histories of young women are subject to as much scrutiny as those of most young men, because they are being interviewed for eligibility to enter the most sacred of Mormon edifices, the temple (a prerequisite both for missionary service and for temple marriage). Unlike meeting houses, chapels, stake centers, or tabernacles (such as the historic one in Salt Lake City with its famous organ and choir, which Mormons and non-Mormons alike are invited to enter for worship, instruction, or entertainment), the temple is a sacred edifice with restricted admission. As the "House of the Lord," it is a place where no unclean thing or person may enter after its dedication to that purpose (the public is often invited to visit a temple prior to its dedication). Even faithful Mormons are not free to enter without a "recommend," which is issued after a searching examination by the proper authorities. Sexual "purity" is a major requirement for admission. Those who have "gone through the temple" are required to don special undergarments of white cotton or nylon with special markings as a reminder and a symbol of the covenants and commitments made in the temple. The most important of these are service to God and humankind, chastity, and faithfulness to marriage vows.[11]

In Mormon theology, there is a continuum from the sacred to the physical, with spirituality encompassing both. The temple wedding ceremony is sacred and private, and so are relations between married couples. Because the human body is a temple, it likewise represents the spiritual and the physical, and its privacy should be respected. Temple garments are designed to encourage modesty. It goes without saying, then, that pornography attacks the very core of the Mormon belief system—not because nudity or the sexual act are inherently offensive, but because their public display violates a sacred space that encompasses both the physical and the spiritual. It is for these reasons that a recent contretemps at the Brigham Young University art museum has been widely misrepresented and misinterpreted. Journalists across the nation had a field day when it was reported that Rodin's famous sculpture "The Kiss" was removed from a Rodin exhibit hosted by the museum as a result of complaints from Mormon visitors. Predictably, there was an outcry that this incident confirmed a widely held belief that Mormons are puritanical. No doubt, some of those who objected were. It is also true that many, and possibly the majority, of Mormons visiting the exhibit did not find the sculpture offensive. Yet it must also be granted that among those who objected, there were some who saw such a display not as obscene, but as violating their fundamental belief that the sacred and the private are inseparable.

Given the realities of human nature, the ideals represented by the temple are not always easily attained, unless Mormons are indeed different from their fellow humans. However, in 2002, 103 temples were in service throughout the world, with several more under construction. Currently, some 60,000 missionaries (including some 8,000 women) who have passed through a temple in preparation for their service spread the message of Mormonism to the far corners of the earth (wherever they are allowed). While it is indeed doubtful that Mormons are moral athletes, some evidence does suggest that "clean living" in close families, regular and committed church activity, and a theology that stresses moral progress both here and in eternity (as well as the close monitoring of behavior) have an influence on sexual morality. For example, whereas the divorce rate for Mormons married outside the temple differs little from that of non-Mormons, the divorce rate for temple marriages is significantly lower than either—though this is qualified by the fact that less than 30 percent of Mormon marriages take place in the temple.

A significant increase in premarital sex suggests that secular morality has made inroads on Mormon sexual behavior. Surveys conducted among Mormon high-school seniors some thirty years ago showed that only 10 percent of males and 18 percent of females reported having had sexual relations— dramatically lower than comparative national statistics at the time. More recent statistics indicate that between 30 to 40 percent of Mormons have engaged in premarital sex. These figures help explain the large percentage of children born out of wedlock—among the highest in the nation.[12]

Thus, an inevitable disparity exists between prescription and behavior. Even temple marriages are not entirely immune from sexual transgression, as evidenced by occasional church trials for adultery. More frequent are cases of fornication that Mormon bishops (ward leaders) are called upon to deal with. Are those guilty of sexual transgressions forever banned from entry into the temple? Not those, according to apostle and church president

Spencer W. Kimball (1973–1985), who avail themselves of the cure to spiritual "disease"—repentance. In a popular bestseller, *The Miracle of Forgiveness,* Kimball has spelled out in considerable detail the steps necessary for transgressors to achieve recovery from sin, making them eligible for full participation in all church activities and blessings, including those available only in the temple. As Kimball pointed out in his introduction, "because of the prevalence and gravity of sexual . . . sins, these receive particular emphasis."[13] First published in 1969, the book has gone through over fifty printings—a clear indication that matters sexual are of great concern to many Mormons.

It is not altogether certain that, had the book been published a generation earlier, it would have met with the same popularity. For the first half of the twentieth century, sexual advice from the pulpit was on the whole rather low-key—a kind of ritual acknowledgment of Mormonism's newly won respectability. World War II appears to have been somewhat of a turning point, as tens of thousands of young Mormon men joined the armed forces and some of its women joined the service auxiliaries. Increased sexual temptation was only to be expected, as well as greater sophistication regarding things of this world, concerns increasingly reflected in General Conference talks and church magazine articles. However, it was not until the 1960s, the heyday of the sexual revolution, that these changes impinged in a major way on Mormon consciousness and behavior. Kimball's book hit the market to fill a real need—to help Mormons confront and cope with anxieties that may have been more pressing and disturbing than those their grandparents had to face in the crisis of modernization accompanying the demise of polygamy. But whereas the postpolygamy generation responded to change by consciously choosing to blend into the cultural mainstream of Protestant America, a significant number of Mormons at the turn of the twenty-first century are expressing doubts and reservations about too close an identification with the values of modern society in a kind of conservative retreat, which is encouraged and enforced by a patriarchal, quasi-authoritarian style of leadership. However, not all Church members find this conservatism appealing, with some continuing to prefer an internalized, self-directed approach to personal morality. Although such tensions are not publicly acknowledged in official church circles, they are aired in unofficial publications promoted and supported by some Mormon intellectuals, such as the quarterly *Dialogue* and the monthly *Sunstone*. The latter also sponsors annual Sunstone symposia, where controversial issues are freely debated, matters sexual among them. These have included discussions of masturbation, birth control, abortion, female sexuality, and same-sex orientation.[14]

Controversial Issues

A consistent theme in these discussions is the apparent contradiction between a Mormon theology that promotes a positive view of sexuality and sexual relations, teaching that sex is a gift of God and eternal, and the pronouncements by some church leaders that stress the negative side of sexual expression. At a recent Mormon women's forum, participants explored the ways in which Latter-day Saint teachings and culture affect members' sexuality, sexual beliefs, and behavior. "How," they asked, "can Mormons meet their sexual needs in positive, responsible, and ethical ways." At a symposium on sexuality, a group of Mormon women read from a collection of personal essays inspired by Eve Ensler's "The Vagina Monologues." It appears that women, rather than men, are articulating their sexual concerns.[15]

Birth Control and Abortion

If some Mormons perceive a harsh and judgmental attitude toward sex emanating from the pulpit, such opinions vary considerably from authority to authority and are not considered doctrine. When it comes to official pronouncements or directives from the highest authorities, in recent years the messages have become more cautious, diplomatic, and tolerant both in tone and substance. For example, birth control has been a matter of discussion and controversy since the early days of Mormonism, but especially in the modern period. "Multiply and replenish" is a motto familiar to all Mormons, and many have heard Brigham Young's admonition that "there are multitudes of pure and holy spirits waiting to take tabernacles. Now what is our duty? To prepare tabernacles [bodies] for them."[16] Some fifty years ago J. Reuben Clark, Jr., a member of the First Presidency, made the grim pronouncement that "as to sex in marriage, . . . the prime purpose . . . is to beget children. Sex gratification must be had at that hazard."[17] Yet a generation later, none other than Spencer W. Kimball wrote: "We know of no directive from the Lord that proper sexual experiences between husbands and wives need be limited to the procreation of children."[18] In 1969, an official pronouncement, a masterpiece of diplomatic circumlocution, essentially left the decision of birth control to the marriage partners themselves. That religiously active Mormons have more children per family than their American Catholic and Protestant counterparts thus appears to be a matter of free choice (recent statistics show 3.5 children per Mormon family, 2.5 children per Catholic family, and 2 children per Protestant family). A nationwide comparison of Mormon and non-Mormon birth rates places the former 50 percent higher than the national average.[19]

In instances where church authorities have appeared heavy handed and intrusive in their attempts to interfere in the private lives of members, they have on occasion backed down. When a church directive instructed stake presidents and bishops to inquire into the sexual practices of individuals being interviewed for temple recommends, one specific question concerned oral sex, with the suggestion that those who engaged in such "perversions" were ineligible for a recommend. The resulting outcry was followed by a quick rescinding of the instruction. It appears that couples were insisting not so much on their right to practice oral sex as to their right to privacy. Even on the question of abortion, the Mormon Church's opposition is not as uncompromising as that of the Catholic Church, leaving the door open to exceptional cases such as rape, incest, danger to the woman's life or health, or severe medical defects of the fetus. In the words of one informed commentator, "the question never has been *if* there were such grounds, but always *which* grounds were legitimate."[20] In contrast, a statement concerning partial-birth abortion is unequivocal in its condemnation of the practice. More recently, all five Mormon senators came out in favor of federal support for stem-cell research, with church leaders assuming a cautious watch-and-wait attitude, in contrast to the categorical opposition of the Catholic Church. Summing up the Mormon Church's attitude toward sexuality and medical ethics, this same commentator remarked that as "new facts have to be accommodated, dated but inapparent [sic] sociocultural assumptions are exposed and eroded."[21]

Race

A telling illustration of this observation is the change in doctrine proclaimed by President Spencer W. Kimball in 1978 that eliminated race as a criterion for membership in the Mormon lay priesthood. Prior to that date, church members of Negro ancestry were not allowed to hold the priesthood. It was a practice that had been introduced in the early days of the Church and justified on the basis of Biblical authority combined with "modern" scriptures introduced by Joseph Smith, and corroborated by nineteenth-century "scientific" evidence. Of course, although the "scientific" and sociocultural underpinnings of the Mormon "Negro Doctrine" had eroded long before 1978, this was not necessarily true in the minds of conservative church members, thus it took somewhat longer to work out an interpretation acceptable to the majority of Mormons.

If it is a truism that race and sex are never far apart, the "Negro Doctrine" is a striking example. According to nineteenth-century Mormon opinion, Blacks were under a curse that went back to Cain, who was punished with a mark (possibly black skin) for having killed his brother Abel. A descendant of Cain, an "Egyptian" woman, was on Noah's ark, thus preserving the curse in post-Diluvian history, which was then reinforced by the curse on Ham (again, black skin) for having looked on his drunken father's nakedness (note the sexual imagery). A major reason for the black skin was to prevent racial intermixture. The taboo of miscegenation was pervasive in antebellum American society. Brigham Young's remedy for miscegenation, if harsh, was self-understood in the cultural context of the period: "Shall I tell you the law of God in regard to the African race? If the White man who belongs to the chosen seed mixes his blood with the seed of Cain, the penalty, under the law of God, is death on the spot."[22] The extremity of the penalty reflected the powerful sexual appeal of Blackness, based in part on a perception of its exotic nature. Whites were more likely to succumb to the temptations of the Black race than to the seductions of members of their own race. Clearly, there was sexual danger in darkness. That Blacks should not be admitted into the "House of the Lord," which represented purity (those who enter the temple are dressed in white), thus had powerful symbolic significance. However, as long as the Mormon kingdom was separate from the world there was little likelihood of racial contamination. It is therefore not surprising that racial/sexual anxieties increased after twentieth-century Mormons were forced to live *in* the world. Thus, it may have been part of their effort to make sure they weren't also *of* the world that Mormons saw themselves compelled to keep African-Americans out of the temple not only symbolically, but also literally. Thus, the groundwork for the clashes during the Civil Rights movement had been prepared decades earlier. Seen from this perspective, President Kimball's revelation of 1978 marks a milestone, not of some incremental change in Mormon consciousness, but of a major intellectual and cultural revolution.[23]

Gender

Because this kind of accommodation has not yet been extended to women, there are those who will no doubt disagree with this interpretation. Mormon feminists were disappointed that their demand that women, too, should be allowed to hold the priesthood was categorically rejected, for reasons that were not all that different from those of the Catholic hierarchy—that the Petrine succession was a male prerogative (Mormons believe that the priesthood had been lost because of apostasy until its restoration by divine messengers, including Peter himself). Feminists were reminded that worthy women not of Black lineage had always been eligible to enter the temple, and that males could not achieve exaltation without them (as indeed women could not without being sealed in eternal marriage to a man). In Mormon theology, a distinction is made between "salvation," which is attained by the individual, and "exaltation," which is reserved for families and is attainable only through the New and Everlasting Covenant. In the kingdom of God, there is a division of labor: women bear children and have the primary responsibility for raising them, whereas men preside over the family as well as the larger units of the kingdom. Yet although women are to be obedient to their husbands, they are not expected to be subservient to them. Women are masters over their own bodies, and sexual relations require their consent. These are some of the reasons why the majority of Mormon women have not been vocal in demanding the priesthood. At the same time, given that the theological impediments appear more historical than substantive, the obstacles standing in the way of full equality for women seem far less daunting than those standing in the way of permitting same-sex relationships in the church.[24]

Homosexuality

In a chapter titled "Crime Against Nature" in his book *The Miracle of Forgiveness*, Spencer Kimball has forcefully articulated the Mormon case against homosexuality and lesbianism (with strong emphasis on the former). He begins the chapter with a brief discussion of the sin of masturbation, unworthy of a young man because it indicates lack of self-control. Worse, "it too often leads . . . to that sin against nature, homosexuality. For, done in private, it evolves often into mutual masturbation—practiced with another person of the same sex—and thence into total homosexuality." "Deviations from normal, proper heterosexual relationships are not merely unnatural but wrong in the sight of God."[25] It follows that homosexual inclinations can be overcome and the sinner's behavior corrected. Those who choose to mend their perverse ways and repent will be forgiven, becoming eligible for all the blessings and privileges available to faithful members of the church. Of course, such beliefs are highly controversial and are in conflict with those of the majority of Mormon gays and lesbians, who prefer to follow an influential body of biological, sociological, and psychological opinion, according to which same-sex orientation is innate and thus not subject to choice or social or psychological conditioning. If this is the case, those Mormons critical of the Church's position ask, how can God demand and/or proscribe behavior for which He has created the precondition? Not surprisingly, a substantial number of Mormons with same-sex orientation have left the church. In the face of such condemnation, it is perhaps more surprising that many gay and lesbian Mormons are struggling to maintain their religious beliefs and their membership in the church. In an anonymous *cri de coeur,* one young homosexual exclaimed: "I have a strong testimony of the gospel. I know the church is true and I want to remain loyal and active. I can only hope that he who welcomed to his side sinners, publicans, and harlots will grant the same grace to me—and that his church will also."[26] For a number of reasons, this isn't likely to happen anytime soon. For one, Mormon conceptions of the purpose of sex are still tied, if not exclusively, to procreation. Also of some importance is the fact that scientific opinion is divided on the "nature–nurture" debate. And a significant portion of the gay and lesbian community has chosen to bypass this issue, arguing for freedom of lifestyle decisions—a position that implicitly cedes the moral high ground to church authorities. For traditionally oriented Mormons, sexual orientation and sexual behavior have taken on symbolic significance in the modern culture wars, in which true Christians must stand united against the ungodly. Although the church leadership has been careful not to be identified with the Christian Right, it has gone to great lengths in recent years to strengthen the church's Christian identity and to downplay the name "Mormon"—not unmindful of the fact that cultural conservatism has a powerful appeal to many church members as well as to conservative Christians critical of Mormon "heresy."

Polygamy

As the church moves into the twenty-first century, important issues concerning sexuality remain unresolved. On the world stage, however, it isn't same-sex orientation as much as the old canard polygamy that still has potential for embarrassment. Although most Americans have learned that "Mormons are just folks down the block" (to quote a leading religious historian),[27] in many parts of the world, even Europe, Mormons are still thought of as those strange people with the many wives. Protestations to the contrary lacked credibility in certain quarters as Utah was preparing for the 2002 Winter Olympics and journalists from around the world reported that more than 40,000 people in the Mormon heartland live in polygamous households (nearly half as many as in late nineteenth-century Utah)—even though they had been officially excommunicated from the Mormon Church. Of course, to put this in perspective, the population of Utah in 1890 was around 208,000, and more than ten times that number as of the census of 2000. Moreover, there is more to it than just the numbers. Although in the nineteenth-century it was only a minority of Mormon households that practiced polygamy, it was the *principle* of plural marriage that defined Mormon culture, even for those who practiced monogamy. Of course, that is no longer the case. Choosing to prosecute a particularly flagrant violation of Utah's anti-bigamy legislation (*State of Utah v. Green*), the state brought enormous attention to Mormonism and polygamy; over a hundred reporters from around the globe covered the trial—the very thing the Mormon Church would have liked to avoid. It may be surprising to some that modern polygamy has the outspoken support of many of the women living in such unions who firmly reject the notion that they are the victims of a patriarchal, oppressive system. Three of these women have collected the personal essays of 100 of their sisters who have or have had polygamous relationships and support the principle of plural marriage.[28] Presentations of their work at a Sunstone symposium and at the Mormon History Association have generated a great deal of interest among mainline Mormon intellectuals.

To the church at large, such intrusions of a past it would prefer to forget or ignore cannot help but cause some discomfort. They bring into the open a contradiction between theory and practice, because plural marriage is still a theological principle even though it is not practiced in this world by the mainline church (some Mormon scholars have called it a "shelf" doctrine). It is ironic that if constitutional protection for plural marriage should ever become a reality (a position advocated by Harvard legal scholar Laurence Tribe, among others), the Mormon Church would be faced with the unpleasant prospect of having to accept the legality of a practice that has become unpalatable to the majority of mainline Mormons. It is even more ironic that should this come about, it would be through the extension of the legal reasoning of *Griswold v. Connecticut* (the legalization of birth control) and *Roe v. Wade* (the legalization of abortion) to the legalization of same-sex relationships.[29]

Conclusion

Much of the preceding discussion was based on the relationship between Mormonism and American culture. However, within the past half century Mormonism has experienced a major demographic shift—from a religion of approximately 1 million members, most of whom lived in the Mormon heartland of the Intermountain West (with church headquarters in Salt Lake City at the center), to a membership approaching 12 million, with approximately 2 million in the heartland, more than 5 million in the rest of the United States and Canada, and nearly 6 million over the rest of the globe. While a leading sociologist's projection of a church membership of 265 million by the year 2080 seems exaggerated, his argument that Mormonism will be the next major world religion is within the realm of plausibility.[30] Of course, among such a large number of cultures, sexual norms and practices are bound to vary significantly. Even if the Church leadership sets a uniform standard of sexual behavior, awareness of and sensitivity to diverse cultural values cannot help but influence the manner in which these are taught and enforced. The effect can be liberalizing, though it can also lead to bureaucratic standardization and then to a kind of routinization that Thomas O'Dea observed as early as 1957.[31]

Perhaps the most telling example of liberalization was the liberalization of racial dogma, which, although a general response to a changing cultural climate, must also be attributed to specific problems connected to the expansion of Mormonism. For example, in the 1960s and 1970s, Mormon missionaries met with rather spectacular success in Brazil, a country with a racially mixed population (primarily African and Portuguese). Local members understandably expected to have access to all the promises and blessings of the Church, such as the New and Everlasting Covenant, including marriage for time and eternity. The demand for a temple thus gained momentum, providing the trigger that led to the lifting of the exclusion of Blacks from the priesthood and from the temple churchwide. Given their belief that sexual identity is determined in the preexistence, and that divisions of gender are clearly and immutably defined, the majority of Mormons in all likelihood will always be affected more by how the church deals with traditional concerns of sexual morality and ethics than with the more divisive problems that have a potential for alienating mainline believers. However, given the belief in continuing revelation by a living prophet, and given its history of resolving complex and contentious issues, the Mormon Church in time may well find solutions to problems—such as the ordination of women and the acceptance of same-sex orientation—that appear insurmountable at the present time.

QUESTIONS FOR DISCUSSION

1. Some scholars have suggested that antebellum American society experienced a "crisis of the family." What do they mean by this? How did Americans attempt to deal with this "crisis"?

2. What is the scriptural basis for Mormon theology? How does it differ from that of mainline American Christianity?

3. It has been suggested that Joseph Smith instituted plural marriage in order to satisfy his sexual appetites. Do you find this explanation sufficient for the complex social system required to make polygamy work?

4. In the presidential campaign of 1856, Republican candidate John C. Fremont proposed the eradication of the "twin relics of barbarism, slavery and polygamy." In what way are these two institutions similar? How do they differ?

5. A prominent American feminist historian once suggested that Mormon polygamy, far from being repressive to women, was in fact liberating. On what grounds could she have made this argument?

6. Define the Mormon concept of "premortal existence." Why is it central to the Mormon philosophy of sex and the family?

7. What is "eternal marriage"? What are its implications for Mormon family practices and sexual conduct?

8. Distinguish between a Mormon "meeting house" and a "temple." How does temple worship influence the sexual morality and conduct of Mormons?

9. Do you regard Mormon sexual mores as repressive? Do you think they encourage prudery and hypocrisy?

10. On what grounds do Mormons disapprove of homosexuality and lesbianism? Does this make them homophobic?

11. If Mormonism as a religion may be seen as socially and sexually conservative and restrictive, how do you explain its success in attracting followers?

RECOMMENDED RESOURCES

Mormon Scripture

The Book of Mormon (Salt Lake City: The Church of Jesus Christ of Latter-day Saints, 2002 — current printing).

The Doctrine and Covenants (Salt Lake City: The Church of Jesus Christ of Latter-day Saints, 2002 — current printing). [Revelations by Joseph Smith and his successors.]

The Pearl of Great Price (Salt Lake City: The Church of Jesus Christ of Latter-day Saints, 2002 — current printing). [A collection of inspired writings and translations, including Joseph Smith's account of the "First Vision," the "coming forth" of the Book of Mormon, and the founding of the church.]

Secondary Sources

Fawn M. Brodie, *No Man Knows My History: The Life of Joseph Smith the Mormon Prophet* (New York: Alfred A. Knopf, 1945; 2d ed., 1971).

David John Buerger, *The Mysteries of Godliness: A History of Mormon Temple Worship* (San Francisco: Smith Research Associates, 1994).

Lester E. Bush, Jr., and Armand L. Mauss, eds., *Neither White Nor Black: Mormon Scholars Confront the Race Issue in a Universal Church* (Midvale, UT: Signature Books, 1984).

Brent Corcoran, ed., *Multiply and Replenish: Mormon Essays on Sex and Family* (Salt Lake City: Signature Books, 1994).

Kathryn M. Daines, *More Wives Than One: Transformation of the Mormon Marriage System, 1840–1910* (Urbana and Chicago: University of Illinois Press, 2001).

Lawrence Foster, *Religion and Sexuality: Three American Communal Experiments of the Nineteenth Century* (New York: Oxford University Press, 1981).

Maxine Hanks, ed., *Women and Authority: Re-emerging Mormon Feminism* (Salt Lake City: Signature Books, 1992).

Klaus J. Hansen, *Mormonism and the American Experience* (Chicago: University of Chicago Press, 1981); see especially chapter 5, "Changing Perspectives on Sexuality and Marriage," 147–178.

B. Carmon Hardy, *Solemn Covenant: The Mormon Polygamous Passage* (Urbana and Chicago: University of Illinois Press, 1992).

Ron Schow, Wayne Schow, and Marybeth Raynes, eds., *Peculiar People: Mormons and Same-Sex Orientation* (Salt Lake City: Signature Books, 1991).

Jan Shipps, *Sojourner in the Promised Land: Forty Years Among the Mormons* (Urbana and Chicago: University of Illinois Press, 2000), 51–97.

ENDNOTES

1. Lawrence Foster, *Religion and Sexuality: Three American Communal Experiments of the Nineteenth Century* (New York: Oxford University Press, 1981); Louis J. Kern, *An Ordered Love: Sex Roles and Sexuality in Victorian Utopias—the Shakers, the Mormons, and the Oneida Community* (Chapel Hill: University of North Carolina Press, 1981).

2. There is need for an up-to-date biography of Joseph Smith, though Fawn M. Brodie's *No Man Knows My History: The Life of Joseph Smith the Mormon Prophet* (New York: Alfred A. Knopf, 1945; 2d ed., 1971), written from a secular humanist perspective, is still worth reading. A more up-to-date account is Richard L. Bushman, *Joseph Smith and the Beginnings of Mormonism* (Urbana and Chicago: University of Illinois Press, 1984), who writes from inside Mormonism as a believer.

3. Scholarly accounts from varying perspectives are Leonard J. Arrington and Davis Bitton, *The Mormon Experience: A History of the Latter-day Saints* (New York: Alfred A. Knopf, 1979), who write from the inside as believers; Klaus J. Hansen, *Mormonism and the American Experience* (Chicago: University of Chicago Press, 1981), who writes from a secular humanist perspective; and Jan Shipps, *Mormonism: A New Religious Tradition* (Urbana and Chicago: University of Illinois Press, 1985), a sympathetic outsider writing from a religious studies perspective.

4. For studies of Mormon "polygamy" I especially recommended Richard S. Van Wagoner, *Mormon Polygamy: A History* (Salt Lake City: Signature Books, 1986), a useful up-to-date survey; B. Carmon Hardy, *Solemn Covenant: The Mormon Polygamous Passage* (Urbana and Chicago: University of Illinois Press, 1992), a brilliant study of cultural transformation; Kathryn M. Daines, *More Wives Than One: Transformation of the Mormon Marriage System, 1840–1910* (Urbana and Chicago: University of Illinois Press, 2001); a superb case study of a Mormon community; and Sarah Barrington Gordon, *The Mormon Question: Polygamy and Constitutional Conflict in Nineteenth-Century America* (Chapel Hill: University of North Carolina Press, 2002), an innovative and illuminating study of constitutional and cultural issues.

5. The most up-to-date general work of RLDS history is Richard P. Howard, *The Church Through the Years* (Independence, MO: Herald Publishing House, 2 vols., 1992–93).

6. The Doctrine and Covenants, Section 132. The D&C contains a collection of major revelations by Joseph Smith, as well as several by some of his successors. Readily available from the church publishing house (Salt Lake City: The Church of Jesus Christ of Latter-day Saints, 2000).

7. M. R. Werner, *Brigham Young* (New York: Harcourt, Brace, 1925); Foster, *Religion and Sexuality*, 181–225. For an overview of Mormon attitudes, see Hansen, 147–178.

8. Jan Shipps, "From Satyr to Saint: American Perceptions of the Mormons, 1860–1960," in *Sojourner in the Promised Land: Forty Years Among the Mormons* (Urbana and Chicago: University of Illinois Press, 2000), 51–97.

9. Unpublished research by the author; Gordon Shepherd and Gary Shepherd, *A Kingdom Transformed: Themes in the Development of Mormonism* (Salt Lake City: U. of Utah Press, 1984); Shipps, "From Satyr to Saint"; Marvin Rytting, "Exhortations for Chastity: A Content Analysis of Church Literature," in Brent Corcoran, ed., *Multiply and Replenish: Mormon Essays on Sex and Family* (Salt Lake City: Signature Books, 1994), 85–102.

10. Romel W. Mackelprang, " 'They Shall Be One Flesh': Sexuality and Contemporary Mormonism," in *Multiply and Replenish,* 47–66; Hansen, "Changing Perspectives on Sexuality and Marriage," in *Multiply and Replenish,* 19–46.

11. David John Buerger, *The Mysteries of Godliness: A History of Mormon Temple Worship* (San Francisco: Smith Research Associates, 1994); Colleen McDannell, "Mormon Garments: Sacred Clothing and the Body," in *Material Christianity: Religion and Popular Culture in America* (New Haven: Yale University Press, 1995), 198–221; Kathleen Flake, "Not to Be Riten: The Nature and Effects of the Mormon Temple Rite as Oral Canon," *Journal of Ritual Studies* 9 (Summer 1995), 1–21.

12. Harold T. Christensen, "The Persistence of Chastity: Built-in Resistance in Mormon Culture to Secular Trends," in *Multiply and Replenish,* 67–84.

13. Spencer W. Kimball, *The Miracle of Forgiveness* (Salt Lake City: Bookcraft, 1969).

14. Armand L. Mauss, *The Angel and the Beehive: The Mormon Struggle with Assimilation* (Urbana and Chicago: University of Illinois Press, 1994).

15. Eve Ensler, *The Vagina Monologues* (New York: Villard, 1998).

16. Mackelprang, *Multiply and Replenish,* 54.

17. Ibid., 53–54.

18. Ibid., 56–57.

19. Tim B. Heaton, "The Demography of Utah Mormons," in *Utah in Demographic Perspective* (Salt Lake City: Signature Books, 1986), 181–93; Tim B. Heaton, "Vital Statistics," in Daniel H. Ludlow, ed., *Encyclopedia of Mormonism* (4 vols., New York: MacMillan, 1992) 4: 1518–36.

20. Lester E. Bush, "Ethical Issues in Reproductive Medicine: A Mormon Perspective," in *Multiply and Replenish,* 183–215.

21. Ibid., 210.

22. Quoted in Hansen, *Mormonism and the American Experience*, 195.

23. Newell G. Bringhurst, *Saints, Slaves, and Blacks: The Changing Place of Black People Within Mormonism* (Westport, CT: Greenwood Press, 1981); Lester E. Bush, Jr. and Armand L. Mauss, eds., *Neither White Nor Black: Mormon Scholars Confront the Race Issue in a Universal Church* (Midvale, UT: Signature Books, 1984).

24. For a representative selection of feminist concerns, see Maxine Hanks, ed., *Women and Authority: Re-emerging Mormon Feminism* (Salt Lake City: Signature Books, 1992).

25. Kimball, *Miracle of Forgiveness*, 78–79.

26. "Solus," in Ron Schow, Wayne Schow, and Marybeth Raynes, eds., *Peculiar People: Mormons and Same-Sex Orientation* (Salt Lake City: Signature Books, 1991), 13.

27. Martin Marty, in Hansen, *Mormonism and the American Experience*, x.

28. Mary Batchelor, Marianne Watson, and Anne Wilde, *Voices in Harmony: Contemporary Women Celebrate Plural Marriage* (Salt Lake City: Principle Voices, 2000).

29. Laurence Tribe, *American Constitutional Law*, 2d ed. (Mineola, NY: Foundation Press 1988), 521–28; Orma Linford, "The Mormons and the Law: The Polygamy Cases," *Utah Law Review* 9 (1964), 308–70, 543–91, 589.

30. Rodney Stark, "The Basis of Mormon Success: A Theoretical Application," in Eric A. Eliason, ed., *Mormons and Mormonism: An Introduction to an American World Religion* (Urbana & Chicago: University of Illinois Press, 2001), 207–42.

31. Thomas F. O'Dea, *The Mormons* (Chicago: University of Chicago Press, 1957).

Chapter 8

The Children of God

Miriam Williams Boeri

One of the more visible and highly publicized new religious movements (NRMs) that emerged during the late 1960s was the Children of God (later known as The Family of Love or The Family). Although the group began as religious fundamentalists intent on following Biblical principles, they gained widespread national attention due to their unorthodox sexual practices and became known in the popular press as a "sex cult." Sociologically, *cult* refers to the beginning stage of a new religion, but some scholars prefer to use the term *new religious movement* instead of cult. The terms cult and new religious movement are used interchangeably in this chapter.

History of the Movement

In order to understand the history of the Children of God, it is necessary to place communal experimentation in historical and social context. The idea of collective living arrangements with alternative social structures is not new to American culture. During the nineteenth century, a number of such communities proliferated, including the Shakers, the Mormons, and the Oneidans. Known as "utopian communities" in the historical literature,[1] these communal groups experimented with a wide variety of sexual social structures. The Shakers practiced celibacy and channeled their sexual energies into frenzied dancing activities; the Mormons promoted the practice of polygyny; and the Oneidans allowed sexual relations with multiple partners, which they referred to as "complex marriages."[2] Many of the followers of these communal experiments claimed to have been seeking perfection; therefore, sexual patterns

160

changed throughout each experiment's history to accommodate both internal and external problems. However, in-depth studies of available records, such as personal diaries and medical data, reveal that sexual relations within the communities were not always considered perfect by their members.[3] So, too, with the Children of God.

The Children of God began in the late 1960s as an evangelical Christian group under the charismatic leadership of David Berg, who later became known among his followers as Moses David ("Mo"). Berg documented the history of the nascent group through numerous writings called the "Mo Letters" (ML).[4] Although these documents are primarily Berg's own perspectives and values, they do provide a source of historical information and insight into the mind of this charismatic leader. Berg was the absolute power figure in the Children of God, and his "formerly repressed, then unbridled sexuality served as the basis for the group's ideology."[5]

Berg was born on February 18, 1919, in California. Both of his parents were evangelists, and young Berg started his evangelical career with his mother, a radio and tent revivalist. He married in 1943 and had four children with his first wife, although he later considered a number of other women to be his "wives" and reportedly sired children who do not bear his legal name.[6] In 1964, he became an evangelical missionary with the Christian and Missionary Alliance, and a few years later, he was in Huntington Beach, California, leading a youth ministry called Teen Challenge. By 1968, Berg and his teenaged children were singing Christian music to the hippies and students who congregated at a coffee house called the Light Club. Here, Berg found a few dozen young people searching for alternative lifestyles and persuaded them to join his family circle as they evangelized the "lost youth of America." Thus began an avalanche of recruitment that grew to include over 100 members within a year.[7]

Berg claimed that his birth was accompanied by a prophecy that he was "filled with the Holy Ghost from his mother's womb, like John the Baptist,"[8] and he followed in his parent's ministry as an evangelist. He was "determined to save tomorrow's youth from their terrible fate as innocent victims of a fiendish, anti-God, social, economic, educational, and religious system which had only driven them to drugs, crime, violence, and the brink of Revolution against their unloving parents."[9] Not until 1968, when Berg and his family moved in with his mother in a small town in California, did he actually form a small following. Starting with a band of 50 young people who joined Berg and his family as full-time members,[10] the group traveled across America and Canada collecting more disciples. Evangelizing on college campuses, in churches, and among the drug addicts and flower children, the group grew steadily. By 1971, there were 1,500 members in the United States and Canada,[11] and by 1973, 2,244 members were living in 180 homes around the world.[12]

Initially, the group supported itself financially with money and material goods donated by new members and provisions procured from local stores and factories. For example, in the New York colony, teams of members were sent to fast food establishments, restaurants, and food markets to ask for donations of food. In other cases, grocery store dumpsters provided colony members with fresh produce and dairy products that were outdated but still edible. In 1973, Berg introduced a new method of obtaining financial resources by distributing his letters on the streets and asking for donations. His writings were carefully selected for the general public and illustrated with cartoons and pictures. This method, known as "litnessing" (witnessing with literature) resulted in a substantially higher level of communal income.

Throughout most of its history, the Children of God members did not work in paid employment. Rules established by Berg demanded that all money received by a member be turned over to the colony leader for communal use. Individual member's needs were met by the colony; members did not have personal money. After expenses for a particular home were paid, the remaining money was sent to a central office in a secret location, which eventually became known as World Services (WS).[13] It is believed that Berg lived at this central colony until his notoriety required that his living arrangement become more carefully concealed. Supposedly, Berg received death threats from a number of angry parents and relatives of the group's members, and it is probable that legal suits against Berg were pursued at various times. Mo Letters revealing the location of Berg's whereabouts were not published and distributed until Berg moved to a new location. Moreover, the vast majority of members never saw their leader, Moses David (Berg), in person, and until his death in 1994, his photo was disguised in all group publications.[14]

Berg, or Moses David, was a charismatic leader in the sense that he was deemed by his followers to be endowed with supernatural and God-given qualities. Sociologist Max Weber conceptualized that new religious movements needed charismatic leaders in order to attract members and maintain a high level of commitment.[15] Charismatic leaders are likely to emerge during times of social unrest and promote revolutionary ideas, as was the case with Berg in the late 1960s. Children of God members were told that Berg was the prophet of God for the end time, as predicted in the Bible, and whether they all accepted this as fact or not, or to what degree it was believed, is not known. However, in order to remain a member of the group, one had to act as if one believed Berg to be the end-time prophet and oracle of God. The leap of faith required for new members, many of whom were college educated, to adhere to such a belief appeared to be an acceptable price to pay in exchange for the revolutionary worldview, total meaning system, brotherhood, community, and love they found in the Children of God social environment.

According to Weber's model, charismatic leadership must eventually be replaced with a more stable system of statuses and roles. Berg developed a rigid leadership hierarchy and organization, establishing a stable economic base and a full-time administrative staff. At the same time, he sustained his charismatic authority through his letters. In a sense, he institutionalized the role of charismatic leader. Even while the Children of God were effectuating a process of routinization, in which the new worldview of the group was institutionalized,[16] Berg remained the source of truth, the interpreter of sacred passages, the prophet, and the ideological leader whose power continued to grow. Any dissenters or voices of protest to his absolute authority were shamed into silence or excommunicated from the group.

Berg placed rings of trusted leaders around him who wielded power at various levels. Those closest to him were under his constant scrutiny and were publicly disgraced through the letters if they disobeyed any aspect of his teachings. The members in this ring included his biological family, their respective mates, and faithful members from the ranks of leadership. A second ring of leaders consisted of those who worked in the headquarters, World Services, whose location was unknown to most members. The next ring of leadership was composed of hand-chosen members with special talents or skills and outstanding obedience to Berg. Leaders at this level facilitated communication between the members scattered around the world and World Services. This ring of leaders changed frequently, with some rising to the next level or falling into the masses of members. The terms used to define these rings of leadership, such as "bishops" or "visiting servants," changed throughout Children of God history. Finally, the lowest ring of leadership consisted of the local leaders who were "shepherds" of individual colonies (homes). Through this structure, Berg was able to maintain complete obedience throughout the group, and dissenters were quickly excommunicated or they defected. Schisms, a common problem among new religious movements, were never allowed to form in the Children of God. Instead, groups of former members formed in different areas of the world. Some continued with Children of God doctrine and practices, whereas others formed completely different communal groups.[17] In addition, some former members became part of the friends of the Children of God, contributing to the group financially but receiving few group publications and little support.

The process by which new members are socialized into a radically different social structure is outlined in Kanter's model of commitment building,[18] which aptly explains the method by which a recruit becomes a committed Children of God member. First, new members are asked to sacrifice former roles and statuses, such as student, a specific occupation, or a social class. They are required to invest all of their time and wealth in the new group. All former relationships are renounced, including marriage and kinship relations. Mortification of the "self" through confessions and public denouncements or physical punishment follow, and a new set of criteria for evaluating the self are established. Finally, surrounded by an aura of mystery, transcendence is achieved through spiritually oriented experiences that provide personal meaning, often transmitted through a charismatic leader, but one that each member shares by association with the group. Adherence to the group's ideology is thus cemented, and any deviation is quickly truncated by group pressure to conform as well as by personal feelings of guilt. Members who obtain positions of leadership and deviate from standards set by Berg were publicly denounced in the Mo Letters, demoted from leadership positions, and excommunicated from the group if their rebellion continued. Ironically, because the majority of members never met Berg personally, feelings of animosity toward leadership were usually directed at leaders who were in closer communion with members; therefore, when these leaders were demoted or publicly disgraced by Berg, many members interpreted this action as further proof of Berg's divine source of authority.

Disciples were only permitted to read the Bible, and each new disciple was required to memorize a large number of selected Bible verses before they were entrusted to read the Mo Letters distributed by the Children of God's publication center at World Services.[19] Some of these publications were never released to the general public, and a few of them have since been recalled and retracted, particularly those relating to child/adult sexual activities. Eventually, the Mo Letters were given equal weight to the Scriptures and considered official instructions for individual and group behavior.[20]

Among the thousands of Mo Letters written by Berg, only a small portion contained explicit sexual material, but these are the letters that will receive the most attention in this chapter. Much of the controversy surrounding the Children of God centers on their sexual practices. As the next section will show, these practices changed over time, ranging from enforced chastity to open marriage. The most infamous practice was "Flirty Fishing" (female members enticing males into the group by offering sex), which substantially increased the membership and income of the group. Due to widespread legal repercussions, charges of adult sexual involvement with minors, and the increased spread of sexually transmitted diseases, "Flirty Fishing" was officially discouraged in 1987.[21] Currently, the Children of God, now known as The Family, has a membership of approximately 12,000 in homes spread across the globe. The location of many homes, particularly of "World Services and Creations," remains a closely guarded secret.[22]

Children of God's Teachings on Sex

Sociologists generally agree that new religious movements, or cults, actively construct a novel worldview.[23] When researchers seek to obtain documentation on official teachings of such groups, they often find that outsiders are permitted to read only selected documents that are not always representative of the full doctrine taught to members. The official teachings of the Children of God/The Family that are open to public view can be read on their current Web site, www.thefamily.com. However, the reader should keep in mind that these "official teachings" might omit those doctrines and documents that the leaders of the group deem inappropriate for public consummation. As a former member, I have access to relatively recent Children of God official teachings through my contact with former members of the group. Although the vast majority of defectors are not willing to appear critical of the Children of God/The Family, they often bring written material with them for their own spiritual benefit during their time of transition from one religious faith or lifestyle to another.[24] It is from the official documents, those written by Moses David (Berg) and those written or published by the new leadership under Maria (Karen Zerby) and her consorts, that I draw from for this section.

Marriage or Sexual Chastity

During the group's early period, chastity was encouraged. Among the "Revolutionary Rules,"[25] only two pertain to intimate and sexual interactions:

> Defile not the temple of the Holy Ghost—no smoking or smooching other than "greeting one another with a holy kiss"—and absolutely no dating without permission. Betrothals only for staff members after months of service and ready to go on their own with team approval.[26]

Despite the fact that the majority of new members during this early period were recruited from the hordes of hippies roaming the California beach towns in search of drugs, music, and free love, the rules appear to have been obeyed with few exceptions. The relatively few children born to nonbetrothed (unmarried) females in a communal group that allowed no form of birth control seems to support the fact that chastity and celibacy were the norm for single members during the early stages of Children of God history. Historically, the group allowed betrothals (marriage within the group) only among trusted members who had lived at least six months in the group; however, mass betrothals, sometimes arranged by leaders the night before the marriage, included recently recruited female members. Females joined the group at a much lower rate than male members, which meant that there were not enough females to be betrothed mates for males, a fact that was to have future repercussions. When two members were betrothed, the "Revolutionary Love-Making Sheet"[27] was handed to the new couple. In this epistle, Berg gave explicit instructions on lovemaking, highlighted with Biblical references. For example:

> **Where:** in bed—Heb. 13:4. On the grass under the trees—SoS 1:16–17 . . . **When:** Ezk. 16:7—the time of love (when you feel like it—day or night—even daily!) Eph. 5:22—wives submit as unto the Lord (even when you don't feel like it) . . . **How:** with words—with much fair speech she caused him to yield, with the flattering of her lips she forced him—Pr. 7:21 . . . **Equipment:** Perfume: the saviour of thy good ointments SoS 3:6 . . . Vaseline: ointments, oils—SoS 1:3 . . . Tissues: for wiping the hands and other parts after coitus (intercourse) and to prevent soiling linens—Pr. 30:20 . . . Wine: stimulates sex—Pr. 104:15 . . . Bread: helps the hungry . . . **Positions:** SoS 1:13 He shall lie all night betwixt my breasts (the man on top, between her legs, is the most usual but not necessary) . . . **How to embrace:** His left hand shall be under my head and his right hand should embrace (hug) me—SoS 2:6, 8:3 (to be firmly clasped in his arms is thrilling to most women) (pp. 80–81).

Sexual Liberation

In contrast to the Children of God's early emphasis on chastity, during the 1970s the group gradually moved toward more libertarian teachings. These changes seemed to parallel developments in the life of the group's leader. In 1970, Berg took an extended trip to Europe and Israel with his personal secretary, Maria, leaving his wife behind in America. Berg retained absolute power over the everyday life of his expanding group through frequent communication. Letters sent by Berg to the group at this time gave evidence of an intimate relationship between the founder/leader and his young secretary. In a letter titled "Old Church—New Church Prophecy,"[28] a metaphorical story depicts the old church as an elderly wife who no longer wants to make love and the new church as a young, eager bride. Illustrations show a handsome, virile, naked man leaving an older woman, who covers her nakedness with a cloth. In the next illustration, the naked man crowns a young, bare-breasted girl in tattered clothes, saying, "I will have a new bride who will love me." In 1970, Berg received ("in the spirit") what became known as the "All Things" revelation that was based largely on the scripture, "All things are lawful unto us" (1 Corinthians 6:12). "All Things" meant exactly what it said, and out of this evolved the fundamental article of faith that all things, including the enjoyment of sexual freedom, were lawful to those who were motivated by love.[29]

According to those who were in high-status positions at that time, leaders in the group had been practicing wife-swapping years before the letter "One Wife"[30] was released to all members. However, "One Wife" was a turning point in the official Children of God teachings on sexuality, and the conventional institution of marriage as a communion between one man and one woman, practiced in the Children of God until that time, was radically altered. "One Wife" stated that:

> We do not minimize marriage ties, as such. We just consider our ties to the Lord and the larger Family greater and more important. . . . If we broke up every so-called marriage in the Revolution [the group], and it did the work good, to make them put God first, it would be worth it . . . God is in the business of breaking up little selfish private families to make of their yielded broken pieces a larger unit—one family. . . . The private family is the basis of the selfish capitalistic private enterprise system and all its selfish evils. The history of communes shows that the most successful communes either abolished all private relationships entirely and required total celibacy, or abandoned the private marriage for group marriage . . . partiality toward your own wife or husband or children strikes at the very foundation of communal living. (pp. 1911–1914)

For many members, these words reinforced what they already felt about communal life and marriage. Married couples who disagreed with the "One Wife" doctrine left the group quietly. Marriages that were already on shaky ground were now given license to dissolve. Husbands who were afraid that their wives would be shared with all men in the group saw their fears materialize sooner than they expected. In quick succession, new Mo Letters arrived demanding that women be sexier ("Revolutionary Women"[31]) and stop wearing bras ("Come on Ma—Burn Your Bra"[32]). In "Revolutionary Sex,"[33] Berg contrasts the "the traditions of men with the laws of God," and writes that the Scriptures permit polygamy and, in some cases, even incest. Members who would not follow the new letters were accused of being "old bottles" that were too brittle to hold the "new wine."[34]

Homosexuality

Rules and norms for sexual interaction changed frequently according to the experiences and whims of Berg. For example, homosexuality was forbidden until a gay male lived in Berg's home and became close to the leader. During that time, homosexual acts between males were permitted selectively but not necessarily encouraged. However, sexual and intimate relationships between women were always encouraged. In "Women in Love,"[35] the scripture saying "all things are pure to him who is pure" (Titus 1:15) was applied to "relationships between two women" but not to those involving two men.[36] In this epistle, Berg writes of male homosexuality that "it makes me sick . . . maybe John had that inclination, but I'm sure Jesus never would have tolerated it"[37]; however, "lesbianism so-called could possibly necessarily be a stop gap, a temporary interim solution to a sexual need."[38] Many years later, Berg would allow homosexual relations between two men. In a letter called "Homos—A Question of Sodomy," Berg writes:

> Merely masturbating each other and sucking each other off—this doesn't really seem any different from having women do it for you. . . . I guess we'll just have to say according to your faith be it done unto you. . . . There's a possibility that God could tolerate some form of it.[39]

A few years later, Berg changed his mind again and writes in "The Devil Hates Sex" that "as far as I'm concerned there are no more sexual prohibitions hardly of any kind, except He [God] sure seemed to hate sodomy and I don't see where he withdrew that."[40] An official publication by Zerby (also known as Maria, the mistress who became leader of the group after Berg's death) states that any kind of sexual activity whatsoever with other men is an excommunicable offense.[41] The frequent reversals on official sexual practices are consistent with Berg's early writings that claim that "all things change"[42] in the Children of God/The Family.

Flirty Fishing (FFing)

Despite numerous Mo Letters that indicated that the group was heading toward an open marriage system, sexual sharing between single and married members did not spread throughout the entire group until a new method of witnessing and recruitment was introduced in a letter called "Flirty Little Fishy."[43] Purported to be a revelation from God, the letter describes Berg's second wife, Maria, flirting in front of men in order to "catch" them and bring them into God's kingdom. The letter is illustrated with a scantily clothed woman in a provocative pose before a man and a nude woman impaled on a hook. The text states:

> Help her to catch him with her fingers of flesh that she might impart unto him Thy Spirit, O Lord, for which he hungers. Oh God, in Jesus Name! Each one of them seek after her, suck of her, dream of her, drink of her. . . . Help her to catch men, be bold, unashamed and brazen, to use anything she has, Oh

God, to catch men for Thee!—Even if it be through the flesh, the attractive lure, delicious flesh on a steel hook of Thy reality, the steel of Thy Spirit.[44]

Berg ends the letter with a plea to all female members:

Are you willing to be bait on God's hook or in his trap? Would you do anything for Jesus to help your Fisherman catch men, even to suffer the crucifixion of the hook or the danger of the trap. . . . How far would you go to catch men—All the way?[45]

Flirty Fishing, known as "FFing" among Family members, soon became a primary method of "winning souls" as well as providing economic support for the group. Berg claims to have been inspired by Biblical scriptures, such as the Gospel of Matthew 4:19, in which Jesus said to his disciples, "Follow me and I will make you *fishers* of men." Children of God doctrine portrayed this method as a missionary practice: "Sex and actual lovemaking (became) a means of witnessing to and showing them (those with whom they wanted to share their faith) a tangible sample and proof of the sacrificial love of God."[46]

In a series of letters called "King Arthur's Knights," Berg recorded the activities of two of his female consorts as they began their seduction of men attending clubs in London using the FFing method. In these letters, Berg instructs Maria on how to entice men, such as "fuck the daylights out of him!" and "grab his dick out of his pants."[47] In January 1977, the Children of God published the "FFer's Handbook," which was described as the complete instruction manual on FFing. Although the group emphasized the divine goodness of human sexuality,[48] within a few years female members were required to receive financial recompense for their "gift of love." The "FFers Handbook" told the FFers that "You've got to catch a few to make the fun pay for itself. So don't do it for nothing." However, the women were instructed not to ask directly for money. In "Does FFing Pay," Berg wrote the FFing girls never received any money for their sexual services but that men who received sexual favors may make a donation to the group:

Not a direct payment to the woman just for a fuck, which causes and makes it crude and about as low as you can get, just like the rest of the world, but if they can feel like they are not just paying a prostitute but that they are actually giving it to the Lord and the work, this I think we would all feel very acceptable.[49]

In due course, World Services began to include statistical data on FFing in their *Family News* newsletters that were distributed to members worldwide. In 1982, Berg writes "we just had the greatest year of FFing we ever had," quoting statistics showing that from 1978 to 1981, "family members had sexual intercourse with outsiders 63,000 times or an average of 15,750 per year, which translates into a monthly average of 1,312."[50] A Family publication in the late 1990s claimed that during the 10 years of FFing as an outreach ministry over 100,000 people were "won to Jesus."[51]

Special FFing homes were established in wealthy European cities such as Monte Carlo, where a number of Family women spent their evenings at nightclubs frequented by the rich and famous.[52] FFing was also used to influence men who held power. Berg wrote, "Our FFers are our most powerful lobbyists. They literally lobby for the Family with government officials and men of influence."[53] Articles in the *Family News* on FFers in various parts of the world include descriptive titles such as "FFing on the French Riviera," "FFing as a Social Escort," "How FFing Solved Our Legal Problems," and "Escorting People to Jesus."[54] Escort services were established in Hong Kong, Australia, and other Eastern locations. Ward writes that "Berg officially put an end to FFing in September 1987, declaring 'all sex with outsiders is banned!—unless they are already close and well known friends!'"[55] A recent Family newsletter reports Zerby giving permission to a handful of members to have sexual relations to people outside the group.[56]

Contraception

From the beginning, the Children of God discouraged contraception. In response to the problem of female members who became pregnant to men who had no intention of joining the Children of God, Berg reconfirmed the group's commitment to unprotected sex and the prohibition on the use of any birth control. Babies conceived during FFing encounters were called "Jesus babies," which Palmer[57] suggests accounted for about 10 percent of total Family births during the period that FFing was practiced. Most of the former female members interviewed reported that they were not allowed to use any form of birth control, including condoms; and a large percentage of FFers reportedly contracted sexually transmitted diseases, which soon spread throughout the group.[58] According to Ajemian (personal communication), a "so-called condom revolution" was instituted when engaging in sex with outsiders after 1987. Former members report that the spread of sexually transmitted diseases, including HIV/AIDS, might have influenced the decision to curtail the practice of FFing and allow the use of condoms.

Children and Sex

By far, the most controversial and debated official teaching of The Children of God/The Family has been its inconsistent teachings on child–adult sex and child sex education. A brief review of the Family childcare publications provides insight into the group's practices regarding children and sex.

History of Childcare

According to the Children of God's own report,[59] "the average number of children for each married woman in The Family is about four, and it is not at all uncommon to find families with eight, nine, ten, or more children." As the number of children born into the group rose rapidly, Berg's oldest daughter, Deborah, became the first "childcare leader" and worked hard to establish clean, safe nurseries and schools in Children of God homes. After Deborah Berg's defection from the group, Berg appointed a series of new childcare leaders, and the children's training as future missionary members became an important focal point of the group.

Berg's new instructions on raising and training children were sent to all Children of God homes throughout the world so that, generally, children were raised with the same norms and values regardless of where they lived. English was spoken in all homes, and children were cared for and taught by members only. During the 1970s, many homes in North America and Europe had nurseries and Montessori schools either within the communal compound or in a separate home dedicated as a "school" for children in the same geographic area.

The Children of God, like many cults, was viewed with suspicion by outsiders. When authorities began to investigate the educational needs of children in the cults in their respective countries, the Children of God established specific model schools and "media homes" for presentation to nonmembers, particularly journalists, researchers, and law enforcement officials. Unfortunately, much of the literature we have on children in cults stems from the scholarly studies by academic observers of these "media homes";[60] the homes observed were far from a representative sample. These schools and children's homes were specifically selected for public viewing, and a greater amount of time and money was spent on these homes compared with those where the majority of children lived. In reality, the education of children depended largely on what individual parents desired for their own children. Concerned parents who had received more than a high-school education before joining the Children of God often taught their own children more advanced subjects than were taught in the communal schools. However, due to frequent moves, even academically conscientious parents were not always able to be near their children. For example, during the 1980s, many adults had to travel extensively on "road teams," selling literature and tapes to support the group while leaving their children in the group schools for weeks or even months without seeing them. The children were told to obey the adults who ran the schools, even when these adults were complete strangers to them. Such circumstances led to recurring accusations of child abuse, including corporal punishment and sexual molestation.[61,62] Although the group's teachings on children's sexuality changed frequently and were seemingly random, a pattern emerged toward more sexual permissiveness within the group, accompanied by greater secrecy toward outsiders.

Berg's Teachings on Sex and Children and the "Book of Davidito"

All children were socialized into the subculture of the Children of God through the Mo Letters, yet there were differences in the degree to which letters pertaining to sex were followed. Questions arose among members over how much the "law of love" (which stated that anything done in love was lawful) should be applied to children and sex. Berg wrote in "Revolutionary Sex"[63] that children should "receive a more thorough sexual education and satisfaction of their desire to know [about sex] in the safer and cleaner confines of their own homes from their own parents and with other like children."

Most adults in the group agreed that children should not have negative attitudes about sexuality and should be free to explore sex with each other, but they questioned whether parents and adult childcare workers should teach the children explicitly about sex.

Such questions were answered in a controversial publication known as the "Davidito Series," or the "Book of Davidito,"[64] which was about a young child raised in Berg's home. Written to provide guidance to Sara, the child's nanny, these letters were distributed to all Children of God members. According to the letters, when Davidito is seventeen months old, he climbs naked into bed with Sara and "crawls on top of her and began hunching away. . . . Berg felt Davidito's little penie and said, 'I never would have believed it if I didn't really feel how hard he really is.' "[65] The series contains a photo of Sara masturbating Davidito, and a passage describes Zerby outside listening at the door while Davidito says, "Sara, now kiss it. . . . Oh, it flopped in your nose!"[66] Family members were told to destroy the Book of Davidito after defecting members exposed the book and the hidden official teachings on childhood sexuality.

Zerby later claimed that the Davidito letters were not written by her and Berg but by the nanny, Sara. However, Berg's views on children and sex were not limited to the Davidito letters. In a series of comic books published by the Children of God called "Life with Grandpa," small children were read the story of how Grandpa Berg taught the children in his home the facts of life. For example, Berg explained that a penis was like a plough and a woman's womb was like a furrow in which the man planted his seed. The comic book was illustrated with drawings of the plough in the soil and the penis in the vagina.[67]

Illustrated series for older children included the "Heaven's Girl" letters in which a female Family teenager is depicted with superhuman powers and an immense love for all men. In this series, the young teen gives sex to older men in order to gain favor for the Christians persecuted during the "Great Tribulation." Heaven's Girl became a role model for many female youth in the group, who were not allowed to read magazines or books, watch TV, or listen to music produced outside the group.

During the late 1970s and early 1980s, most group homes in North America and Europe did not openly teach children sex following the model depicted in the Davidito letters. Many former members who exited the group during this time did not report excessive sexual activity among children. However, testimonies of mothers who were in the group with their children[68] and from adolescents who were raised in the Children of God[69] suggest that the Davidito letters gave adults who desired sexual activity with children the freedom to do so. As one mother of six put it, the Children of God "set us up to live with an abuser and a pedophile . . . because in the cult we were taught that acts of pedophilia were okay."[70]

After the Davidito series was officially disfavored, training in child sexuality focused on sex between children and teens of the same age. Zerby wrote in "Flirty Little Teens Beware"[71] that "this is the very thing the system would like to use against us—sex with minors, which they always term child abuse although in our loving Family there would be very little possibility of genuine abuse." But the "system" was already investigating the Children of God's sexual practices with children. In the late 1980s and early 1990s, group homes in Argentina, France, and Australia were raided by law enforcement officials, and children were taken from the homes for questioning and inspection. The most concentrated investigation came in Britain during the early 1990s when a grandmother of a child in the Children of God asked that the court grant her custody, claiming the group practiced sexual child abuse. The British case, known as the Ward case, and continuing from February 1992 until October 1995, illustrates the difficulty of assessing cult practices. Crucial evidence brought before the court was the testimony from young members who had been sent to training camps established for the Children of God's own rebelling teens.

Teen Camps and the Ward Case

During the late 1980s, many of the children in the Children of God/The Family were becoming teenagers. Despite the intense socialization practices of the group and almost complete isolation from outside influences, the teens in The Family, like many adolescents, rebelled against their parents' way of life. Their rebelliousness resembled that of other adolescents in form, but not in content. Whereas teenagers in mainstream Christian denominations rebel by violating rules against premarital sex, Children of God adolescents might refuse to share sexually or complain about the long hours of witnessing. Achieving a required level of commitment to the group among second-generation members is reported to be a problem for many communal utopias.[72] In an attempt to control problem youths and to reindoctrinate teens who rejected the Children of God's teachings, the group, like many Christian denominations, established teen camps around the world, albeit with very different rules than those typically seen in Christian camps. Van Zandt[73] writes that the camp structures protected the young people from sexual pressures by establishing "sharing schedules" in which adolescents were paired up for the night; other researchers document sexual exploitation of young girls by older men.[74]

Kent and Hall[75] describe increasing adult control over the young people's physical, mental, and sexual activities. Teens at the camps were required to work all day, seven days a week, on chores such as busting old cement and laying new cement; cutting grass with sickles and gathering it up; transporting scrap metal, bricks and dirt; and cleaning septic tanks, with adults watching every second. Mandatory "word classes" and devotional readings were daily events, and "confessional reports" had to be written every evening. Punishment for any sign of rebellion against this regime included solitary confinement, public beating with a paddle, and sexual advances by adults.[76]

In addition to the interviews collected by Kent and Hall,[77] stories of sexual exploitation of children were documented during the Ward court case in England,[78] in which the custody of a child in the Children of God was disputed. The story of Berg's granddaughter, Merry (called Mene in the group), attracted much of the court's attention. Merry, who lived in Berg's home while she was an adolescent, appeared before Lord Justice Ward to recount her story. Merry claims that she was made one of Berg's lovers when she was only eleven years old,[79] and her poignant account of sexual abuse at the hands of her grandfather, including fondling and oral sex, was included in the final judgment statement.[80]

Before Lord Justice Ward issued his decision on the child custody case,[81] Berg died of a heart attack and Zerby, his mistress, filled his position. Following a confessional statement from Zerby denouncing sex with minors and retracting much of the literature, Lord Justice Ward issued his final judgment in 1995. The child in question would remain a ward of the court, but, if certain conditions were met, the mother, a current member of the Children of God / The Family, could have care and control of her son while living in a Family Home.

Based largely on Zerby's statements, the final decision to allow the child to remain with the cult has been used to support the argument that child abuse does not exist in the Children of God / The Family. However, according to James Penn, a high-level Children of God leader who defected in 1998, and as revealed in recent publications by The Family, it appears that the statements made by Zerby to the court did not accurately portray all the beliefs and practices of the group concerning children and sex.

Penn,[82] a co author of many of Zerby's publications when he was in the group, contends that the statement to the judge "contained significant lies and deliberate deceptions in that it failed to acknowledge that Mo, Maria [Zerby], and Peter had intentionally promoted adults having sexual contact with minors." See http://www.geocities.com/magicgreenshirt/[83] for a complete account. In 1993, Zerby wrote that Berg's radical doctrines should be defended and that "if someone were to specifically ask us if any intimate contact between an adult and a minor is inherently wrong, abusive and bound to cause psychological harm, we would have to honestly answer 'no.'"[84] Zerby justifies the previous deception to the judge, saying that "the problem was that we didn't know how much we could say without putting the Family at legal risk . . . we had to be careful and try to protect the Family."[85] She suggests that the Family will eventually have to take a public stand and say that adult/child sexual relations are not immoral, but merely illegal, and she blames the context of illegality on the Devil, who "has just got the whole world hood-winked about this."[86] After allegedly communicating with Berg in the spirit world, Zerby instituted the doctrine of "Loving Jesus," whereby members have sex with Jesus while masturbating and imagining Jesus as a male with a penis and oneself (male or female) as female with a vagina.[87]

The Ward case and its aftermath illustrate the difficulty scholars have in interpreting nonmainstream religions and their readings fairly. As one of the most controversial new religious movements, the Children of God received much attention in academic debates. Considering the immense amount of misinformation that has been employed to vilify marginal groups throughout history, most academics are cautious when writing about deviant behavior within any particular group, and many have criticized theories of brainwashing and research methods that involve the collection of testimony from apostates. For example, in a recent chapter in *The Encyclopedia of Criminology and Deviant Behavior,* Dawson[88] writes that "claims of sexual deviance are used today to discredit unconventional religions," including the Children of God/The Family. Yet, such caution may risk obscuring or downplaying real violations of members' rights that occur in some new religions. When empirical studies and participant observation research support the likelihood that human rights have been systematically violated within secret and totalistic societies, such reports should not be hidden from academic scrutiny merely because they go against the current trend in scholarly literature. Scholars should not act as judges; neither should they withhold findings that do not appear to be politically correct.

The fascinating aspect of the Children of God was their encouragement of nontraditional sexual relationships within a traditional Christian belief system. The Children of God, growing out of the sexual revolution of the 1960s, incorporated sexual liberation into its religious doctrine. This radical environment provides researchers with a natural experimental social setting in which to examine the effects of this legacy. The reality of free sex was far from blissful for many of its practitioners. Schwartz and Rutter[89] contend that the sexual revolution often gave men an opening for sexual opportunism. The social environment of the Children of God/The Family appears to have given men sexual opportunity with both women and children. One result of this free-sex environment is evident. The culture created by eliminating sexual constraints appears to have profited males more than females, particularly adult males. Children and women, although living in a "free-sex" environment, did not always feel free to choose whom to love. As one woman revealed, "it broke down and men started to want just sex and not for love."[90] Currently, in the Children of God/The Family, sex, love, and religion have been merged by Zerby, the female leader who continues Berg's idealization of sex but without the male sexual drive.

QUESTIONS FOR DISCUSSION

1. Describe the methods the Children of God/The Family used to recruit new members. What strategies were employed to increase commitment to the group? How did sex become part of the strategies used by the Children of God? How did the use of sex change over time? Do you see similarities between these strategies and those employed in other social groups, such as churches, work places, or social clubs? How are those strategies different?

2. Researcher David Van Zandt produced an excellent ethnography of living in a cult through his study as a covert participant in the Children of God (see *Living in the Children of God,* 1991). During his period as an alleged "member," he felt guilty about his undercover position and decided to tell the cult leaders that he was actually an academic researcher. They allowed him to continue in the group as a researcher and

an overt participant; however, Van Zandt admits that he was no longer privy to inside information and subsequently was not able to experience the everyday life of a typical cult member. What are your views about conducting research as a covert participant and as an overt participant? Do you think a researcher who is an overt participant can be fully knowledgeable of the sexual activities discussed in this chapter? Are there ways that one can conduct covert participant observation without ethical concerns? If so, discuss how.

3. Define the concepts of "brainwashing," "apostates" and "apologists" as they relate to cult research. If these terms are unfamiliar, ask your instructor for more information on these terms. What are your views on the contradictory stories told by current members and former members of new religious movements? Design a research method that would produce the most valid findings on the cult phenomena discussed in this chapter.

RECOMMENDED RESOURCES

Books

Davis, Deborah. 1993. *The Children of God: The Inside Story.* Grand Rapids, MI: Zondervan Publishing House. Deborah Davis is Linda Berg, the daughter of Moses David Berg, the founder of the Children of God. After her defection/excommunication from the Children of God, along with her second husband and a few of her children, Davis wrote this exposé of her life with her father and as a leader of the Children of God.

Van Zandt, David. 1991. *Living in the Children of God.* Princeton, NJ: Princeton University Press. This is an excellent qualitative study of Van Zandt's dissertation research on the Children of God. The author first posed as a covert participant of the cult and later revealed his position as a researcher. It covers the middle period of the Children of God before Flirty Fishing spread to all the group's homes.

Williams, Miriam. 1998. *Heaven's Harlots.* New York: William Morrow & Co (now HarperCollins). This book, by a former member of the Children of God, describes the history of Flirty Fishing and one woman's fifteen-year experience in the Children of God.

Video

The Love Prophet and the Children of God. Produced by Abbey Jack Neidik and Irene Angelico of DLI Productions in association with CFCF 12 and Knowledge Network TV, Ontario. This hour-long documentary covers the history of the Children of God through the Mo Letters, pictorial archives, and interviews with current members, former members, and academic researchers.

Internet

www.thefamily.org: This is the official site of the Children of God/The Family. It provides a wealth of information that the group offers for public viewing.

http://countercog.excult.org: This site, developed by a former member, provides access to a number of recent Children of God documents, Mo Letters, and references on the Children of God, including the full Lord Justice Ward judgment.

www.voy.com/14107/: This site, coordinated by a former member, provides references on the Children of God, testimonies from former members, an active bulletin board, and links to other ex-Children of God sites.

www.exfamily.org: Latest new website for ex-members.

www.geocities.com/magicgreenshirt: This site, created by a recent defector from the Children of God/The Family who held a position of leadership, exposes the inside processes of recent Children of God operations.

ENDNOTES

1. Foster, Lawrence. 1991. *Women, Family, and Utopia: Communal Experiments of the Shakers, the Oneida Community, and the Mormons.* Syracuse, NY: Syracuse University Press.

2. Kephart, William M., and William W. Zellner. 1998. *Extraordinary Groups: An Examination of Unconventional Lifestyles,* 6th ed. New York: St. Martin's Press.

3. D'Emilio, John, and Estelle Freedman. 1997. *Intimate Matters: A History of Sexuality in America,* 2d ed. Chicago: University of Chicago Press.

4. The fact that the letters were not distributed equally to all members or to the public is an important point. Not only did many new members not have access to all of the beliefs and behaviors of the group, but the media and scholars were given very limited access to these letters and other group publications. Unfortunately, some scholars believe they have unlimited access to all literature, but as numerous defectors from the top strata of leadership reveal, there are always publications that remain secret.

5. Kent, Stephen A. 1994. "Lustful Prophet: A Psychosexual Historical Study of the Children of God's Leader, David Berg." *Cultic Studies Journal* 11(2): 135.

6. Personal communication with the author.

7. Bainbridge, Williams Sims. 1997. *The Sociology of Religious Movements.* New York: Routledge.

8. Berg, David. 1972. "Survival: the True Story of Moses and the Children of God." Mo Letter 172: 124, p. 130 (found in *The Basic Mo Letters,* 1976, published by the Children of God, Geneva, Switzerland).

9. Ibid.

10. Full-time status meant "forsaking," or leaving behind, everything and everyone that was part of one's previous life, a process known as "burning your bridges."

11. Chancellor, James D. 2000. *Life in the Family: An Oral History of the Children of God.* Syracuse, NY: Syracuse University Press.

12. Ward, The Right Honourable Lord Justice Alan. 1995. "W 42 1992 in the High Court of Justice. Family Division. Principal Registry in the Matter of ST (a Minor) and in the Matter of the Supreme Court Act 1991." October 19: 295 pp.

13. From the late 1970s to 1990s, the money and reports were sent to various post boxes in Switzerland.

14. Berg was often depicted as a lion in group publications because he was "the Lion of Judah."

15. Roberts, Keith A. 1990. *Religion in Sociological Perspective,* 2d ed. Belmont, CA: Wadsworth Publishing Company.

16. Roberts, Keith A. 1990. *Religion in Sociological Perspective,* 2d ed. Belmont, CA: Wadsworth Publishing Company.

17. Caparesi, Cristina, Mario Di Fiorino, and Stephen A. Kent. 2002. *Costetti ad Amare: Saggi sui Bambini di Dio/The Family.* Forte dei Marmi, Italy: Centro Studi Psichiatria e Territorio.

18. Kanter, Rosabeth Moss. 1972. *Commitment and Community: Communes and Utopias in Sociological Perspective.* Cambridge: Harvard University Press.

19. All World Services publications were generally released with a code that identified the letter or article for distribution among only disciples (DO), disciples and friends only (DFO), and the general public (GP). Many of the letters were published with a date that precedes the actual release of the letter to the worldwide group.

20. Millikan, D. 1994. "The Children of God, the Family of Love, The Family." In *Sex, Slander and Salvation: Investigating the Family/The Children of God,* edited by J. R. Lewis and J. G. Melton. Stanford, CA: Center for Academic Publication.

21. Chancellor, James D. 2000. *Life in the family: An Oral History of the Children of God.* Syracuse, NY: Syracuse University Press.

22. Ward, The Right Honourable Lord Justice Alan. 1995. "W 42 1992 in the High Court of Justice. Family Division. Principal Registry in the Matter of ST (a Minor) and in the Matter of the Supreme Court Act 1991." October 19: 295 pp.

23. In Merton's model of Anomie, these groups would fall in the rebel category. Merton, Robert K. 1938. Anomie and Social Structure. *American Sociological Review* 3:672–682.

24. The process of role exiting is thoroughly analyzed in a book by Ebaugh (1998). Helen Rose Fuchs *Becoming an Ex: The Process of Role Exit.* Chicago: University of Chicago Press.

25. Reading the Mo Letters, it is difficult to know when a Bible passage stopped and when Berg's interpretation began. For example, the "Revolutionary Rules" (Berg 1972, ML S), the official rules for new members of the Children of God who joined in the early 1970s, described the "new revolutionary's" life. One rule describes the dress of a member: "The appearance of a revolutionary depends largely on the field of battle. 'To the Jew as a Jew, the Greek as a Greek, the Roman as a Roman'—or the hippie as a hippie" (Berg 1972, ML S:93).

26. Berg, David. 1972. "Revolutionary Rules." Mo Letter S:93 (in *The Basic Mo Letters,* 1976, published by the Children of God, Geneva, Switzerland).

27. Berg, David. 1969. "Revolutionary Love-Making Sheet." Mo Letter No. N (in *The Mo Letters: Volume I,* 1976, published by the Children of God, Geneva, Switzerland).

28. Berg, David. 1969. "Old Church—New Church." Mo Letter No. A (in *The Mo Letters: Volume I,* 1976, published by the Children of God, Geneva, Switzerland).

29. Ward, The Right Honourable Lord Justice Alan. 1995. "W 42 1992 in the High Court of Justice. Family Division. Principle Registry in the Matter of ST (a Minor) and the Matter of the Supreme Court Act 1991." October 19: 295 pp.

30. Berg, David. 1973. "One Wife." Mo Letter No. 249 (in *The Mo Letters: Volume II,* 1976, published by the Children of God, Geneva, Switzerland).

31. Berg, David. 1973. "Revolutionary Women." Mo Letter No. 250.

32. Berg, David. 1973 "Come on Ma—Burn Your Bra." Mo Letter No. 286.

33. Berg, David. 1973. "Revolutionary Sex." Mo Letter No. 258 (in *The Mo Letters: Volume II,* 1976, published by the Children of God, Geneva, Switzerland).

34. Berg, David. 1973. "Old Bottles." Mo Letter No. 242 (in *The Mo Letters: Volume II,* 1976, published by the Children of God, Geneva, Switzerland).

35. Berg, David. 1973. "Women in Love." Mo Letter No. 292 (in *The Mo Letters: Volume II,* 1976, published by the Children of God, Geneva, Switzerland).

36. Ibid., 2327.

37. Ibid., 2334.

38. Ibid., 2335.

39. Berg, David. 1978. "Homos—A Question of Sodomy." Mo Letter No. 719: 21.

40. Berg, David. 1980. "The Devil Hates Sex—But God Loves It!" Mo Letter No. 999: 118.

41. World Services. 1995. "The Love Charter." Zurich, Switzerland.

42. Berg, David. 1970. "All Things Change, But Jesus Never!" Mo Letter No. 6 (in *The Mo Letters: Volume I,* 1976, published by the Children of God, Geneva, Switzerland).

43. Berg, David. 1974. ML 293 (in *The Mo Letters: Volume II,* 1976, published by the Children of God, Geneva, Switzerland).

44. Ibid., 2341.

45. Ibid., 2347.

46. Ward, The Right Honourable Lord Justice Alan. 1995. "W 42 1992 in the High Court of Justice. Family Division. Principle Registry in the Matter of ST (a Minor) and the Matter of the Supreme Court Act 1991." October 19: 295 pp.

47. Berg, David. 1974. "King Arthur's Knights." Mo Letter No. 505: 18.

48. Saliba, J. A. 1994. "Scholarly Studies on the Children of God/The Family: A Comprehensive Study." In *Sex, Slander and Salvation: Investigating the Family/The Children of God,* pp. 165–180, edited by J. R. Lewis and J. G. Melton. Stanford, CA: Center for Academic Publication.

49. Ward, The Right Honourable Lord Justice Alan. 1995. "W 42 1992 in the High Court of Justice. Family Division. Principle Registry in the Matter of ST (a Minor) and the Matter of the Supreme Court Act 1991." October 19: 295 pp.

50. Berg, David. 1982. Mo Letter 1083: 83.

51. World Services. 1996. "The Family: Women in The Family." Zurich, Switzerland.

52. Williams, Miriam. 1998. *Heaven's Harlots: My Fifteen Years as a Sacred Prostitute in the Children of God Cult.* New York: William Morrow and Company.

53. Berg, David. 1984. Mo Letter No. 1755: 20.

54. World Services. 1985. *Family Encyclopedia.* Zurich, Switzerland.

55. Ward, The Right Honourable Lord Justice Alan. 1995. "W 42 1992 in the High Court of Justice. Family Division. Principle Registry in the Matter of ST (a Minor) and the Matter of the Supreme Court Act 1991." October 19: 295 pp.

56. World Services. 2001. "Good News 911." Zurich, Switzerland.

57. Palmer, Susan J. 1994. "Heaven's Children: The Children of God's Second Generation." In *Sex, Slander and Salvation: Investigating the Family/The Children of God,* pp. 1–26, edited by J. R. Lewis and J. G. Melton. Stanford, CA: Center for Academic Publication.

58. Boeri, Miriam Williams. 2002. "Women After the Utopia: The Gendered Lives of Former Cult Members." *Journal of Contemporary Ethnography* 31(3): 323–60.

59. World Services. 1996. "The Family: Women in The Family." Zurich, Switzerland, p. 11.

60. Lewis, J. R. and J. G. Melton (eds.). 1994. *Sex, Slander and Salvation: Investigating the Family/The Children of God.* Stanford, CA: Center for Academic Publication.

61. Kent, Steve A., and Deana Hall. 2000. "Brainwashing and Re-Indoctrination Programs in the Children of God/The Family." *Cultic Studies Journal* 17: 1–23.

62. Boeri, Miriam Williams. 2002. "Women After the Utopia: The Gendered Lives of Former Cult Members." *Journal of Contemporary Ethnography* 31(3): 323–360.

63. Berg, David. 1973. "Revolutionary Sex." Mo Letter No. 258 (in *The Mo Letters: Volume II,* 1976, published by the Children of God, Geneva, Switzerland), 1345.

64. World Services. 1982. "The Story of Davidito." Zurich, Switzerland.

65. Ward, The Right Honourable Lord Justice Alan. 1995. "W 42 1992 in the High Court of Justice. Family Division. Principal Registry in the Matter of ST (a Minor) and in the Matter of the Supreme Court Act 1991." October 19: p. 65.

66. World Services. 1982. "The Story of Davidito." Zurich, Switzerland, p. 457.

67. Ward, The Right Honourable Lord Justice Alan. 1995. "W 42 1992 in the High Court of Justice. Family Division. Principal Registry in the Matter of ST (a Minor) and in the Matter of the Supreme Court Act 1991." October 19: p. 65.

68. Boeri, Miriam Williams. 2002. "Women After the Utopia: The Gendered Lives of Former Cult Members." *Journal of Contemporary Ethnography* 31(3): 323–360.

69. Kent, Steve A., and Deanna Hall. 2000. "Brainwashing and Re-Indoctrination Programs in the Children of God/The Family." *Cultic Studies Journal* 17: 1–23.

70. Boeri, Miriam Williams. 2002. "Women After the Utopia: The Gendered Lives of Former Cult Members." *Journal of Contemporary Ethnography* 31(3): 323–360.

71. Zerby, Karen. 1989. "Flirty Little Teens Beware." http://countercog-excult.org

72. Smith, William L. 1999. *Families and Communes: An Examination of Nontraditional Lifestyles.* Thousand Oaks: Sage Publications.

73. Van Zandt, David E. 1991. *Living in the Children of God*. Princeton, NJ: Princeton University Press.

74. Kent, Steve A., and Deanna Hall. 2000. "Brainwashing and Re-Indoctrination Programs in the Children of God/The Family." *Cultic Studies Journal* 17: 1–23.

75. Ibid.

76. A more detailed description of the teen camps can be read in Kent and Hall's excellent article on accounts from former teen members. For example, a particularly disturbing scene of a public paddling was described by four of the teens who had lived at the Philippine home, in which a young man was spanked bare-bottomed publicly before his peers until he begged for mercy. In a teen program in England, a young woman was "beat so hard with the stick [that her] buttocks were cut and her knickers covered with blood" (Kent and Hall 2000:18). Accounts can also be read at the former member Web sites listed in the Resource section of this chapter.

77. Ward, The Right Honourable Lord Justice Alan. 1995. "W 42 1992 in the High Court of Justice. Family Division. Principal Registry in the Matter of ST (a Minor) and in the Matter of the Supreme Court Act 1991." October 19: 295 pp.

78. Kent, Steve A., and Deanna Hall. 2000. "Brainwashing and Re-Indoctrination Programs in the Children of God/The Family." *Cultic Studies Journal* 17: 1–23.

79. Bunshun, Shukan. 1992. "Un etudiante de 19 Ans Temoigne, Les Abus Sexuels Oue J'ai Vue Dans La Secte-Realite Effrayante de la 'Famille d'Amor' " 5e Pertie d'une Campagne de Poursuite Approfondie. Tokyo. Translated into English by Alpha Omega Co. Ltd.

80. Kent, Steve A., and Deanna Hall. 2000. "Brainwashing and Re-Indoctrination Programs in the Children of God/The Family." *Cultic Studies Journal* 17: 1–23.

81. More detailed information on the court case can be obtained by referring to the full judgment found at www.countercog.excult.org (see Resource section).

82. Penn, James. 2001. "No Regrets." Available at http://www.geocities.com/magicgreenshirt.

83. Magic Green Shirt refers to a Berg letter by the same title that describes teens telling the "truth" during the tribulation.

84. Penn, James. 2001. "No Regrets." Available at http://www.geocities.com/magicgreenshirt.

85. Zerby, Karen. 1993. "Summit '93 Mama Jewels! #2. For Summit Use Only!" www.geocities.com/magicgreenshirt.

86. Kent, Steve A., and Deanna Hall. 2000. "Brainwashing and Re-Indoctrination programs in the Children of God/The Family." *Cultic Studies Journal* 17: 1–23.

87. Zerby, Karen. 1995. "Loving Jesus" 311 GN 662.

88. Dawson, Lorne L. 2001. "Religious Cults and Sex." In *Encyclopedia of Criminology and Deviant Behavior, Volume III*, edited by Clifton D. Bryant. Brunner-Routledge, p. 323.

89. Schwartz, Pepper, and Virginia Rutter. 1998. *The Gender of Sexuality*. Thousand Oaks: Pine Forge Press.

90. Boeri, Miriam Williams. 2002. "Women After the Utopia: The Gendered Lives of Former Cult Members." *Journal of Contemporary Ethnography* 31(3): 323–360.

Chapter 9

Islam

Larry Poston

Islam finds its origin in the teachings of the Prophet Muhammad (570–632 C.E.), who was born and raised in Mecca, Arabia. Orphaned at a young age and raised in humble circumstances, Muhammad became an exemplary businessman, married well, and at mid-life began to devote himself to meditation and spiritual searching. The angel Jibril (Gabriel) appeared to him and revealed a new Scripture, which became known as the Qur'an ("the Recitation").

Many of the teachings and narrative accounts of the Qur'an are similar to those found in the Jewish Tanakh and the Christian New Testament, but they differ in several fundamental ways as well. The Muslim scriptures contain a great deal of law, some history, some specifically religious doctrine, and some poetry. All of the concepts of the Qur'an are considered to be inspired by God, and they are thus to be obeyed without question.

Muhammad's teachings were not initially accepted by most of his countrymen, and he was forced to move to Medina, a neighboring town, in 622 C.E. There he developed a following and eventually returned to Mecca, establishing it as the chief holy place of Islam. Making a pilgrimage to Mecca to circle the Ka'ba, a formerly pagan shrine that Muhammad cleansed of idols, has become an intrinsic part of the Muslim faith.

After Muhammad's death, his successors were called *caliphs* ("representatives"), although a dispute over how such successors should be chosen led to the division of Islam into the *Sunnis* (who form a majority of today's Muslims) and the *Shi'ites* (a minority group recently famous for their fundamentalist revolution in Iran). The first caliph began a series of military campaigns (*jihads*) that, during the first 100 years of the religion's existence, resulted in the spread of the Muslim faith across North Africa and into Spain in the West and to India in the East. This expansion was followed by a long period of consolidation and maintenance that has continued until relatively recently. Over the course of more than a thousand years, Islamic beliefs and practices were established and developed, many of which were influenced by or blended with the customs of the various cultures that the Muslims came in contact with during the jihads. Among these "blendings" were ideas regarding sexuality.

The period from 800–1200 C.E. is known as the "Golden Age" of Islam. Most of what Westerners call the "liberal arts and sciences" were developed by Muslims during this period while the West was in the midst of what is commonly known as the "Dark Ages." Indeed, the European Renaissance was sparked by Crusaders who returned to Europe with philosophical knowledge, scientific expertise, and medical know-how taken from Middle Eastern Islamic culture.

During this same historical period, the Mongol invasions devastated the Muslim world. These conquests were interpreted as a judgment of God upon the Muslims' presumptuousness in "dabbling with worldly studies." Such an interpretation of historical events had profound effects on the Muslim view of the purpose of earthly life, leading to a decision on the part of many to abandon the liberal arts and sciences and to concentrate exclusively on Quranic and theological studies. These effects are still seen today in the division that exists throughout the Islamic world between Muslims who desire to adopt the worldview and acquire the technological advances of the modern West and those who oppose and seek to destroy such advances. The Muslims who belong to the latter category are attempting to return to a more fundamentalistic version of their faith, meaning that they wish to see the teachings of the Qur'an and the traditions (*hadith*) of Islam interpreted literally and followed exactly as they were written. They also desire to see this form of Islam spread over the whole earth, turning humankind from the "evil" of the modern world to a life of righteousness and peace.

Currently numbering 1.2 billion persons—a fifth of the world's population—and increasing rapidly due both to a high birth rate and conversion, Muslims are a force to be reckoned with. In the United States, they are tied with or have already surpassed the adherents of Judaism for the position of the second largest religion in America.

Sex in Islam

At least two generations of Westerners have formed their views of Muslim sexuality through literary works such as E. M. Hull's *The Sheik,* which has been billed as "the most passionate romance of all time." Hull's heroine, Diana Mayo, is kidnapped and raped by a desert chieftain who is presented as the epitome of Muslim manhood.

> "Who are you?" she gasped hoarsely.
>
> "I am the Sheik Ahmed Ben Hassan . . ."
>
> "Why have you brought me here?" she asked, fighting down the fear that was growing more terrible every moment.

He repeated her words with a slow smile. "Why have I brought you here? Bon Dieu! Are you not woman enough to know?" . . .

For the first time she had been made conscious of the inferiority of her sex . . . where every moment she was made to feel acutely that she was a woman, forced to submit to everything to which her womanhood exposed her, forced to endure everything that he might put upon her—a chattel, a slave to do his bidding, to bear his pleasure and displeasure . . . he was pitiless in his arrogance, pitiless in his Oriental disregard of the woman subjugated. He was an Arab, to whom the feelings of a woman were non-existent.[1]

This passage is typical; Muslim males are regularly portrayed as lustful, brutal chauvinists for whom women are nothing more than a means of satisfying their sexual desires and their bearing children. It is widely known that Muhammad had as many as eleven wives—making him somewhat unique among the founders of the world religions, the rest of whom were celibate or monogamists—and the fact that many adherents of Islam still allow and even recommend such practices as polygamy and female circumcision serves only to confirm and reinforce the stereotype.

Are such portrayals and images truly characteristic of the Muslim masses or are they exceptional, practiced only by a minority but seized upon by Western media in order to shock or titillate? Are the practices mentioned above intrinsic aspects of the Islamic religion or cultural items retained by people after converting to Islam? This chapter will explore the Quran's teachings regarding sexuality and will include an overview of how these teachings have been applied in the course of Islamic history.

Sexuality in the Qur'an and the Hadith (Traditions)

As in the case of the Jewish Tanakh and the Christian New Testament, the Qur'an's treatment of sexuality is generally limited to *prohibitions of illicit practices.* Perhaps the most that can be said from a "positive" standpoint is that "according to Quranic philosophy there is nothing wrong with sex if it is used for procreation within the marital framework and not merely for enjoyment and pleasure."[2]

This view is typical of conservative Muslim thinking. The Qur'an makes it clear that the created order is to be viewed in strictly pragmatic terms: "Nor for idle sport did We create the heavens and the earth and all that is between!" (Surah 21:16). Sex is included in "all that is between"—it was not intended by God primarily for human pleasure. In keeping with this view of life, marriage in Islam is generally conceded to exist as an institution primarily for the *control* and *limitation* of one's sexuality. While such a view would appear completely alien to most modern Americans and Europeans, it is interesting to note that some of the most detailed explications of this idea have been penned by Western converts to the Muslim faith. Consider, for example, the following quotation from a woman born and raised in New York but who currently resides in Pakistan as a member of a polygamous family:

In Islam marriage is a *contract* which aims to legitimatize sexual relations and create the foundation of a healthy family atmosphere for the rearing of the children . . .

the teachings of Islam, in forbidding sexual relations outside of marriage, put this prohibition into practical effect by making marriage, divorce, and remarriage as easy as possible so that there can be no excuse for illicit relations.[3]

Marmaduke Pickthall, a British convert, holds a similar view: "In marriage there is no merging of personalities. . . . They have simply entered into an engagement for the performance of certain duties toward each other . . ."[4] From their writings, it becomes clear that converts to Islam relish this strictly functional orientation toward marriage and sexuality due to their disenchantment with Western romanticism, a concept believed to produce a view of marriage that is too idealistic. Ethnic Muslims view the relation of sex to marriage similarly, but tend to speak of it in even more mechanistic or legalistic terms, such as the following quotations illustrate.

> . . . marriage is a mechanism for the moral and mutually beneficial control of sexual behavior and procreation. Islam regards sexual activity as an important and perfectly healthy drive of both males and females . . . it is not shameful and should not be denied to members of either sex. Lack of sexual satisfaction is believed to cause personality maladjustments and to "endanger the mental health and efficiency of the society."[5]
>
> The justice of women's sexual servility is derived from the notion of marriage as a legal contract between a man who pays and provides for his wife, thereby producing a set of obligations upon her. The obligations include satisfaction of his sexual needs.[6]

In keeping with the establishment of a strictly functional sexuality that has as its object procreation rather than pleasure, the Qur'an commands premarital chastity. "Let those who find not the wherewithal for marriage keep themselves chaste . . ." is the stern requirement of Surah 24:33. The hadith (traditions) amplify this command: "The Messenger said, 'Young man, those of you who can support a wife should marry, for it keeps you from looking at strange women and preserves you from immorality, but those who cannot, should devote themselves to fasting, for it is a means of suppressing sexual desire.'"[7]

Technically, these rulings have implications for both genders, although historically the Muslim female has been made to bear the greater responsibility for maintaining chastity. Although the Qur'an directs its warnings toward the male as apparently having the predominant sex drive, "Muslims have always believed that female sexuality is potent with a predilection to create havoc and chaos in the male," says Yvonne Haddad. "Thus it is necessary to control the woman in order to preserve order and well-being in society."[8] Consequently, social practices appear to have a double standard that has been noted by many. Typical is the following observation by Douglas and Davis:

> The male attempts to engage unmarried females in sexual behavior which he would not tolerate in a female blood relative and which he is likely to take as indicative of immorality in a fiancee . . . he may decide not to marry a girl because she has given in to his sexual advances, despite the fact that he promised marriage as part of the process of persuading her to become intimate.[9]

Traditionalists do not find the requirement of premarital chastity to be restrictive but believe that marriage relationships are enhanced by this restriction. It is believed that premarital loss of virginity produces psychological effects that are detrimental to proper marital adjustment. Limiting sexual intercourse to the confines of marriage serves to "strengthen the institutions of marriage and the family by making them carry benefits that could not be achieved elsewhere."[10] In other words, marriage would not be attractive or desirable if sexual encounters were available through more casual social contacts. And if the institution of marriage becomes unimportant and is abandoned, the security necessary for the proper raising of children is lost. Consequently, marriage must be endued with a special "charm," while at the same time avoiding the unrealistic romanticism so prevalent in Western society. This goal is achieved through specific Muslim practices and traditions, such as the strict separation of the genders:

> In the Muslim village, young people of the opposite sex are separated from the age of puberty or before. If they are to realize a sexually successful marriage in the village, the possibilities for familiarity must be limited and the aura of mystery and excitement engendered by marriage candidates of the opposite sex preserved . . . [this] is a much more logical underlying purpose for segregation than the [mere] need to curb sexual promiscuity.[11]

The expectation that a woman has kept her virginity until marriage is part and parcel of the Muslim wedding ceremony. Whereas most Western couples would be aghast at the thought of being followed to the wedding chamber by crowds of guests who will cheer them on while the first intercourse takes place, this is still the common practice in the Muslim heartland (i.e., Saudi Arabia, Egypt, Syria, Lebanon, etc.). The guests will not disperse until after the "displaying of the sheet," a ceremony in which the linens upon which the sexual act took place are held up so that the bloodstains left by the rupturing of the hymen may be seen by all.

Of course, in times past as well as in times present, couples have engaged in premarital sexual experimentation. When such occurs, "legal virginity" can still be maintained in various ways. Douglas and Davis note three such means. First, the couple may engage in sexual practices that do not involve penetrative intercourse. Second, in situations where the husband has been the only premarital lover, he may cut himself on the wedding night, staining the sheet on behalf of his wife. (A small vial of chicken blood prepared beforehand may also be used to produce the necessary results). And third, in situations where the girl has engaged in intercourse unbeknownst to her husband, she may have a doctor insert sutures at the vaginal opening in such a way that they will tear and produce bleeding during the first occurrence of penetration.[12]

The Qur'an provides for strict punishment of both fornication (i.e., premarital intercourse) and adultery (extramarital intercourse). Surah 24:2 states: "The woman and the man guilty of adultery or fornication—flog each of them with a hundred stripes. Let not compassion move you in their case, in a matter prescribed by Allah, if ye believe in Allah and the Last Day. And let a party of the believers witness their punishment." Although not as harsh as the Hebrews' stipulations for punishment of a girl found not to be a virgin on her wedding night (see Deuteronomy 22:13–21), the social consequences in Islamic contexts are sufficiently dire to make public incidents exceedingly rare. Indeed, publicity regarding one's real or alleged promiscuity is highly undesirable due to the stipulations of Surah 24:3: "Let no man guilty of adultery or fornication marry any but a woman similarly guilty, or an Unbeliever; nor let any but such a man or an Unbeliever marry such a woman: to the Believers such a thing is forbidden." Those who indulge in premarital intercourse are thus considered to be in a class all their own—an underclass, not worthy of association with the religiously upright.

The Qur'an also provides limitations for those with whom one may enter into a marriage union:

> Prohibited to you are—your mothers, daughters, sisters, father's sisters, mother's sisters, brother's daughters, sister's daughters, foster-mothers, foster-sisters, your wives' mothers, your step-daughters under your guardianship, born of your wives to whom ye have gone in—no prohibition if ye have not gone in—wives of your sons proceeding from your loins, and two sisters in wedlock, at one and the same time . . . (Surah 4:23)

Lois Lamya al-Faruqi, a Temple University professor who before her death was one of the leading commentators on Islam in the West, remarked that this list fulfills two major purposes: "to prevent the biological effects of inbreeding, and to guard against excessive familiarity between sexual partners. Such familiarity is regarded as cause for sexual indifference in the partners . . . Marriage with someone as close as a mother, sister, daughter, or aunt would result, in most cases, in denial of sexual gratification for the marriage partners."[13] The reason that such gratification cannot be experienced with a close relative is that there has been no opportunity for the "mystery" and "excitement" described previously to exist in relationships with persons one has been acquainted with for a number of years.

The next verse (4:24) makes it clear that "all others are lawful," though it is once again stipulated that one's desire for marriage must be chaste. Lust must never be a motivating factor. As Abdullah Yusuf 'Ali notes in his commentary upon this passage: "Marriage in the original Arabic is here described by a word which suggests a fortress (*hisn*); marriage is, therefore, the fortress of chastity."[14]

Within the marriage relationship, the husband has the right of sexual access to his wife (or wives). Two hadith are often quoted in this connection, the first being that "when a woman spends the night away from the bed of her husband, the angels will curse her until morning." The second informs us that "Allah's messenger said: 'By Him in whose hand is my life, when a man calls his wife to his bed and she does not respond, the one who is in heaven is displeased with her until he [her husband] is pleased with her."[15] A more considerate view, however, is held by the Qur'an, which states in Surah 2:223 that "Your wives are as a tilth unto you, so approach your tilth when or how you will; but do some good act for your souls beforehand; and fear Allah, and know that ye are to meet Him in the Hereafter . . ." 'Ali comments regarding this passage that

> Sex is not a thing . . . to be treated lightly, or to be indulged to excess. It is as solemn a fact as any in life. It is compared to a husbandman's tilth: it is a serious affair to him; he sows the seed in order to reap a harvest. But he chooses his own time and mode of cultivation. He does not sow out of season nor cultivate in a manner which will injure or exhaust the soil. He is wise and considerate and does not run riot. Coming from the simile to spiritual beings, every kind of mutual consideration is required . . .[16]

Thus, while misogyny certainly exists within Muslim families—just as it exists among the adherents of all religious faiths—in actuality it is quite limited, and, when it does occur, such practices violate the scriptural precepts of the Islamic religion.

Contemporary Issues

With respect to specific issues in contemporary Islam, five relate directly to Muslim sexuality. These are polygamy, *mut'ah* (temporary) marriages, birth control, homosexuality, and female circumcision.

Polygamy

There is no disagreement among Muslims that polygamy (or polygyny, as some prefer) is permitted in the Qur'an. The phrase in Surah 4:3 that is quoted in support of this practice is "Marry women of your choice, two, or three, or four . . ." This passage is considered by all to allow Muslim males to be married to a maximum of four wives at the same time.

Those who interpret this passage to grant general permission for multiple marriage appear mainly to be males, who place the most positive spin possible upon the institution. Yvonne Haddad, for instance, cites Abbas Mahmud al-'Aqqad as claiming that polygamy "lifts [a woman] from her condition of humiliation, grief, and squalor to a noble state of matrimony in which she experiences purity, dignity, and honor."[17] She also quotes 'Ali 'Abd al-Wahid, who holds that "polygyny appears only in distinctly advanced societies . . . many sociologists believe that the practice will increase and will be adopted by other societies as they become modern and progressive."[18] Marmaduke Pickthall insisted that since in an Islamic marriage "the woman retains her own personality, her own opinion and initiative, her own property and her own name in the case of polygamic as of monogamic marriage . . . it therefore does not very greatly matter from her point of view, whether monogamy or polygamy be the prevailing order of society . . ."[19] And with the current focus on women's rights, some will go to great lengths to demonstrate that polygamy actually empowers women: "Polygyny is one of the manifestations of the liberation of woman, empowering her will, since the man does not marry other wives without her permission."[20] Advocates of plural marriage bemoan the fact that in modern Islamic societies, marriages are now delayed, polygamy prohibited, and divorce and remarriage made difficult. "Muslims have taken a very natural religion and gradually made it very hard for themselves. The changed sexual behavior has meant introduction of sexual abuse, including frequent masturbation, homosexuality, and unhappy marriages."[21]

Detractors, however—who have included such notables as the modern reformer Muhammad Abduh—do not find the Quranic passage cited earlier to be as clear as it might appear. Even so conservative a document as the Constitution of Iraq under Saddam Hussein pointed out that the permission for four wives is preceded by the phrase "If ye fear that ye shall not be able to deal justly with the orphans. . . ." This condition is taken to mean that polygamy is permitted only in situations where there is a surplus of young, marriageable females—the kind of situation that exists in connection with large-scale warfare or natural catastrophes in which children are left parentless and wives husbandless. Plural marriages would thus be a means of providing food, shelter, and clothing for orphaned or widowed females; in other words, a welfare system. It is argued that in circumstances where warlike or catastrophic conditions are not extant, polygamy should not be countenanced by Muslims.

Others point out the phrase that follows the main text: "But if ye fear that ye shall not be able to deal justly (with them), then only one . . . that will be more suitable, to prevent you from doing injustice." Their argument is that polygamy is permitted only if a man has the means to meet the needs of a plurality of wives economically, psychologically, and sexually. If he is unable to keep two, three, or four wives equally supplied in each of these areas, he must limit himself to a single spouse. Those who adopt this argument believe that the number of Muslim males who can fulfill these conditions for more than one wife are extremely few.

From the perspective of Westerners, objections to polygamy usually arise from a vestigial Puritanism that assumes that the institution is motivated by a desire for multiple sexual partners. This assumption is not completely unfounded. Phil Parshall, for instance, remarks that "a teacher of Islam with three wives has told me, 'God has made this provision [i.e., polygamy] for those of us who have sexual needs of a new wife every ten years. This is much better than being like a Christian televangelist who went to prostitutes to fill his physical desires.'"[22] But the majority of Muslims are adamant that such is not the teaching of true Islam. Lois al-Faruqi commented that "as an excuse for sexual promiscuity, the practice is unconditionally condemned . . ."[23] Asghar 'Ali Engineer—an award-winning academician and commentator on Islamic religious and social issues—states that he "does not agree with those who tend to justify polygamy on the basis of biology."[24]

Mut'ah Marriage

Closely related to plural marriage is *mut'ah*, or temporary marriage. During some of the earliest conflicts in Islamic history, married soldiers were given permission by Muhammad to enter into temporary liaisons with unmarried women for the purpose of satisfying the warriors' sexual desires. Not to be confused with prostitution—which is unlawful in Islam—the *mut'ah* was an actual marriage involving a legal contract. Quranic justification is seen in Surah 4:24: "Except for these, all others are lawful, provided ye seek them in marriage with gifts from your property—desiring chastity, not lust." Thus according to an interesting process of reasoning, the *mut'ah* was designed to *preserve* the chastity of married soldiers, who were accustomed to being able to satisfy their sexual desires at any time with their wives. It was believed that for such men, the temptation to avail oneself of prostitutes would be too great to withstand, and temporary marriage was the best available solution. Because the Qur'an allows more than one wife, adding an additional "short-term" wife was not a problem.

The hadith are clear on the issue: "Narrated Jabir bin Abdullah and Salama bin al-Akwa: 'While we were in an army, Allah's Apostle said, 'If a man and a woman agree to marry temporarily, their marriage should last for three nights, and if they like to continue, they can do so; and if they want to separate, then they can do so.'" According to Engineer, the Sunnis hold that the Prophet prohibited this form of marriage after having allowed it during certain battles; it was never meant to be a normative practice.[25] The Twelver Shi'ites, however, claim that it was never prohibited and may still be practiced today. Indeed, one of the most recent sources of permission was a decree issued by the Ayatollah Khomeini during his reign in Iran: "A woman may legally belong to a man in one of two ways; by continuing marriage or temporary marriage. In the former, the duration of the marriage need not be specified; in the latter, it must be stipulated, for example, that it is a period of an hour, a day, a month, a year, or more."[26] While most modernists consider this institution to be nothing more than a tawdry attempt to legalize prostitution, traditionalists hold it to be as much a part of Islam as polygamy.

Birth Control and Homosexuality

Must intercourse always allow for the possibility of pregnancy to result? Most scholars claim that Islam has traditionally permitted at least the form of contraception known as '*azl*, or *coitus interruptus*. The medieval jurists made it clear that this procedure could only be used with the permission of the wife, because she has rights both to children and to sexual fulfillment. Modernists tend to expand this permission to include any contraceptive device that does not induce an abortion, stating that "Islam considers lack of money and the inability to bring up more children properly to be valid reasons to employ contraceptives."[27] With respect to abortion, the overwhelming majority of Muslims are opposed to the practice in nearly all cases, though there exist some schools that believe that it may be used before 120 days of pregnancy have elapsed: "Only after this time does the spirit enter the fetus, causing it to be formally created."[28]

Many traditionalists, however, insist that any form of birth control violates the very purpose of God's creation, citing the following hadith: "Narrated Ibn Muhairaz: 'I entered the Mosque and saw Abu Said al-Khudri and sat beside him and asked him about al-Azl (*coitus interruptus*) . . . we asked him about it and he said, 'It is better for you not to do so, for if any soul till the Day of Resurrection is predestined to exist, it will exist.'" In other words, one must never seek to prevent the possibility of a new life being formed, for in doing so one may be defying the will of the Creator God.

It is for this reason that a majority of Muslims condemn homosexuality, for there is no possibility for life to be created from homosexual acts. Quranic support for this condemnation is found in Surah 26:160–175, which contains the Islamic version of the story of Lot. In a discourse with the men of his town, the patriarch makes the following statement: "Of all the creatures in the world, will you approach males, and leave those whom Allah has created for you to be your mates? Nay, you are a people transgressing all limits!" The remainder of the text speaks of God's destruction of these homosexual offenders.

Muslims deny that anyone is born with a predilection toward homosexuality; it is instead considered a sinful choice made by men and women who degrade and corrupt themselves by indulging in such acts. Each of the five Islamic schools of law condemns homosexuality, though they vary in their prescriptions for the punishment of offenders. In some Muslim nations (Egypt, for instance), a practicing homosexual is subject to a punishment of 100 lashes (the same penalty as for adultery), whereas in Iran and Afghanistan, homosexual acts are punishable by death. In such environments, an openly gay lifestyle is not an option.

However, a nascent "gay rights" movement has emerged within Islam, spearheaded by groups with names such as Queer Jihad, al-Fatiha, and BiMuslims, all of which are seeking to gain acceptance for their sexual preferences from the Muslim community at large. The relative anonymity of the Internet has made possible an increasing number of forums and chatrooms such as MuslimGayMen, Iman, QueerNet GayMuslims, QueerArabWomen, and TransMuslims.

Female Circumcision

Clitoridectomy (female circumcision) is an issue that in many respects is more difficult to approach than any of the others we have discussed. Whereas modernists in both the West and in Muslim countries have tended to attribute the preceding issues to patriarchalism and chauvinism, it is questionable whether one can classify female circumcision in this way, because it is women who are among the ritual's most ardent supporters and who usually perform the operation on other women.

Nothing in the Qur'an speaks specifically of this subject—either positively or negatively—nor is it part of the accepted traditions of the faith. It is practiced, however, in every Muslim country in the world with the exception of Turkey and Iran, and it has found its way into some of the Muslim communities in North America and Europe, despite its illegality in all Western nations. Historians consider the procedure to be an example of a pagan ritual being absorbed into a new culture; such mixings invariably occur when individuals of different civilizations encounter one another. Psychologists of religion have deduced that older women retain and champion the practice as a means of exercising power over younger females or because of a mean-spirited desire to see all women subjected to the same degree of humiliation—a case of "since I had to endure it, so must you." However, current events reveal that the issue cannot be reduced to such black and white terms, and the following example illustrates just how complex the discussion can become.

In 1979, female genital mutilation (FGM) was declared illegal by the Egyptian government, the result of three decades of intense lobbying by opponents of the practice. The procedure had actually been forbidden in state-run hospitals and medical clinics since the early 1950s; thus the 1979 declaration was an attempt to flush out and eliminate the unlicensed practitioners who had sprung up throughout the country. This attempt was far from successful, however, and in 1994 CNN in conjunction with an International Population Conference aired a documentary that highlighted this issue. It was at this point that the issue of nationalism reared its head. The fact that CNN—a Western agency—had the temerity to criticize a Middle Eastern cultural practice offended many who had previously been staunch opponents of it, causing them instead to become fierce *advocates* of the ritual. The rector of Al-Azhar University—the oldest and most distinguished Muslim college in the world—issued a legal decree to the effect that *both* female and male circumcision were requirements for sincere adherents of Islam, and in a flash, nearly all of the progress made over four decades toward eliminating FGM was wiped out. Consequently, "the major political issue of modern Egypt in both rural and urban areas, is now no longer Islam, but female circumcision."[29]

The situation is made more complex by the fact that the term "female circumcision" (or *khitan* as it is called in Arabic) is used to describe a variety of surgical operations. For some, female circumcision is limited to the removal of the prepuce, or covering, of the clitoris. This procedure is considered to be the exact equivalent of male circumcision, and it is claimed that a woman's sexual pleasure is actually heightened through such surgery because the nerve endings in the clitoris acquire greater exposure and become more sensitive. More common, however, is the removal not only of the prepuce, but of the entire clitoris (a process known as *excision*). Yet a third level involves removal of the clitoris, the labia minora, and (sometimes) most of the labia majora as well (*infibulation*). It is these latter operations that are by far the most controversial, because they fundamentally alter a woman's ability to enjoy sexual intercourse.

But in what way this ability is altered is a major point of discussion. Conventional Western wisdom assumes that the purpose of the more radical procedures is to *reduce* or *eliminate* the pleasure a female can derive from sexual intercourse, and medical studies available from the World Health Organization show that infibulated women exhibit an increase in vaginal and urinary tract infections, chronic pelvic infections, vulval abesses, sterility, incontinence, depression, anxiety, sexual disfunction, and obstetric complications connected with childbearing.

Eliminating sexual pleasure does indeed appear to be the motivation of many Muslims—both male and female—who support the practice. In research conducted in the Middle East, Fernea found among the justifications for FGM the following: "it controls the sexuality of women who are more highly sexed than men;" "women need this natural curb . . . [because] left to their own uncircumcised devices, they would run wild, become promiscuous, and thus ruin the bloodlines, the family structure that keeps society together;" "circumcision makes women more attractive to men."[30] Opponents consider these arguments to be absurd, because there is not a shred of historical or anthropological evidence that uncircumcised women—certainly the majority of the female population of the world—"run wild, become promiscuous, or ruin bloodlines."

But some proponents have argued that as in the case of the first level of *khitan,* so the more radical surgical procedures serve to *increase* a woman's capacity for sexual pleasure. It is claimed that most women experience orgasm through stimulation of the clitoris, usually either before or after intercourse. The act of penetrative sex by itself does not regularly—or in some cases ever—result in the female reaching a climax, because a woman's chief "pleasure center" is the clitoris rather than the vagina. It is argued that when the clitoris is removed, the female's focus of sexual pleasure is relocated to the vagina, and since vaginal orgasms are held to be much more intense than those involving the clitoris, the woman's ability to enjoy the sex act is vastly improved. Testimonies regarding these views are limited, because sexual intimacy is not a regular topic of discussion within Muslim contexts, but apparently there is enough "underground" information circulating among Muslim women to make the case for a positive view of the practice. Consequently, the debate is certain to continue for the foreseeable future.

Conclusion

Due to the nature of the issues discussed in this chapter, it may appear to some readers that the Islamic view of women and sexuality presented by Hull in *The Sheik* is not really so farfetched after all. But it would be a mistake to judge the topic of sex in Islam solely on the basis of the controversy that surrounds such practices as polygamy and female circumcision. A number of positive items must be mentioned as well.

It may come as a surprise to many that a large number of Western converts to the Muslim faith are females who are attracted to the religion specifically because of its view of women. Marcia Hermansson, for instance, has written that the typical female convert is "a woman in her 20s who found in Islam the structure she missed in a liberal, *laissez-faire* home where no standards were set and she was told to 'be herself.' Such a woman is drawn to accept a totally observant Islam consonant with the dress and behavior norms advocated by the current 'Islamic movement . . .' "[31] These women find in Islam what they have not experienced in contemporary Western society. Convert Wadiah al-Amin, for instance, has remarked that "the most influential aspect of Islam . . . was its emphasis on family life and role definitions. It had a nice order, something I lacked most as a person."[32] And Amina Benjelloun states in the account of her conversion to Islam that "there is guidance in the Qur'an for every aspect of my public and private life. There is comfort in it in times of trial and distress, and encouragement to be the best I can possibly be as a human being and a woman. Through Islam I discovered my true value, my value as a woman . . . I discovered that being a woman is something very special and I was glad I was a woman."[33]

Testimonies regarding conversion experiences include those of former feminists who had tired of or become disillusioned with the agendas of secularist women's organizations. Many had first turned to Christianity and Judaism, but found that the feminist movements within these faith systems were indistinguishable from their secular counterparts. Islam appeared to be the perfect alternative, giving opportunity for the individual "to be a woman again." Carol Anway, who came face to face with these issues when her daughter converted to Islam, has included a number of case studies in her book *Daughters of Another Path: Experiences of American Women Choosing Islam* 1995.

It is ironic that while many female "outsiders" find the traditionalism and conservatism of the Muslim view of women to be highly attractive, many within Islam feel repressed and relegated to a form of "second-class citizenship." For this reason, one finds what might be considered a nascent feminism among Muslims in certain countries. This movement is presently limited to the more highly educated members of the Islamic countries that are considered to be "liberal" in their accommodation of global society. Publicity in the Muslim world regarding the experiences of some of the more noted Islamic feminists (such as Taslima Nasrin, a Bangladeshi writer who was forced to flee to Sweden when she was threatened with death for her remarks about the Qur'an) have prevented the feminist movement from making the kind of progress seen in the West. In more repressive societies, such as Saudi Arabia and Iran, any such rhetoric remains underground by necessity and runs the constant risk of repression. However, many are nonetheless optimistic with regard to prospects for future advances.

We find thus that with respect to a basic approach to sexuality, Muslims have much in common with both Judaism and Christianity. All three celebrate sexuality as a divinely ordained part of human life, but warn of the potential danger that exists when sexual drives are allowed free and undisciplined expression. All three set strict limitations with respect to sexual intercourse: It is to be confined to the marriage relationship. The majority of the adherents of all three have a negative view of homosexuality, considering it to be a sinful practice. And all three are characterized by a broad spectrum of views on the part of their adherents concerning the role of women in relation to men.

Muslims differ from the other "People of the Book," however, in that their faith allows for both polygamous and temporary marriages. Also, although not directly taught by either the Qur'an or the traditions, female circumcision is practiced by a significant number of the religion's adherents.

Perhaps the greatest difference between Islam and its related faiths is the fact that whereas in Judaism and Christianity sexuality ceases at the end of earthly life, the eternal reward of the righteous Muslim male includes sexual relations with the *houris*, described in several places in the Qur'an as "chaste women; restraining their glances, with big eyes of wonder and beauty . . ." (37:48); "chaste women restraining their glances, companions of equal age . . ." (38:52); "we shall join them to Companions, with beautiful, big, and lustrous eyes . . ." (44:54); "like unto Pearls, well guarded . . ." (56:23); "maidens, chaste, restraining their glances, whom no man or Jinn before them has touched . . . fair companions, good, beautiful" (55:56, 70); "Round about them will serve youths of perpetual freshness . . . We have created their Companions of special creation, and made them virgin-pure and undefiled, beloved by nature, equal in age . . ." (56:17, 35–37). Although not all Muslims interpret these passages in a strictly literal sense, most commentators have combined them to form a picture of female "companions" who are physically beautiful, submissive virgins, a number of which are allotted to each male as a reward for good deeds performed in this life. Sexuality for the Muslim, then, transcends human mortality and continues for an eternity of paradisiacal bliss.

QUESTIONS FOR DISCUSSION

1. Many Muslim scholars claim that sexual intercourse may only be engaged in for purposes of procreation. How might this claim be defended? For what reasons might it be criticized and/or denied?

2. Is the claim of a "double standard" in Islam with respect to males—that they may lose their virginity while females are expected to maintain their own—logically consistent? Why or why not?

3. What benefits might the veiling and seclusion of women—as required in certain Muslim sects—have for preserving the sanctity of sexual relations? What disadvantages might exist with respect to these practices?

4. Is the marriage practice of "displaying the sheet" merely an embarrassing anachronism in the modern world or can the institution and all that it implies serve—as Muslims claim—to enhance the "mystery" and thus the desirability of marriage?

5. It is maintained by some writers and commentators that the Muslim view of paradise with its portrait of beautiful, submissive virgins for every righteous male is a strong motivating factor for suicide bombings and other terrorist activities leading to martyrdom. What are your thoughts regarding the mental state of one who is willing, as it were, to "die for sex?"

6. With respect to such institutions as polygamy and female circumcision, should Westerners seek to impose their own beliefs on other societies or should they be tolerant and respectful of cultural differences? On what basis might distinctions of "good" or "bad" be made between various kinds of cultural practices?

7. Given that females outnumber males in every society, is polygamy an institution that should be accepted (and even recommended) in cultures that make few—if any—provisions for single females to live on their own?

8. Whereas a Western female finds it nearly impossible to imagine sharing her husband with another female, could her objections be merely the result of her own enculturation? In other words, would a woman who has lived her entire life in a polygamous family or culture have the same objections or fear the same consequences as a Western woman?

9. Can the idea of *mut'ah,* or temporary marriage, be defended from the standpoint of pure pragmatism, or should the practice be considered nothing more than an attempt to skirt the prohibitions of Islam against prostitution?

10. What measures might Muslims living in Europe or America be forced to take in order to maintain their traditional religious beliefs and practices with respect to sexuality?

RECOMMENDED RESOURCES

Anees, Munawar A. 1989. "Genital Mutilations: Moral or Misogynous?" *Islamic Quarterly* 33:101–117. An exploration of the various viewpoints taken by Muslims with respect to female circumcision.

Athar, Shahid (ed.). (n.d.). *Sex Education: An Islamic Perspective.* [Online]. Available: http://islam-usa.com/s1.html. [2002, January 14]. A comprehensive Web site dealing with nearly every conceivable topic under the rubric of "sexuality" from a Muslim perspective.

Burstyn, Linda. 1995. "Female Circumcision Comes to America." *Atlantic Monthly* 276, no. 4:28–35. An excellent article dealing with the issues of when a religious practice is imported into a country that practices a constitutionally mandated separation of church and state.

Esposito, John L. 1982. *Women in Muslim Family Law.* Syracuse, NY: Syracuse University Press. A work that takes up the issue of sexuality from the standpoint of Islamic law.

Farah, Madelain. 1984. *Marriage and Sexuality in Islam: A Translation of al-Ghazali's Book on the Etiquette of Marriage from the Ihya'.* Salt Lake City: University of Utah Press.

Al-Ghazali (d. 1111) is considered the "St. Augustine" of Islam. This work contains a classical Islamic view of sexuality as it is still understood by most conservative Muslims today.

Haeri, Shahla. 1989. *Law of Desire: Temporary Marriage in Shi'i Iran.* Syracuse, NY: Syracuse University Press. A detailed treatment of the concept of *mut'ah* marriage as it is currently practiced in Iran.

Many Wives. (n.d.). [Online]. Available: http://www.mukmin.com/channels/ myfamily/pages/Dealingwith/Polygamy/index.php3. [2002, January 14]. An extensive Web site that covers several aspects of polygamy, with subtitles such as "The System," "Its Virtues," "Effects on Family," "Among Wives," "Being Responsible," and "Common Concerns."

Murray, Stephen, and Will Roscoe, eds. 1997. *Islamic Homosexualities.* New York: New York University Press. A work dealing with the nascent gay movement within Islam.

Sex. (n.d.). [Online]. Available: http://www.themodernreligion.com/sex.html. [2002, January 14]. Another comprehensive Web site that deals with a variety of sexual issues as seen from a conservative Muslim standpoint.

Smith, Robyn Cerny. (n.d.). *Female Circumcision: Bringing Women's Perspectives into the International Debate.* [Online]. Available: http://www. lawlib.utoronto.ca/ Diana/fulltext/smit.html. This Web site examines the issue of female circumcision from the perspectives of women from all around the world, most of whom live in Muslim countries.

Swanson, Mark N. 1984. "A Study of Twentieth-Century Commentary on Surat al-Nur (24): 27–33." *Muslim World* 74 (July–October):187–203. This passage from the Qur'an is one of the most extensive treatments of women's issues, including issues of sexuality. This article summarizes the spectrum of commentaries on this passage that have appeared in recent history.

ENDNOTES

1. E. M. Hull, *The Sheik: A Novel* (New York: A. L. Burt Company, 1921), pp. 57, 91–92.

2. Ali Asghar Engineer, *The Rights of Women in Islam* (New York: St. Martin's Press, 1992), p. 100.

3. Maryam Jameelah, *Islam Versus Ahl al-Kitab: Past and Present* (Lahore, Pakistan: Mohammed Yusuf Khan and Sons, 1978), p. 306.

4. Muhammad Marmaduke Pickthall, *Islamic Culture* (Lahore, Pakistan: Feroz Sons, 1927), p. 137.

5. Lois Lamya Ibsen Al-Faruqi, "Marriage in Islam," in *Perspectives on Marriage: A Reader*, edited by Kieran Scott and Michael Warren (New York: Oxford University Press, 1993), p. 399.

6. Afsaneh Najmabadi, "Feminism in an Islamic Republic," in *Islam, Gender and Social Change*, edited by Yvonne Yazbeck Haddad and John L. Esposito (New York: Oxford University Press, 1998), p. 68.

7. Yvonne Yazbeck Haddad, "Islam and Gender: Dilemmas in the Changing Arab World," in *Islam,* edited by Haddad and Esposito, p. 26, n. 48.

8. Ibid., p. 17.

9. Douglas A. Davis and Susan Schaefer Davis, "Dilemmas of Adolescence: Courtship, Sex and Marriage in a Moroccan Town," in *Everyday Life in the Muslim Middle East,* edited by Donna Lee Bowen and Evelyn A. Early (Indianapolis, IN: Indiana University Press, 1993), p. 88.

10. Al-Faruqi, "Marriage," p. 408.

11. Ibid., p. 401.

12. Davis and Davis, "Dilemmas," pp. 85–88.

13. Al-Faruqi, "Marriage," pp. 400–401.

14. 'Abdullah Yusuf 'Ali, *The Holy Qur'an: Text, Translation and Commentary (New Revised Edition)* (Brentwood, MD: Amana Corporation, 1989), p. 192, n. 538.

15. Haddad, "Islam and Gender," p. 29, n. 116.

16. 'Ali, *The Holy Qur'an,* p. 90, n. 249.

17. Haddad, "Islam and Gender," p. 13.

18. Ibid.

19. Pickthall, *Islamic Culture,* p. 145.

20. Haddad, "Islam and Gender," p. 13.

21. Ali Nawaz Memon, *The Islamic Nation* (Beltsville, MD: Writers Inc. International, 1995), p 53.

22. Phil Parshall, *Inside the Community* (Grand Rapids: Baker Book House, 1994), p. 170.

23. Al-Faruqi, "Marriage," p. 402.

24. Engineer, *Rights,* p. 22.

25. Ibid., p. 24.

26. Ayatollah Ruhollah Khomeini, *Sayings of the Ayatollah Khomeini* (New York: Bantam Books, 1980), p. 94.

27. Donna Lee Bowen, "Pragmatic Morality: Islam and Family Planning in Morocco," in *Everyday Life,* edited by Bowen and Early, p. 96.

28. Ibid.

29. Elizabeth Warnock Fernea, *In Search of Islamic Feminism* (New York: Doubleday, 1998), p. 271.

30. Ibid., p. 274.

31. Marcia K. Hermansson, "Two-Way Acculturation: Muslim Women in America Between Individual Choice (Liminality) and Community Affiliation (Communitas)," in *The Muslims of America,* edited by Yvonne Yazbeck Haddad (New York: Oxford University Press, 1991), p. 193.

32. Wadiah Al-Amin, "Islam Gave Me a Sense of Dignity," *Islamic Horizons* (September 1979): 8–9.

33. Aminah Benjelloun, "Why I Am a Muslim," *Islamic Horizons* (September 1984): 6.

Chapter 10

Sex and Religion: Concluding Reflections

Christel Manning and Phil Zuckerman

When we first conceived the idea for this book almost three years ago, we didn't realize what a hornet's nest we were stepping into. From our choice of which religious traditions to cover, to which authors would write them, to how each tradition should be addressed, readers are likely to have strong reactions to the topic of sex and religion. Some conservative readers may feel that such a text should stick to explaining the teachings of each religion and avoid cultural, historical, or sociological issues. They may argue that by indulging the views of those who criticize or ignore institutional teachings, we are legitimating those critiques, which reflects a liberal bias typical of academics. Some liberal readers may feel that this book does not sufficiently address various critiques of a given tradition or that it ignores the experience of particular individuals or groups oppressed by the tradition, thus legitimating the oppressor, reflecting a conservative bias. For example, some readers of earlier drafts of this volume felt that the Christianity chapter gives short thrift to Protestantism; some felt that the Hinduism chapter should say more about dowries; and that the Islamic chapter should include more on feminism. Some Mormon readers felt that their religion should have been covered as part of Christianity and not in a separate chapter. Some members of the Children of God felt that the chapter on their religion dwells too much on the controversies surrounding their late leader. In hindsight, we should have expected such controversy: both religion and sex have become highly politicized, so the intersection between the two is likely to be explosive.

Because of the controversial nature of the topic, it is impossible to address all such questions and critiques. However, we would like to conclude the book with a brief reflection on two important critiques that are likely to be made of this book. One pertains to feminist scholarship; the other to the study of new religious movements.

Questioning Majority Religion

The first critique is that a book such as this one should be more critical/ skeptical, especially with respect to the patriarchal religions dominant in Western society, Judaism and Christianity. The chapter on Christianity, for example, suggests that most Christian churches view divorce negatively and refers to the harmful impact of divorce on children to explain that view. The chapter does not discuss how oppressive past restrictions on divorce were, especially to women, or what women gained from more liberal divorce laws—which may seem to some readers to legitimate the traditional view of divorce. Other readers may feel there is insufficient discussion of Pope John Paul II's opposition to contraception and women's ordination, especially when compared to the author's positive comments about John Paul II speaking out against degradation of women in Third World countries. Similar arguments could be made with respect to the Judaism chapter. While it mentions aspects of orthodoxy that discriminate against homosexuals, the discussion is pointedly neutral, giving no expression to the continuing pain and suffering of those affected by that discrimination. The chapter does discuss the problems of women whose husbands refuse to grant them a get, but it may seem to some readers to minimize those problems by suggesting that the rabbis are working to resolve them.

Silence, according to this argument, implies complicity. As Carol Christ and Judith Plaskow point out in their now classic work, *Woman Spirit Rising*, one of the first tasks of feminist scholarship in religion was to "break the conspiracy of silence" about women's experience in religion.[1] When a book engages in more description than critique of a patriarchal institution, it tends to understate how institutional teachings affect deviant individuals or how dominant institutions oppress deviant groups. Members of dominant institutions (e.g., white, heterosexual, male Protestant college students) are often oblivious to such oppression (e.g., what it feels like to be a gay Catholic or a Muslim in a mostly Christian society). This is a book written by mostly Western authors of mostly Jewish and Christian upbringing and is likely to be read by an audience of much the same background. Some feminist critics may argue that the authors, therefore, have a responsibility to engage in more critical reflection on these traditions.

Protecting Minority Religion

The second critique is the flipside of the first: that this book is overly critical and presents too negative a view of religions holding minority status in Western society, such as Mormonism, Children of God, and Islam. The Mormon chapter, for example, does not mention positive female experiences of polygamy or discuss polygamy as a First Amendment issue, but it does include an extended discussion of the church's race restrictions. Thus it may seem to some readers to confirm common prejudices against Mormonism as a racist and sexist religion. Similarly, the chapter on the Children of God may seem to legitimate common stereotypes of this group as a dangerous cult. The chapter does not acknowledge that some women enjoyed Flirty Fishing, and it does not describe the persecutorial environment that makes it highly unlikely for groups like the Children of God to be cleared of charges.[2] Finally, the Islam chapter cites many examples of teachings that would seem by Western standards to oppress women and only briefly discusses the Islamic feminism and gay rights movements; to some readers it may not do enough to counter Western stereotypes of Islam as hopelessly misogynistic.

Minority religions, according to this argument, need to be sympathetically described rather than unfairly evaluated by the moral standards of the majority. Too many people already think of all new religions as dangerous cults. Too many already think of Mormons as, using the words of one of our students, "those folks in Utah who go door to door and practice polygamy." Too many Americans already associate Islam with terrorism and the oppression of women. No religion should be singled out as being alternative because doing so brands it as deviant, which is oppressive. And, in describing minority religions, special care needs to be taken to contextualize beliefs and practices that deviate from the mainstream. A book by mostly Western authors written for Western readers has a special responsibility to be empathetic, or to use the words of the late Ninian Smart, "walk a mile in the moccasins" belonging to a person of another religion.[3]

A Question of Power

Both of these critiques raise questions that we as editors had to ask ourselves and our authors, realizing that they are part of a debate that we could contribute to but ultimately not resolve. Although seemingly opposite, at the heart of both arguments is the question of power: The power to define what is a "major" or "world" religion and what is "alternative," and, within a given religion, what is traditional or orthodox and what is not. The power to determine what is normal and what is deviant, which teachings correspond to the natural diversity among people and which are oppressive and discriminatory, what is right and what is wrong.

It should not be surprising that the intersection of sex and religion raises power issues, or that feminist scholars and those studying new religions continuously run up against the question of power. Patriarchy is by definition an institution that gives one sex power over another, and religions have historically acted to legitimate that power. Many first-generation new religions have been attractive to women because they offer more flexible gender roles (Shakers, Christian Science, early Pentecostalism, etc.).[4] Indeed, one of the most common ways for members of dominant religious institutions to discredit new religions is to brand them as sexual deviants, which then justifies their persecution.[5] Early scholars who addressed the question of power when studying women or new religions were often ridiculed by the academy as engaging in unscholarly (i.e., not objective) work and promoting a personal agenda. Yet it is now widely acknowledged that silence about power serves to legitimate existing power arrangements.

As the editors of this book, we concur with much in both critiques. Power is important. Writing is political. So-called objective writing often does collude in the oppression of deviant individuals and nonmainstream groups. We acknowledge that, as academics, we have more access to knowledge, and therefore power, and that as educators, we have a responsibility to use that power in an ethical manner. More specifically, as experts we should make an effort to be more critical of dominant institutions (because the default is not to be) and to be more empathetic with nonmainstream movements (again, because default is not to be). This is why we instructed our authors to be self-conscious of the default position: to be sure to cover major critiques within the tradition and to make sure that sympathetic information is included, especially for traditions that readers are likely to have negative stereotypes about. There is a danger, however, of traveling too far in the nondefault direction, which can cause distortions that are just as oppressive, only to different people.

The Dilemmas of Deconstructing Power

Feminist critics filled an important gap in the scholarship on religion by focusing on women's experiences and demonstrating that entire traditions have been framed from a male perspective. Thus, seemingly neutral texts and rituals were, in fact, not neutral, but had the effect of excluding and oppressing women: gendered language (describing both God and normative humanity as male), Jewish ritual circumcision, the exemption of from the minyan, the Passover text, Catholic altar boys, the prohibition of contraception, and even the veneration of Mary all reflect assumptions and influence behavior in ways that affirm patriarchy.[6] Feminist critics should also be commended for seeking to rebuild what they had torn down, suggesting ways of reforming and reconstructing the traditions: gender-neutral language, naming rituals for girls, feminist Haggadahs, altar girls, and the ordination of rabbis and priests. The problem for the feminist effort is that many people, including women, like their religion the way it is.

Some women affirm the traditional teachings of what feminists would call patriarchal Christianity and Judaism—not because they are afraid to express dissent, lack alternatives, or have internalized a negative, powerless self-image, but because they have found ways to interpret the tradition so that it actually empowers them. These women, mostly members of fundamentalist or evangelical Christian or Orthodox Jewish communities, have begun to add their voices to the literature on women in religion. Thus the huge volume of feminist scholarship critical of Judaism and Christianity published in the 1960s and 1970s was followed in the 1980s and 1990s by a spate of books, mostly by sociologists, interviewing women in these traditions.[7] They assert that the so-called patriarchal traditions actually value, even celebrate, feminine roles and responsibilities such as menstruation or motherhood more than more liberal traditions. They resent the assumption that they are oppressed and see the feminist critique as an elitist theory that does not reflect the lived experience of the majority of ordinary women.

A similar argument can be made with respect to scholars of new religions. The popular media—the source for most Americans' understanding of minority religion—has historically been sensationalist and overwhelmingly negative.[8] Coverage occurs only when the group is involved in controversy, dramatizing ways in which its beliefs and practices deviate from mainstream "Judeo-Christian" society. Thus most people know that the "Moonies" conduct arranged marriages and that their leader went to jail; they do not realize that the Unification church is a Christian sect that teaches from the Bible. They know that the "Hare Krishnas" wear orange robes and that some gurus were accused of sexual harassment; they do not realize that worship of Krishna is an ancient Hindu tradition, and that ISKCON provides a religious community to many Indian immigrants. In fairness, media coverage of mainstream religions can be equally sensationalist, yet most people have sufficient personal experience with such religions to arrive at a more balanced picture.

Given the prejudices people have about new religions, sociologists engaging in more systematic research are doing important work.[9] By collecting empirical data disputing brainwashing theory (which is mostly based on anecdotal evidence) and showing that converts to new religions typically make an active decision that meets their personal needs at that time;[10] by conducting participant-observation in seemingly exotic cults such as Wicca, Santeria, or the Moonies (rather than relying on the usually negative accounts of ex-members) and recounting the ordinariness of the participants (sane, middle-class folks with jobs and kids);[11] by critically investigating how government treats new religions (e.g., judges giving permission to kidnap and "deprogram" converts; Federal Agents' invasion of Waco) and proving discrimination;[12]—sociologists have gone a long ways toward normalizing new or foreign religions, which in turn helps ensure that their members are treated fairly.

Sociologists are to be commended for encouraging people to refrain from judgment of alternative religions by the standards of those who happen to be in the majority. The problem arises when members of the minority religion engage in abusive or oppressive conduct. As Miriam Williams puts it in her chapter on the Children of God, scholars' reluctance to vilify new religions "may downplay real violations of members' rights that sometimes occur" in such groups. She and other critics argue that in the current academic climate of political correctness, ex-members who report negative experiences often feel that their testimony isn't taken as seriously as that of members. They point out that researchers do not usually have full access to information because alternative religions, like any organization seeking to make a positive impression, engage in information management. Thus researchers are sometimes reading only selected texts, participating in model communities or events, and interviewing trained respondents. The result may be that domestic violence or sexual abuse is ignored—at the expense of the victims.[13] Women and children who were sexually abused by male cult leaders such as David Koresh (leader of the Branch Davidians at Waco) or David Berg (leader of the Children of God) resent having their experience dismissed as mere rationalizations for their defection. They see scholarly defenses of unusual sexual practices as elitist theorizing that does injustice to the lived experience of actual participants.

We have tried in the editing process of this book to do justice to both sides of these debates. Although each author has brought a particular slant to his or her topic, each chapter provides sufficient information on various perspectives on controversial issues for readers to draw their own conclusions. This is not a feminist text, nor is it a representative study of new religions. Our intent was not to deconstruct the patriarchal structure of dominant religions, nor to foster more empathy for alternative sexual practices in minority religions.[14] Rather, we sought to introduce the readers to teachings and practices and controversies surrounding them, in the hope that they would raise questions and use the resources provided to seek more answers.

ENDNOTES

1. Carol Christ and Judith Plaskow, eds. 1979, 1992. *Womanspirit Rising: A Feminist Reader in Religion* (San Francisco: Harper Collins).

2. James Richardson. 1991. "Cult/Brainwashing Cases and Freedom of Religion." *Journal for the Scientific Study of Religion* 24(2): 163–79.

3. Smart, Ninian. 1993. *Religions of Asia* (Englewood Cliffs, NJ: Prentice Hall).

4. Susan Jean Palmer. 1994. *Moon Sisters, Krishna Mothers, Rajneesh Lovers: Women's Roles in New Religions* (Syracuse, NY: Syracuse University Press); Catherine Wessinger, ed. 1993. *Women's Leadership in Marginal Religions: Explorations Outside the Mainstream* (Urbano and Chicago: University of Illinois); Marion Goldman. 2002. *Passionate Journeys: Why Successful Women Joined a Cult* (Ann Arbor, MI: University of Michigan).

5. Lawrence Foster. 1981. *Religion and Sexuality: Three American Communal Experiments of the Nineteenth Century* (New York: Oxford University Press).

6. Christ & Plaskow, ibid.

7. Christel Manning. 1999. *God Gave Us the Right: Conservative Catholic, Evangelical Protestant, and Orthodox Jewish Women Grapple with Feminism* (New Brunswick, NJ: Rutgers University); Debra Kaufman. 1991. *Rachel's Daughters: Newly Orthodox Jewish Women* (New Brunswick, NJ: Rutgers University); Lynn Davidman. 1991. *Tradition in a Rootless World: Women Turn to Orthodox Judaism* (Berkeley: University of California); R. Marie Griffith. 1997. *God's Daughters: Evangelical Women and the Power of Submission* (Berkeley: University of California); Brenda Brasher. 1998.

Godly Women: Fundamentalism and Female Power (New Brunswick, NJ: Rutgers University).

8. See Philip Jenkins. 2000. *Mystics and Messiahs: Cults and New Religions in American History* (New York: Oxford University Press).

9. For an excellent overview of sociological research on new religions, see Lorne Dawson. 1998. *Comprehending Cults: The Sociology of New Religious Movements* (New York: Oxford University Press).

10. Roger Strauss. 1979. "Religious Conversion as a Personal and Collective Accomplishment." *Sociological Analysis* 40(2): 158–65; James T. Richardson. 1985. "The Active vs. Passive Convert: Paradigm Conflict in Conversion/Recruitment Research." *Journal for the Scientific Study of Religion* 24(2): 163–69.

11. Eileen Barker. 1984. *The Making of a Moonie: Choice or Brainwashing* (Cambridge: Oxford University Press); Margot Adler. 1986. *Drawing Down the Moon: Witches, Druids, Goddess Worshippers, and Other Pagans in America Today* (Boston: Beacon Press).

12. Stewart Wright, ed. 1995. *Armageddon in Waco: Critical Perspectives on the Branch Davidian Conflict* (Chicago: University of Chicago Press). See also James T. Richardson. 1995. "Legal Status of Minority Religions in the United States." *Social Compass* 42(2): 249–64. Richardson has researched and published extensively on the subject of government and media bias against new religions. For a good overview of his work, see Lorne Dawson, *Comprehending Cults.*

13. Robert Balch. 1996. "Sex, Slander, and Salvation: Investigating the Family/ Children of God." Book Review. *Journal for the Scientific Study of Religion* 35(1): 72; Robert W. Balch and Stephan Langdon. 1998. "How the Problem of Malfeance Gets Overlooked in Studies of New Religions: An Examination of the AWARE Study of the Church Universal and Triumphant." In *Wolves within the Fold: Religious Leadership and Abuses of Power,* edited by Anthony Shupe (New Brunswick, NJ: Rutgers University Press).

14. For readers interested in such a treatment, see Patricia Beatty Jung et al. 2001. *Good Sex: Feminist Perspectives from the World's Religions* (New Brunswick, NJ: Rutgers University Press) for a feminist approach, or Susan Palmer, *Moon Sisters,* for an approach sympathetic to new religions.